D0204850

Self-understanding in childhood and adolescence

Self-understanding in childhood and adolescence

WILLIAM DAMON

Brown University

DANIEL HART

Rutgers University

The right of the
University of Cambridge
to print and sell
all manner of books
was granted by
Henry VIII in 1534.
The University has printed
and published continuously
since 1584.

CAMBRIDGE UNIVERSITY PRESS

Cambridge
New York   Port Chester   Melbourne   Sydney

Published by the Press Syndicate of the University of Cambridge
The Pitt Building, Trumpington Street, Cambridge CB2 1RP
40 West 20th Street, New York, NY 10011-4211, USA
10 Stamford Road, Oakleigh, Victoria 3166, Australia

First published 1988
First paperback edition 1991

Printed in Canada

Library of Congress Cataloging-in-Publication Data

Damon, William, 1944–
Self-understanding in childhood and adolescence / William Damon
and Daniel Hart.
    p.   cm. – (Cambridge studies in social and emotional
development)
Bibliography: p.
Includes index.
ISBN 0-521-30791-0 (hbk.)
1. Self-perception in children.   2. Self-perception in teenagers.
3. Self.   I. Hart, Daniel.   II. Title.   III. Series.
BF723.S28D36   1988
155.4'18 – dc 19   87-37556
                                                   CIP

British Library Cataloguing in Publication applied for

ISBN 0-521-30791-0 hardback
ISBN 0-521-42499-2 paperback

Contents

Preface   *page* vii

1 Introduction   1

2 Previous developmental theory and research   18

3 A developmental model of self-understanding   53

4 The self-understanding interview and scoring procedures   77

5 Understanding the self-as-object   87

6 Understanding the self-as-subject   123

7 Self-understanding and adolescent mental health
  (with Mira Zamansky Levitt)   139

8 Self-understanding in a Puerto Rican fishing village
  (with Nydia Lucca)   158

9 Self-understanding and social cognition   171

References   191
Author index   199
Subject index   202

Preface

This book reports the results of a six-year investigation into the development of self-understanding. It represents a collaborative effort in which the two authors joined to explore the self-conceptions of children and adolescents from a developmental perspective. We had been troubled by a nondevelopmental bias in prior self-concept research and wished to take a new look at this central area of social cognition. In so doing, we extended a research program on children's social-cognitive development that began with studies described in *The Social World of the Child* (Damon, 1977). In the present investigation we took as our main concern the cognitive aspects of personal identity. We also expanded the age range of study to include early and late adolescence as well as childhood.

We consider the present work to be a necessary complement to the initial work on social understanding. *The Social World of the Child* explored children's understanding of the social relations and regulations that define their participation in society. The focus was on friendship and authority (childhood's key peer and parental relations), justice, social rules, and conventions of sex role and etiquette. These relations and regulations are the integrating forces of children's social life, the interpersonal fabric of their social networks. The present book explores the opposite side of the social coin.

As children work out their social relations and standards of conduct, they also distinguish themselves from others as a means of establishing the unique bases of their own individuality. This requires sorting out for themselves both the general and the particular features of their own personal identities. Psychologically this task is as much a requirement of "personhood" as is the more other-oriented process of social understanding. Efforts to distinguish oneself from others are implemented cognitively by self-understanding. Social understanding and self-understanding, then, are the two complementary intellectual functions implicit in social development.

The complementarity of social understanding and self-understanding is an interpenetrating one in which the two constantly inform one another. Social relations by definition include the self, and one's view of any social transaction is colored by how it affects one's self-interest. Likewise, self-understanding is to some extent based on one's observations of the self in relations to others, and it also owes a large debt to one's perceptions of others' attitudes toward oneself. But the overlap between social and self is by no means complete. There are many social realities external to the self that one must grasp in order to function socially. Conversely, one's sense of self-identity always retains a privileged core of personal experience and belief that no social influence can fully determine.

Our hope is that the social and self-understanding studies, when taken together, will sketch a rounded (though still preliminary) picture of both social-cognitive functions as they develop. Between the two investigations, the first author wrote a more general account of children's social development that sets these social-cognitive functions in the context of growing behavioral and affective processes (Damon, 1983a).

In the present book we encounter some complexities unique to the concept of self. For one thing, the self is more than just another social concept and cannot be contained within the differentiating function of social development. The self is relational as well as individualistic, subjective as well as objective, and multifaceted as well as unified. Such dualisms are puzzling to say the least, and they do not stop here. Above all is the almost incomprehensibly dualistic conviction on which all self-awareness rests: The self retains its essential identity over time and circumstance while potentially being susceptible to every conceivable sort of change.

Our challenge, then, was to capture such dualisms in our investigation, and to determine what they mean to the developing child and adolescent. We admit at the start that we only partially succeeded. Our approach was grounded on William James's multidimensional self theory (James, 1961/ 1892), in which many of the most prominent dualities (subjective–objective, stability–change) are represented in his distinction between the "me" and the "I." As we shall explain later in this book, our progress was largely confined to the "me." Nevertheless, through an approach originally suggested by Mead (1934), we did manage to make some indirect inroads into the "I" by studying it through an aspect of the "me," the understanding of core self-experiences. This beginning is at least more encouraging than that heralded by James, who himself despaired of ever studying the "I" in an empirical and nonspeculative way.

To say that there are general dualisms permeating all persons' self-awareness is not to say that all persons think about these dualisms in the same way. In fact, the central focus of this book is the regular pattern of differences that can be traced to developmental trends in self-understanding during the childhood and adolescent years. Our aim is to describe these patterns as much on their own terms as possible, much as was done in *The Social World of the Child*, much as anthropologists strive to impart the uniqueness of a particular culture's perspective.

The anthropologist Clifford Geertz, just prior to outlining some radical variations in how personhood is defined across cultures, notes that the category of "person" is nevertheless a fundamental referent for everyone (Geertz, 1973). People may differ widely in their beliefs about the essence of human nature and yet still share a common orientation to humans as a special class of creature. "At least some conception of what a human individual is, as opposed to a rock, an animal, a rainstorm, or a god, is, so far as I can see, universal" (Geertz, 1973, p. 126).

Within the general class of persons, the self is yet another universal distinction. In one way or another, people everywhere accept and enforce self-grounded notions like individual responsibility, reward, and sanction. But this does not at all imply that people everywhere draw the boundaries between self and other *in the same way*. Clearly some cultures refrain from making self–other separations that seem normal, and perhaps even inevitable, to many Western cultures (LeVine and White, 1986). Such variations no doubt are guided by the general social-cultural, cognitive, and personality functions that any form of self-understanding must serve.

In this book we investigate the way in which such functions are played out in the contemporary American setting of Worcester, Massachusetts. We are aware that the self–other boundary is drawn differently elsewhere, and that this may lead to cultural variations in the nature of self-understanding as well as in its developmental trajectory through childhood and adolescence. But we also believe that the universality of self-understanding's social and personal functions will lead to some comparability across diverse settings. We have an opportunity to empirically examine this issue on a small scale in Chapter 8.

The introductory first chapter begins with a discussion of the semantic boundaries of the construct "self-understanding." We compare and contrast it to related constructs like "self," "self-concept," and "self-esteem." We offer a definition of self, drawn largely from William James and his followers, in order to establish the range of substance and experience that self-understanding deals with. This approach provides a rationale for later developmental assessments of our subjects' self-statements, in much the same way as any "task analysis" enables the assessment of cognitive problem-solving responses. In Chapter 1 we also discuss our view of why self-understanding requires its own developmental analysis. Our position is that self-understanding poses special conceptual problems for the child quite unlike any other concept, social or otherwise. It therefore has domain-specific properties that diverge even from closely parallel concepts like the understanding of other persons. We therefore follow a "partial structure" approach to exploring this concept and its relations to other domains of knowledge. Finally, we discuss the central problem of conceptual stability in beliefs about the self, and we explain why a developmental approach can help resolve this hotly contested issue in social psychology.

Chapter 2 presents the results of a literature review of previous empirical research on self-understanding. Sources are drawn from biological, personality, and social-cognitive approaches. The purpose of this chapter is twofold – to acknowledge the body of literature that we draw on in composing our own developmental model; and to identify the contributions, omissions, and contradictions in the existing literature that make clear the issues to be addressed in the present investigation.

In Chapter 3 we explain the developmental model that we shall be testing in the remainder of the book. This multidimensional theoretical model encompasses all aspects of the self, from the self-as-subject to the self-as-object. It includes the subject's understanding of the following self-dimensions: one's personal characteristics; the processes by which the self is formed; one's personal agency over future changes; one's self-interest; and one's self-evaluation. The model describes developmental progressions within each of these aspects of self and relates these developmental progressions to one another. The chapter discusses in detail the logic behind this model and the assessments that can be made on the basis of it.

Chapter 4 presents a new clinical interview on the self, designed for use with subjects ranging in age from early childhood to late adolescence. Techniques for administering this interview to such a broad age-range are discussed. In addition, we offer an overall discussion of the rationale for using a clinical interview approach for basic research in social-cognitive development.

In Chapter 4 we also describe our techniques for scoring the self interviews. We present selections from our coding manual and discuss principles that we used to construct the coding scheme. We also describe the guideline that we followed in coding interviews for the studies in this book. Interjudge and test–retest reliability figures for these scoring procedures are presented in Chapters 5 and 6.

Chapter 5 reports results from a series of cross-sectional and longitudinal studies. The focus of this chapter is the "me" aspect of self-understanding, the self conceived as object. The main database is a 4-year longitudinal study with 52 boys and girls. These children ranged in age from 4 to 14 at the beginning of the study, and from 8 to 18 by the final testing. In addition, we have an initial cross-sectional database of 120 children in this age range. Analyses of these data reveal age trends and transitional patterns in subject's self-understanding development. Our discussion of these trends assesses how these data fit our theoretical model. We also shall discuss the implications of these data for general models of transition in social-cognitive development.

The research reported in Chapter 5, 7, 8, and 9, like almost all previous empirical work done on self-conception, focuses primarily on the self-as-object (James's "me"). This is because young subjects more readily speak about their characteristics than about such elusive issues as the self's awareness of its own agency, continuity over time, and distinctness from others, all of which comprise the self-as-subject (James's "I"). In Chapter 6, however, we present an exploratory study into how children and adolescents develop an awareness of these processes. As far as we know, this chapter presents the first systematic empirical look at developmental trends in this central component of self-understanding.

Chapter 7 explores the relation between patterns of adolescent self-understanding and two fairly prevalent mental health problems of youth. In two studies of self-understanding involving respectively a sample of anorexic girls and a sample of boys with conduct disorders, deviations from normal patterns of adolescent self-understanding were observed. Their significance to adolescent adjustment problems is discussed.

Chapter 8 presents a study of self-understanding in a Puerto Rican fishing village. To provide a cross-cultural comparison, our self-understanding interviews were translated into Spanish and given to 48 children, ages 8 through 14, living in a small fishing village on the southern coast of Puerto Rico. The interviews were then scored with our scoring manual (although one new coding category had to be devised for this sample in order to capture the full range of their statements). The results revealed a mixed pattern of similarities and differences between the Puerto Rican sample and the mainland American sample.

Developmentally, the Puerto Ricans followed the same progressions in their self-conceptions as did the mainland U.S. children, and were neither ahead nor behind the mainland children in the majority of their self-reasoning scores. They emphasized, however, aspects of the self seldom mentioned by the mainland children, such as their familial obligations and their community memberships. Further, they deemphasized characteristics that were of high priority for the mainland children, such as their psychological orientations and preferences, their comparative abilities, and their relative popularity. We draw from the anthropological literature to explain these patterns and to identify the kinds of socialization experiences that could account for them.

In Chapter 9, the results from three studies contrasting conceptions of self with other social concepts will be discussed. In the first study, moderate empirical associations are established between self-understanding and the social concepts studied in *The Social World of the Child*. In the second study, self and other interviews were given to 40 boys and girls between the ages of 5 and 10 years. Self and other interviews were scored by comparable criteria drawn from the self scoring manual. The pattern of results revealed some similarities but also some striking developmental differences between the two concepts, as predicted from our theoretical model. Implications of these findings for social-cognitive development in general are drawn.

Some material in this book has appeared previously in journals and book chapters. An early version of the Chapter 2 literature review was published in *Child Development* (W. Damon and D. Hart [1982], "The development of self-understanding from infancy through adolescence," *Child Development* 53: 481–64). Portions of Chapter 5 and Chapter 9 were published in two *Social Cognition* articles (W. Damon and D. Hart [1986], "Stability and change in children's self-understanding," *Social Cognition* 4: 102–18; and D. Hart and W. Damon [1986], "Developmental trends in self-understanding," *Social Cognition* 4: 388–407). Another portion of Chapter 9 appeared in R. Leahy, ed. (1985), *The Development of the Self*, Orlando, Fla.: Academic Press (Copyright © 1985 by Academic Press). The Puerto Rican study in Chapter 8 was first reported in D. Hart, N. Lucca-Irizarry, and W. Damon (1986), "The development of self-understanding in Puerto Rico and the United States," *Journal of Early Adolescence* 6: 293–304.

We are grateful to many sources of help and support during the course of this investigation. Karen Pakula and Jaye Shupin collaborated with us in all phases of pilot testing, manual construction, data collection, and data analysis. Beth Riesman, Beth Rosenbaum, and Michael D'Ascenzo also assisted with the data collection. Julie Maloney contributed valuable ideas and empirical assistance to our sections on the self-as-subject. Mary O'Regan helped with the early phases of data analysis. The research reported in this book was made possible, in part, by grants to William Damon from the Spencer Foundation and to Daniel Hart from the Rutgers Research Council. The data presented, the statements made, and the views expressed are solely the responsibility of the authors.

1 Introduction

Understanding oneself is a fundamental human concern that starts early and continues throughout life. The toddler searching for familiar facial features in a mirror, the teenager brooding over a friend's teasing remark, and the philosopher working through abstract verbal puzzles about personal continuity are all captured by the same intriguing problem – the nature of self. The problem attracts not only intellectual curiosity but the deepest sorts of emotional response. For a conceptual exercise, it bears more than the usual cognitive risks and rewards, for it provides the material for self-judgment and evaluation.

Thoughts and attitudes about oneself form a conceptual system that we call "self-understanding." This system's domain encompasses all the considerations that an individual uses to define the self and distinguish the self from others. Included among these considerations may be (depending on the individual) physical and material qualities (e.g., size, possessions), activities and capabilities (e.g., hobbies, talents), social or psychological characteristics (e.g., manners, habits, dispositions), and philosophical beliefs (e.g., moral values, political ideology).

Further, self-understanding can extend beyond the definition of one's current characteristics to the consideration of one's past and future life directions. It may include notions of how one changes or remains the same over time. Included too may be conceptions of the processes accounting for personal changes, and beliefs about one's own role in shaping or guiding these processes. It even may include reflections on one's own consciousness of selfhood.

As part of its task of distinguishing self from others, self-understanding incorporates one's self-interests and how these may differ from the interests of others. Self-understanding also draws connections between the interests of self and others, defining ways in which mutual self-interests may overlap. Finally, self-understanding includes evaluative insights that provide the cognitive bases for self-esteem, shame and guilt, and personal identity.

In self-understanding, however, unlike other conceptual systems, the self must do the understanding of itself. This situation leads us commonly to make reflexive statements like "I am mad at myself," or "I don't know myself very well." In such seemingly contradictory dualisms, "I" and "myself" are both part of the same "self" that is being understood. As we shall see, philosophers like William James developed intricate schemes to deal with this unique complexity.

Such complexities in self-understanding also have caused social scientists to take some problematic routes exploring this fundamental psychological system. Some investigations have chosen to conflate the meanings of the words self, self-concept, person, and personality, often using them interchangeably in the same analysis. Others have chosen to avoid the construct "self" entirely, denying its independent status as a construct or placing it in its own kind of black box. Because we find neither type of solution adequate for a comprehensive developmental study, we shall attempt in this introduction to draw some semantic boundaries between various related constructs of the self system.

"Self-understanding" disentangled from "self"

In its role as a cognitive organizer of one's life experience, self-understanding provides a sense of continuity across the complexities of context and changes of time. It offers a basis for considering one's jumble of personal experiences as one connected life rather than as many disconnected fragments. Not coincidentally this essential sense of personal continuity is precisely the function that has been assigned to the generic notion "self" by generations of philosophers and psychologists (Allport, 1942; Parfit, 1971; Nozick, 1981; Blasi, 1986). This raises a difficult though critical question that we must address at the outset: Is there a legitimate distinction to be made between "self" and "self-understanding"; or is there so much redundancy between the two that they should be collapsed for the sake of parsimony?

An important tradition within social psychology favors such collapsing (Sarbin, 1952; Epstein, 1973). The argument is that the notion "self" adds nothing to the notion "self-concept" (or self-understanding, as we choose to call it). This is because, the argument goes, "self" is nothing more than the theories that individuals hold about themselves. It is a cognitive–affective construction whose referent is neither observable nor verifiable by anyone else.

Social psychologists point out that the notion "self" typically refers to the personal experience of individuality. The nature of this experience, therefore, is determined mainly by the subject, and is not matter for consensual validation. We cannot, for example, dispute the fact of a person's claiming to have a Napoleonic experience, because whether or not a person feels like Napoleon is ultimately subjective. We may try to persuade him otherwise, perhaps with some effect but perhaps not. We also can step back and objectively determine that the person is not physically the same person as Napoleon, and even that he has a different personality than Napoleon. These are matters for which we can assemble objective evidence. But the self remains a personal construction. Others may offer feedback but cannot determine how the feedback will be interpreted or incorporated.

Because individuals have final definitive power over the natures of the self-experience, many social psychologists believe that self should be treated as nothing but a constructed psychological concept. Just as we have concepts of the weather, of clothing, of love, we have concepts of self. But unlike other concepts, self-concept remains in essence wholly personal and individually defined. Therefore, the referent of self-concept (the self) is no more than the individual's cognitive representation of it. As psychologists, the argument goes, our best choice is to study this cognitive representation (the self-concept) and dispense with the invented (or, at any rate, the redundant) referent (the self).

Sarbin (1962) has been a leading advocate of this position, now widely shared in the social-science community. His position is that the notion of self plays an essential role in organizing our personal experience for us, just as any concept enables us cognitively to manage some segment of the world. Treating "self" in these terms means focusing on the representation rather than the referent. When we analyze human conceptions of God, for example, we need not argue about the nature of God, or even about whether God exists. A similar approach can be used in a psychological analysis of self. In an influential statement, Sarbin wrote:

> The interbehavioral field of the human can include perceptions and cognitions referable to objects in the external world, and perceptions and cognitions referable to his own body, his own statuses, and so on. . . . The self is one such cognitive structure or inference. . . . The self (in common with other cognitive structures) is subject to continual and progressive change, usually in the direction from low-order inferences about simple perceptions to high-order inferences about complex cognitions. (Sarbin, 1962, p. 12)

As a scientific approach, Sarbin's position has obvious advantages in practicality and parsimony. Considering the self to be no more than a concept avoids the problem of trying to study those other aspects of self (if they exist) that may be unobservable. Philosophers have long recognized this problem. Early in the eighteenth century, Hume wrote: "For myself, when I enter most intimately into what I call *myself*, I always stumble on some particular perception or other, of heat or cold, light or shade, love or hatred, pain or pleasure. I never catch *myself* at any time without a perception, and never can observe anything but the perception" (Hume, 1738/1978, p. 252). Hume's statement anticipates a tradition of social theorists (William James for one) who, whatever their beliefs about the nature of self, despaired of ever capturing its essence in a scientifically objectifiable manner.

From our own viewpoint, Sarbin's strategy of collapsing self and self-concept provides a convenient approach, because our experimental interest in any case lies solely in the latter. But, however convenient, this approach comes with certain blinders that must inevitably limit the investigatory vision. The main problem is that, in any strategy where a concept is examined apart from its referent, there can be no true index of the concept's adequacy. That is, if we have absolutely no independent notion of what a "self" is (or even if it exists), how can we determine the quality of an individual's cognitive representation of self? This problem is especially acute for a developmental analysis, where comparisons of adequacy must be made and progress assessed.

The Sarbin solution, as indicated in the quoted excerpt, is to use very general and abstract terms ("high-order"; "complex") to accomplish developmental comparisons of self-concepts. Such terms can be used as an index of any sort of developmental change, from that in cellular systems to that in social organizations. In our own writings on social cognition, we have always opposed such an approach (Damon, 1977, 1979, 1983; Hart and Damon, 1986). Like many other developmental psychologists today, we believe that more is learned from analyses that focus on the special conceptual problems posed by the variety of domains, social and cognitive, that constitute human knowledge (Feldman, 1980; Fischer, 1980; Turiel, 1983; Gardner, 1983; Sternberg, 1984).

As for the concept of self, we share Alston's objection that removing its referent distorts its true status as a concept (Alston, 1977). For the self is not exactly an invented fantasy, like a cartoon figure; nor is it an article of pure faith, like God. Rather, it is a set of experiences that people commonly report, however unreliably. Even if we decide not to study those experiences directly (a choice that we have indeed made in our own investigation), their existence endows their cognitive representations (which we do choose to study) with a core substantive reality.

These self-experiences also can provide us with guidance concerning how to explore and assess their cognitive representations in self-understanding. Accordingly, we believe that our investigation in self-understanding is better informed by an initial consideration of the experience of self than by allowing the self to be wholly swallowed up by its conceptual manifestation.

What is self-understanding the understanding of?

If the notion of "self" cannot be confined to the self-concept, what exactly is the extent of its boundaries? We emphatically state that these boundaries do not coincide with the holistic notions of "person" or "personality." We make this claim emphatically because we believe that a disturbing confusion in certain psychological writings, particularly within the psychoanalytic and ego psychology traditions, has been the conflating of these constructs. If "self" is to mean "person," there is no need for it as a special construct. It can serve an important function only if it is taken to mean a unique aspect of the person not captured by any other construct.

Here we turn to the self theory of William James, still the classic psychological analysis of this elusive concept. James's framework, with some more recent modifications to be discussed, has shaped our investigation from its inception. When we explore the self-understanding of children and adolescents, we focus in large part on their understanding of the experiential territory that James mapped out a century ago.

James divided the self into two main components, the "me" and the "I." The "me" aspect is "the sum total of all a person can call his" (James, 1961/1892, p. 44). The primary elements of the "me" are what James called the "constituents." These constituents are the actual qualities that define the self-as-known. They include all the material characteristics (body, possessions), all the social characteristics (relations, roles, personality), and all the "spiritual" characteristics (consciousness, thoughts, psychological mechanisms) that identify the self as a unique configuration of personal attributes.

James analyzed his three primary constituents in terms of their nature and relation to one another. His suggestion was that each individual organizes the constituents of the "me" into a hierarchical structure that assigns differential value to each of the various material, social, and spiritual constituents. James's assertion was that all individuals hierarchize the basic constituent "me" categories similarly, with "the bodily me at the bottom, the spiritual me at the top, and the extra-corporeal material selves and the various social selves between" (p. 57).

When James writes of individuals organizing their "me" constituents into hierarchies, he is of course referring to individuals' cognitive representations of the "me" aspect of self. This is the place of self-concept in James's theory. As such, it presents a fairly comprehensive notion. It suggests a self-concept that incorporates all aspects of the self that one can objectively know, either through one's own observations or through feedback from others.

For our purposes it is important to note here that this Jamesian version of a self-concept, however comprehensive, did not imply any developmental component. Although James admitted to some individual variation in how the "me" constituents were formulated, he did not recognize the possibility that their hierarchical interrelations might vary significantly across individuals or within one individual over time. Thus, James foresaw no need for developmental comparisons between modes of "me" organization.

James's introduction of the second major aspect of self, the "self-as-I," drives his theory deep into the heart of the self's exclusive domain. For the "I" incorporates precisely those experiential features of self that elude all other constructs. The "I" more than any other aspect of the person requires a special "self" notion to express.

The essence of the "I" is its subjectivity. This translates into an awareness of several core features of individuality, among which are: (1) an awareness of one's agency over life events; (2) an awareness of the uniqueness of one's life experience; (3) an awareness of one's personal continuity; and (4) an awareness of one's own awareness.

The power of James's theory lies in its systematic integration of these four components into a single psychological theory of the self-as-subject. As we later note, other philosophical approaches have highlighted one or the other of these self features, but few have envisioned their interconnections within the subjective experience of individual identity. For this reason, we were drawn to James's framework as our own starting point.

James presented the "I" as the "self-as-knower," the aspect of self that initiates, organizes, and interprets experience in a subjective manner. Individuals are aware of the "I" through four types of experience: agency, distinctness, continuity, and reflection (these are simply other terms for the four "awarenesses" that we just mentioned). Each of these experiences has profound consequences for the individual, particularly in creating the sense of personal identity.

From the sense of agency derives a belief in the autonomy of the self, a conviction that one actively structures and processes one's own experience. From the sense of continuity derives stability of self: As James wrote, "Each of us spontaneously considers that by 'I' he means something always the same" (p. 63). From the sense of distinctness from others derives individuality: "Other men's experiences, no matter how much I may know about them, never bear this vivid, this peculiar brand" (p. 71). From reflection derives the self-consciousness that shapes the personal identity's eventual meaning to oneself.

The "I" and personal identity

For James, the continuity and distinctness components of the "I" coordinate to establish one's sense of personal identity. For James this seemed a serious matter with the gravest of personal consequences. James believed that "the worst alterations of the self" are associated with disruptions in identity fostered by a loss of continuity and distinctness (1948, p. 207).[1]

That contemporary philosophy, drawing more on logical discourse than on psychological analysis, has rediscovered many of these Jamesian insights is noteworthy. This strain of recent philosophical thought has emerged from a lively debate about the essence of personal identity (Shoemaker, 1963; Parfit, 1971a; Williams, 1973; Swinburne, 1973–4; Wiggins, 1980; Nozick, 1981). The debate seems to be resolving itself in a Jamesian fashion, which we take as one sort of conceptual validation of his framework.

A common problem within this debate is the hypothetical brain transplant. There are many variations of this problem. If Person A and Person B switch brains, which body then contains the true Person A? If Person A's brain could be split in two so that both halves could fully regenerate, and if half is then donated to Person B, who then retains the identity of Person A? If Person A has a split-brain operation, and if both halves survive and fully regenerate to create two new people, how can we tell which is Person A (or are both)? What if the original Person A then dies – does this change our assessment? What if one of the persons has characteristics that are more similar to those of Person A, such as Person A's appearance, or all of Person A's memories? Do these considerations make a critical difference for the identities of Person A or B? If not, do other considerations make a difference?

In general, the point of contention is what exact quality or qualities account for the essence of an individual's personal identity. To test various positions, a number of possible personal transformations (including near destruction) have been imagined in order to determine whether identity is still maintained under such conditions. This strategy makes possible a logical determination of the necessary and sufficient conditions for the establishment and survival of personal identity.

Philosophers have advanced a number of solutions to this problem, ranging from ones centering on the material presence of brain and body matter to ones centering on memory and the experience of selfhood (Williams, 1970; Shoemaker & Swinburne, 1984). From our reading of this literature, the experience of selfhood positions seem to be winning the day (Parfit, 1971a, 1971b; Nozick, 1981; Shoemaker & Swinburne, 1984). Further, selfhood is increasingly discussed in terms of dimensions like continuity and distinctness. The following statement by Derek Parfit is an example of this trend: "Judgments of personal identity have great importance. What gives them their importance is the fact that they imply psychological continuity" (Parfit, 1971b, p. 12).

From a psychological viewpoint, perhaps the most appealing solution within this tradition is that proposed by Nozick. According to his "closest continuer" theory (Nozick, 1981), the sense of personal identity over time is based on two determinations: first, whether the future self is causally related to the present self, and second, whether the future self is unique. For a person to believe that she will be the same person five years from now, she must suppose that the person who she will be in the future will develop out of the person that she is now. She also must believe that she will grow into one and only one person in the future. Thus, in Nozick's view, a belief in self-continuity combines with belief in self-distinctness to create the experience of personal identity.

The personal importance of the identity experience goes far beyond the logical niceties through which scholars debate this philosopher's riddle. People have great emotional stakes in the belief that each maintains one and only one identity defining the essence of one's existence. The common expression of this emotional stake is the pervasive sentiment that one never wishes actually to become another person despite the relative disadvantage of one's situation in comparison with that of the other. One might wish to exchange *conditions* with someone who is richer, more powerful, healthier, luckier, and so on; but one rarely, if ever, expresses the wish to *become* the other. We sense that becoming another would result in the loss of one's status as a unique individual, and thus in the loss of existence itself. So, like philosophers, we "persons-on-the-street" hold dear the notion of personal identity. For all of us, self-continuity and uniqueness provide some plausible conceptual pillars in support of this notion.

The "I" and the existential self

As we have suggested, however, even well-worked and compelling philosophical positions like Parfit's or Nozick's lack the range of James's self theory. In these cases what is missing are the two other Jamesian dimensions of self-as-subject – agency and reflection. Some contemporary philosophers stress precisely these dimensions (e.g., Sartre, 1947), but they belong to a tradition that focuses on the *existential* functions of self-as-subject rather than on the *personal identity* functions. Consequently, their tradition emphasizes agency and reflection at the expense of continuity and distinctness. In one recent psychologically oriented statement of this position, Blasi (1986, p. 18) writes: "The self is that aspect of the person which is experienced, in that lived awareness that accompanies any intentional actions, as the agentic center of the actions and as other than, or opposite to, the actions' objects and their other causes, and from which originates the experience of identity with oneself that characterizes reflection."

We see, therefore, components of the Jamesian theory of self incorporated throughout modern philosophical thought, but James's own version remains by far the most comprehensive. It presents the subjective self (the "I") as a coordinated, fourfold experience of agency, continuity, distinctness, and reflection. In addition, it includes an objective self (the "me") that forms the basis of self-concept. We take note of the many overlaps between James's vision and more recent philosophical analysis, but our research in self-understanding is guided more by the broader sweep of the former.

Our answer, therefore, to the question that began this section is that self-understanding is the understanding of the self as generally outlined by William James and his followers. Does that mean that, with James, we focus simply on the "me" as the embodiment of "self-as-known"? For, after all, James solved the problem of self-concept by consigning it to the objective self and leaving the self-as-subject (the "I") in the realm of the practically unknowable.

Here we depart somewhat from James's approach. In his own writings, James advocated avoiding the "I" for the purposes of empirical study because of the "I"'s indeterminate nature. Of course, observing or characterizing a phenomenon that is totally subjective and, as a result, may change unpredictably from moment to moment is difficult. Also, unlike the somewhat circumscribed nature of the "me" (which consists of a definable collection of definitions that one and others construct for one's self), the "I" enters into all of a person's interactions with the world. It determines the very meaning of all life events, because it influences a person's interpretation of every encountered person, place, or experience and even provides itself with a reflection on itself. James's conclusion was that inquiry into the "I" was best left to philosophy or religion, and that psychologists interested in self-concept should focus on the "me."

But some years later, George Herbert Mead proposed an important modification to James's position (Mead, 1934). Mead's modification suits our present purposes well, because it grants some access to the subjective self for the study of self-understanding. Mead suggested approaching the "I" through the "me" by studying individuals' *knowledge* of both their objective and subjective selves. This, of course, is not the same as studying the actual *experience* of the subjective self. But it does broaden the domain of self-understanding beyond the circumscribed "me" to include at least conceptual knowledge of the "I." Another way of expressing this idea is to say that the Jamesian "me" in this new definition becomes a bit enlarged in order to incorporate some vital intellectual sense of the "I."

In this most comprehensive definition, which we shall adopt as the framework of our investigation, self-understanding is an individual's knowledge of the self-as-object as well as of the self-as-subject; of the self-as-known as well as of the self-as-knower; of the "me" as well as of the "I." The reason that we adopt the term "self-understanding" rather than "self-concept" is to make this inclusiveness clear; for traditionally self-concept has referred solely to the James's "me" (with James himself setting the precedent).

In other words, self-understanding in our usage starts with an individual's self-definition, the domain of the Jamesian "me." But it also includes the individual's conception of the self-as-subject, in particular the individual's understanding of his or her agency, continuity, distinctness, and reflection. It does not, however, include the actual "I" itself, because the self-as-subject extends well beyond the realm of self-understanding to the entire domain of psychological functioning. This definition of self-understanding as a person's conceptions of objective and subjective self is the definition that we shall use throughout this book.

We have thus far discussed the distinctions and the common features between a number of related concepts: self, person, personality, self-concept, and self-understanding.

In scientific writing it is critical to use each of these constructs for its own unique semantic purposes, noninterchangeably with any other. It is also critical to coordinate these constructs so that the specific meaning of each is informed by the precise meanings of the others.

This need is particularly true in distinguishing between "self-understanding" and its referent "self." The reason that we have spent so much space in this chapter defining these two constructs is that we wish to show that our methodological choices in this investigation are not at all arbitrary. Rather, our questionnaires and coding schemes are based on a certain formulation of the "self" and "self-understanding" territory, a formulation that we believe to be conceptually sound. Unlike the perennial graduate school joke about the construct intelligence and the IQ test, we decidedly do *not* take self-understanding to be definable only as something that is measured by the Damon–Hart self-understanding instrument.

Self-understanding and social cognition

There is a tendency in psychology to polarize approaches to intelligence into two camps: One assumes the interconnectedness of all forms of knowing and the other assumes the particularistic nature of all information. The former looks for structure, positing general principles of cognitive organization, whereas the latter performs task analyses, inferring content-specific rules of learning.

In actuality, however, much of the interesting work in cognitive psychology ascribes fully to neither camp, but rather ranges across a middle position between the two. We place in this "middle ground" all approaches that recognize specificity with divergent domains of knowledge while at the same time looking for general organizing principles within and across domains. Only these approaches can be called "interactional," for they are the only ones committed to the assumption that the knowledge is shaped *both* by features of the environment and by features of the cognizing subject.

Such approaches are well represented in the contemporary developmental literature. Gardner's "multiple intelligences" work, Sternberg's "tripartite theory," writings by Fischer, Feldman, Turiel, and others all reflect attempts to sort out specificity from generality in cognitive development (Fischer, 1980; Feldman, 1980; Turiel, 1983; Gardner, 1983; Sternberg, 1984). Even Piaget, whose theory for many has seemed synonymous with the notion of holistic structure, was very much an interactionist in this regard. He wrote: "I must emphasize that (cognitive) systems are merely partial systems with respect to the whole organism or mind. The concept of structure does not imply just any kind of totality and does not mean that everything is attached to everything else" (Piaget, 1967, p. 143).

We make this point because, when analyzing self-concept, cognitive psychology has treated it much like any other aspect of social (or, for that matter, nonsocial) cognition. Analyses of self-understanding have been limited to dimensions that apply to the understanding of other persons, or even to the understanding of the world in general. The result has been a host of studies showing that self-concepts, like other concepts, become more complex, abstract, differentiated, organized, and so on, with development.

This perspective can be useful, and we shall review the most informative of these studies in the next chapter. But self-understanding cannot be adequately captured without a focus on the particular features of this unique cognitive system. Although it is necessary for us to realize the ways in which self-understanding overlaps with other areas of social and non-social cognition, we must not lose sight of the ways in which it occupies a special place among human intellectual activities.

To begin with, there are important differences between social and non-social cognition; and self-understanding lies firmly within the realm of social cognition. Further, among social concepts, self-understanding is unique for both functional and structural reasons. Being a social concept, self-understanding does indeed share certain features common to all social concepts; and, being a concept, it shares certain other (less immediate) features common to concepts in general. But it also embodies thought processes not available in any other form of knowledge.

The distinction between social and nonsocial cognition, until recently a strange notion to cognitive psychology, is finally becoming accepted, at least within the developmental community. In large part this is because the past decade has seen a host of new research findings on children's social concepts. At first, the awakened interest in children's social cognition was spurred by developmentalists wondering how well the great theoretical insights established by cognitive psychology apply to children's reasoning about their everyday lives. Accordingly, researchers operating within the frameworks of Piaget, Bruner, Vygotsky, Werner, Simon, and others created a lively field of "social-cognitive development." This field has flourished particularly in the areas of children's conceptions of persons, social relations (like friendship or authority), societal institutions (like government or money), moral rules, others' perspectives, and children's referential communication skills (Shantz, 1983).

Although these recent studies in social cognition have borrowed in design and analysis from prior work on intellectual growth in general, many new findings have required revision of, or even departure from, the old models. In fact, many have come to agree that the study of social understanding cannot be derived from the study of logical or nonsocial reasoning (Peters, 1974; Turiel, 1975, 1983; Glick & Clark-Stewart, 1978; Damon, 1979, 1983; Feldman, 1980; Gardner, 1983). Rather, it seems that a model of social cognition demands its own unique categories, functional rules, and other specifically defined principles of conceptual organization. This approach is necessary if the model is to capture those features of social interaction that are substantially different from physical interaction.

For example, one such feature that distinguishes social from physical events is the mutuality of conduct and communication between persons.

Unlike inanimate objects, other people have the capacity intentionally to establish relations with one another. In the intentional relations, persons share perspectives and coordinate interpersonal interactions. From the earliest days of life, the child recognizes and begins to operate in the context of this intentionally relational aspect of social life (Bruner, 1973; Trevarthen, 1974, 1977; Damon, 1983b). Consequently, the focus of social-cognitive research has become increasingly relational, directed at interpersonal transactions rather than at static social "objects" (Youniss, 1975; Damon, 1977, 1983b; Selman, 1980; Fischer, 1980; Butterworth & Light, 1982; Shantz, 1983).

All of this has resulted in great strides forward in the study of social cognition, though at uneven paces. Not all aspects of the social world have been given the same attention. In particular, the self has been relatively neglected by research in social-cognitive development. As Brim wrote a decade ago (and the situation has changed only marginally since), "When one turns to the child development research literature to read about the origin and development of the young child's theories of self in relation to the world, it yields little" (Brim, 1976, p. 245). Some exceptions will be reviewed in the next chapter, but by and large Brim's statement remains fairly accurate.

For progress to be made in self-understanding research, it will be necessary to recognize the common and distinct features of this conceptual system as compared with other aspects of social cognition. Certainly there are legitimate comparisons to be made between understanding self and understanding others, just as there are radical differences, as we will discuss in Chapter 9. For now we note that we assume self-understanding to be unique among social concepts in two ways – functional and structural.

Functionally, as discussed earlier in this chapter, self-understanding serves as the cognitive representation of personal identity. It provides the conceptual basis for one's status as a unique individual within the social network. In this sense, self-understanding serves a differentiation function more naturally than other social concepts. Unlike, for example, concepts of relations (like friendship or authority) or of regulations (like social rules, conventions, or justice), all of which rationalize one's connection to others within a social network, self-understanding explains one's distinctness.

In so doing, self-understanding supports individuation, which stands with socialization as one of the two main pillars of social development (see Damon, 1983a, for a further discussion). It provides a necessary complement to the integrating forces of collective living. To make this crucial contribution, self-understanding must work in a special way.

Self-understanding's special mode of operation is defined by its unique structural features. The most salient of these is the "I"–"me" dualism described earlier in this chapter. Alone among social concepts, self-understanding necessarily revolves around notions of "reflexivity": the self must be understood both as the subjective knower and as the object of knowledge. We have already indicated how this peculiar characteristic of self-understanding creates the conceptual conditions for personal identity and individuation.

Beyond this central dualism, several other features distinguish self-understanding from other social concepts. There are also features that provide important links, particularly to the understanding of persons in general. We shall discuss both types of features in greater depth in Chapters 3 and 9. For now we shall simply let stand our general assertion of self-understanding's uniqueness as a conceptual system.

Self-understanding and self-esteem

In this book we define self-understanding as one's cognitive representation of self, self-interest, and personal identity. It is well recognized, by us and many others, that self, self-interest, and personal identity all have important affective components as well. In fact, psychological research generally has stressed the affective components of self-concept in lieu of the cognitive ones, especially developmental self-concept research. Studies of children's self-conceptions by and large have been dominated by a focus on self-esteem (Wylie, 1979; Harter, 1983). In such studies, the concern is with the positive or negative valence of a child's self-regard, rather than with how the child defines and understands the self.

Because self-esteem is an affective orientation, it has been measured in psychological studies with a view to its direction and strength. Does a child value the self positively or negatively, and how much so? Psychological measurement of children's self-conceptions, therefore, have been largely quantitative in character.

But the intellectual basis of self-concept, self-understanding, is a cognitive activity that must be assessed in qualitative terms. People do not simply harbor a "positive" or "negative" understanding of themselves: rather, their beliefs about self have a substance and a shape. Asking "how much" understanding a person has does not approach the critical question of *how* the self is understood. Without an account of the cognitive processes that people use in construing the nature of self, there can be no satisfactory analysis of self-concept.

Why have psychologists so often chosen to approach the study of children's self-concept through an affective and quantitative dimension like esteem rather than through a qualitative cognitive framework like understanding? Part of the answer lies in psychologists' unfortunate preference for dimensions that can be easily reduced to numbers rather than to descriptive categories. Another, and more justifiable, part of the answer is the long-standing assumption among child psychologists and educators that children's self-feelings are implicated in children's social relations, school performances, and mental health (Rosenberg, 1979). Mainly because of this practical issue, child psychologists have operationalized self-concept through the quantitative measurement of self-esteem.

Accordingly, the field of child psychology abounds with self-esteem scales. Some (e.g., Rosenberg, 1965) tap children's global assessments of their own self-worth, as reflected by how strongly children agree or disagree with statements like "On the whole I am satisfied with myself." Others (e.g., Coopersmith, 1967; Piers & Harris, 1969) assess children's feelings about a series of designated self-attributes, some specific and some general ("I am popular"; "I am a good person"). In a gesture toward developmentalism, some scale designers have been careful to select items that are comprehensible across a broad age range, thus avoiding a common earlier mistake of applying adult-appropriate items to populations of young children (Wylie, 1974).

But none of the existing self-esteem scales allows for variations in the meaning of self. The conceptual basis of children's self-evaluations differ from individual to individual, and is certain to change dramatically in the course of development. No self-esteem measure, as currently constructed, is prepared to recognize this variation. Consequently, self-esteem scales can do little more than assess a child's feelings about an indeterminate "something" of unknown meaning.

This failing has borne ill results; for, despite the seemingly central role of children's self-esteem, psychologists have not succeeded in using it as a strong predictor of anything else. Wylie concludes her definitive review of the self-concept literature with the complaint that "the most impressive thing which emerges from an overview of this book is the widespread occurrence of null or weak findings" in studies relating self-esteem to achievement, interpersonal relations, and a host of other antecedent or consequent variables (Wylie, 1979, p. 690). This assessment is particularly true in child studies. Wylie points out that these nonfindings fly in the face of our widely shared intuitive beliefs that self-regard is importantly connected with many aspects of adaptation to life. In this area, she writes, "theory and conventional wisdom very confidently predict strong trends" (Wylie, 1979, p. 690).

What, then, has interfered with what should be a straightforward attempt to establish empirical relations between self-esteem and other critical life variables? Wylie herself suspects the methodological inadequacies inherent in existing self-esteem scales. We agree, but identify the culprit more specifically as lack of attention in such scales to the changing conceptual bases of self for the growing child. Self-esteem measurement requires a developmental model to ensure that the test items in its inventory reflect the manner in which the concept of self is reorganized over time. Failing such a model, there can be no valid assessment of self-esteem, and consequently no illuminating empirical studies. Self-esteem can be neither assessed nor studied independently of self-understanding, as generations of child psychologists have attempted to do.

A developmental approach to self-understanding

A developmental model of self-understanding is important for many reasons beyond the valid assessment of self-esteem. As noted earlier, contemporary writers on cognitive development have argued that all social concepts must be analyzed on their own terms if they are to be properly understood (Damon, 1977, 1979; Feldman, 1979; Fischer, 1980; Flavell & Ross, 1981; Gardner, 1984). The concept of self is a fundamental organizer of one's social world. It alone provides one with the conceptual means for distinguishing oneself from other in society. In this way, it establishes the cognitive grounds for an individual's unique role, status, and position in the social network – in short, for personal identity, as analyzed within psychology most prominently by Erikson (1950, 1968).

Though not the whole of personal identity, self-understanding provides its rational underpinnings. Like self-esteem, personal identity has important affective components that go beyond the conceptual understanding of self. And, as with the self-esteem literature, most writings on identity formation have emphasized its affective components to the expense of its cognitive ones.

Erikson, for example, uses words like "sense," "will," "resolution," and "emotional orientation" in describing the process of identity formation. James Marcia defines it as "a dynamic organization of drives, abilities, beliefs, and individual history" (Erikson, 1968; Marcia, 1980). Stressing the dynamic and affective properties of identity in this way has provided personality theorists with a means for explaining normal and disturbed behavioral patterns, but it has left unanswered many developmental questions. In particular, we still know almost nothing about how children come to understand the complex experience of their own individuality, or about how the nature of this understanding changes with development.

How does a child organize the many diverse features of self (if indeed the child even recognizes them all)? How can a child grasp the notion that the self changes constantly yet still retains its identity over time; that it is shaped by external forces while still under one's own control; that it is known as an object at the same time as it is known as a subject? How does the young child's understanding of these difficult enigmas change as the child's conceptual capacities grow? These questions can only be answered by a developmental approach to self-understanding.

A developmental approach begins with an analysis of the cognitive processes that constitute self-understanding and proceeds to outline their developmental course. The personal-identity literature has shown us some affective and behavioral outcomes of these cognitive processes, but has left the processes and their development unexamined. Such an examination is the purpose of the present book.

A developmental approach to self-understanding has several implications. First, of course, it means looking to age trends as a primary data source, and we shall do so in both cross-sectional and longitudinal studies. Second, it also means qualitative rather than merely quantitative analyses of these age trends. We have discussed elsewhere why this is necessary for social-cognitive study generally (Damon, 1977). In the present work, we more fully explicate the issue in Chapter 3, where we present our stage model for self-understanding development.

Finally, a developmental perspective must focus on organization and reorganization over time. With such a focus, developmentalists have shown that apparent discontinuities in behavior or thought really can be seen as systemic stability (Jessor, 1983; Sroufe & Rutter, 1984). In social-cognitive study, one technique that allows investigators access to organizational features of thought is the clinical interview, especially when it is linked to scoring procedures based on organizing principles of thought. We shall discuss these matters more fully in Chapter 4. In our own investigation we use such techniques to pursue the stability amidst change that characterizes self-understanding development during childhood and adolescence.

Note

1 Like Erikson long after him, James saw adolescence as the period of life during which identity meets its critical test through such a threatened loss. James himself was acutely aware of the affective implications of this test. He described his own lifelong search for identity as (in his case) an especially difficult struggle to maintain a sense of continuity and distinctness (James, 1910).

2 Previous developmental theory and research

Self-understanding has been studied many times in developmental psychology, under titles like "self-awareness," "self-knowledge," "self-recognition," "self-concept," or (as we noted in Chapter 1) "self." Often such studies have been driven by purposes and assumptions quite different from our own social-cognitive perspective. A few, on the other hand, have used an explicitly social-cognitive approach, directly paving the way for our own investigation. We have made extensive use of both types of earlier work, in some cases because the contrasts have helped us sharpen our own approach and in other cases because the actual insights have contributed to the developmental model of self-understanding that we shall present in Chapter 4. In the current chapter we discuss this background material, beginning with developmental approaches differing from our own and then reviewing the small body of prior social-cognitive studies.

Psychoanalytic writings

Of all branches of psychological theory, psychoanalysis is the most sensitive to the interplay between cognition and affect. Consequently, most psychoanalysts refuse to distinguish between "self" and "self-concept," choosing instead to refer to a composite self with both a reflective awareness and an array of energized traits. Although, as discussed in Chapter 1, we believe it essential to distinguish self and self-concept from one another, we nevertheless have found certain psychoanalytic writings on the self to be informative for our own self-understanding work. Our debt to Erikson's theory is clear from Chapter 1. But an even more detailed psychoanalytic model of self-development can be found in the work of Margaret Mahler (Mahler, Pine, & Bergman, 1975).

Mahler has described the development of self and self-awareness as a process of separation and individuation over three main phases and several

18

subphases. At the outset, during the "normal autistic" phase (0 to 2 months), the infant has little knowledge of, and little sensitivity to, the external world. The infant's awareness is dominated by internal sensations and tensions arising from physiological needs. The infant mistakenly believes that the gratification of all these needs stems directly from actions of the self. By the end of this phase, however, the infant learns to distinguish need reductions resulting from internal regulations from those that are a consequence of something outside of the self.

Mahler called the second step in self-development the "symbiotic phase" (2 to 5 months). According to Mahler, "the essential feature of symbiosis is hallucinatory or delusional somatopsychic (omnipotent) fusion with the representation of the mother and, in particular, the delusion of a common boundary between two physically separate individuals" (Mahler et al., 1975, p. 45). The infant in this phase includes the mother within its boundaries of self, due to the depth of its physiological dependence and affective involvement with the mother. Accompanying the growing attachment to the mother is the gradual turning outward toward the world of the perceptual system. The infant is increasingly becoming attuned to the sights, smells, and sounds of the surrounding environment.

The final step in Mahler's developmental sequence is called the "separation–individuation" phase (6 months and older), which is divided into three subphases. In the first subphase, "differentiation," the infant becomes markedly more alert, attentive, persistent, and goal directed than before. It is possible for the first time to witness the first tentative steps in the lengthy process of constructing a self-perimeter that does not include the mother:

The beginnings of the infant's awareness of separation can be observed in such behavior as pulling at mother's hair, ears, and nose, putting food into the mother's mouth, and straining the body away from mother in order to have a better look at her. This is in contrast to the earlier mode of simply molding into mother when held. . . . By six or seven months the infant's tactile and visual exploration of the mother's body has clearly started the child's differentiation of self from mother. (Mahler et al., 1975, p. 54)

In Mahler's view, the mother's style of interacting with the child determines whether this initial differentiation occurs at a developmentally appropriate time. She offers some clinical vignettes like the following to illustrate her claim:

We also observed children who had a rather unsatisfactory symbiotic relationship because of the mother's great ambivalence toward her child and toward her own role as a mother. . . . These infants, as if compensatorily, knew (differentiated from) their mothers rather early; their relationship improved when greater distance made it more comfortable and when new sources for pleasure in their growing autonomy and in the outside world became available. (Mahler et al., 1975, p. 59)

Like many psychoanalysts, Mahler sees ideal developmental progress as difficult to obtain without appropriate maternal care, which in turn is difficult to provide if the mother is beset by emotional conflicts. Thus, although the infant can demonstrate resilience, deviations from the ideal developmental path are fraught with danger.

The "practicing subphase" (from 12 to 18 months) follows the differentiation subphase. During this phase, Mahler believes "The toddler takes the greatest step in human individuation. He walks freely with upright posture" (Mahler et al., 1975, p. 71). Walking upright enables the child to expand his or her sphere of exploration greatly and also contributes to the infant's growing sense of personal competence and autonomy.

Walking also allows the child to move away from the mother more readily. Mahler claims that in her observations of the first steps of children, almost all first steps are directed *away from* the mother. The child ventures away from the mother to explore the world and practice independence, but returns on a regular basis for "emotional refueling." Walking away from the mother provides the infant "the elated escape from fusion with, from engulfment by, mother" (p. 71), whereas return to her after short periods of separation "reassures him that mother will want to catch him and swoop him up in her arms" (p. 71).

The next step in the individuation–separation process is the third subphase, "rapprochement" (from 18 to 24 months). The growth of autonomous functioning, more frequent and more distant trips away from the mother, and the development of more sophisticated cognitive functioning contribute to the child's delineation of a self separate from the mother. Also characterizing rapprochement, however, is a fear of this independence and separateness. Cognitive development brings with it, in addition to a growing awareness of separateness between self and mother, an awareness of the self's profound limitations.

According to Mahler, the sense that the self is ill-prepared to face the world on its own leads the infant to attempt to retain its psychic fusion with mother, in order to share the mother's omnipotence. This subphase, then, is an emotional roller coaster for the child: Development leads both to growing independence and to an instinctive fear of it.

Again the mother plays a central role in the healthy development of her infant's self-awareness. The mother must be able to endure the child's emotional ups and downs. To encourage the child's independence, the mother must be able to handle her own feelings of rejection that may result from her child's growing self-reliance. Without this encouragement, Mahler believes it may be difficult for the infant to successfully master the central conflict of the rapprochement subphase.

The fourth and final period of the separation–individuation process is called the "consolidation of personality" subphase that is brought about by "emotional object constancy." For our purposes here, the critical defining characteristic of this subphase is the infant's final attainment of a positive image of self separate from that of mother.

Contributing to this development is the development of object permanence and mental representation in the Piagetian sense. With the development of mental representations, the child is able to develop and maintain stable images of self and other. This capability better enables the child to endure periods of physical separation from the mother, because the mental image can be substituted for direct emotional satisfaction. The child's clear separation from the mother in combination with this ability to manage one's thoughts and feelings through mental representations permits the child to develop an initial image of self that serves as the basis for the development of personality and individuality.

Mahler's model provides us with a graphic description of the challenges and achievements of early self-knowledge. It offers some intriguing insights and many hypotheses worth testing. Mahler's own writings, however, have been criticized on a number of empirical and conceptual grounds. Empirically, her claims suffer from a dearth of replicated (or replicable) observations. Discerning the exact basis on which Mahler assigns infants to the different phases and subphases is difficult. Nor does Mahler present information (quantitative or otherwise) regarding the sequential nature of the self phases, their empirical relation to age, or their association to other early psychological processes.

Consequently, evaluating Mahler's overall model is difficult. Harter (1983) has suggested that Mahler's theory reveals more about what the mother does to foster the child's development of self than about the process of self-development. Even in this regard, however, the types of interactions that are presumed healthy or not healthy for the child are described in such global terms that it seems impossible to specify unambiguously their behavioral manifestations. Further, many of Mahler's more specific claims regarding maternal care and consequent developmental outcomes appear to be wrong (Campos et al., 1983).

Most important for our present purposes, Mahler and her co-workers apparently experienced problems in reliably identifying particular patterns of behavior that reveal progress through their hypothesized phases of self-development. Thus, they were unable to develop rating scales or coding schemes to assess such progress and test the empirical relations presumed in Mahler's theory (Mahler et al., 1975).

Biologically oriented approaches

In recent discussions, Jerome Kagan (1981) has attributed the initial emergence of self-awareness to inborn biological mechanisms that mature late in infancy. Kagan's biological view strongly deemphasizes the importance of the social environment in the genesis of the child's capacity for self-knowledge.

Basic to Kagan's position is the postulate that self-knowledge naturally arises in the child as a result of neurological maturation and its consequent impact on psychological functioning. Hence, self-knowledge is seen as a maturational inevitability as opposed to a social-interactional achievement. Although Kagan's view has not garnered much empirical support as of this writing, the growing influence of biological approaches in developmental psychology suggests that confirmatory research will be attempted before long.

Kagan's theory – an attempt to link the growth of self-awareness to the structure of the brain and to the changes that the brain undergoes with age – was spurred by the following kind of observation. In a study of late infancy, Kagan and his co-workers observed a reaction on the part of twenty-month-old infants that they had never seen in younger infants. Unlike younger infants, the older ones cried when observing an experimenter perform a behavior so complex that it would be impossible for the infant to imitate it.

According to Kagan, the infants realized that they were not capable of repeating the action, became frustrated, and then cried. Younger infants, unaware of their own capabilities, did not cry when they observed the behavior because they did not know before trying that they were incapable of repeating it. Kagan believes that this sort of developmental phenomenon requires a maturational explanation, because there is (to him) no obvious interactional feedback that could explain how twenty-month-old infants acquire the ability to anticipate their own capacities and incapacities.

Kagan believes that there are a few underlying skills whose growth during infancy is responsible for self-awareness. First, like Mahler, Kagan believes that representational abilities are critical: Without mental symbols to represent absent objects, the self could not be known, because it is seldom seen. Second, Kagan believes the ability to hold these symbols in active memory is also essential:

A central change characteristic of this period of growth is the ability to sustain ideas and action plans. The psychological stage on which schemata interact and guide action does not collapse every half-minute or so. As a result, the child does not forget the goals he is pursuing, he asks his mother for help if he is unsuccessful, and he smiles upon attaining a self-generated goal. Perhaps what we have been calling self-awareness is better regarded as the capacity to hold cognitive representations on the stage of active memory. (Kagan, 1981, pp. 138–9)

To explain the development of representation and of the ability to maintain mental representations in active memory, Kagan points to three neurological changes that occur at approximately the time that self-knowledge appears. First, Kagan suggests that the development of the neurons, more specifically the dendrites that conduct impulses to the cell body, are not mature enough in early infancy to support mental representation and its active memorization. Second, myelination of the association areas and intracortical plexuses is too incomplete to allow these two skills to emerge. Kagan implicates the infant's later acquisition of mature neuronal density (neurons per unit volume) in the development of these skills. Physiological studies have shown that this normally occurs at about 15 months.

Kagan takes pains to distinguish his biological view of self-knowledge development from the social-interactional approach that we shall elaborate later in this chapter and throughout the rest of this book. Consistent with his biological view, Kagan claims that the genesis of self-awareness is a relatively rapid acquisition once neurological development has advanced sufficiently. The fact that most psychologists assume self-awareness to be a lifelong process reflects nothing more than a cultural artifact, Kagan suggests. Western bias, he writes, commonly produces scientific resistance to claims for the rapid emergence of important skills: "Western scientists prefer to impose gradualism on all instances of change" (Kagan, 1981, p. 145).

Kagan's admission that self-knowledge at times may be affected by social interaction is very different than saying that it arises from it (a claim made by Baldwin, Mead, and their contemporary followers). Here Kagan distinguishes the acquisition of a basic capacity from environmentally induced variations in that capacity. For example, although variations in mother–child interactions can make one 2-year-old typically speak in five-word sentences and another in single words, it does not follow that these same events create the basic capacity for speech. To claim this, Kagan writes, would be to imply that an infant who experiences no social interaction will not grow psychologically, despite observations like Buhler's (1930) report of swaddled Albanian children who quickly attained normative milestones when they were unbandaged (pp. 141–2). In like fashion, Kagan suggests that the genesis of self-awareness is not dependent on social-environmental conditions, but rather that it is an inevitable consequence of neuronal maturation.

Whether Kagan offers his biological theory as an adequate explanation in itself or merely as an antidote to the biases he perceives in Western developmental psychology is difficult to discern. In either case, there are several significant problems with his theory. Specifically, there is little evidence to connect the cognitive developments noted by Kagan to the neurological changes he offers as responsible for the changes. For instance, although dendrites have relatively few branches at birth in the human infant and undergo rapid branching in infancy, dendritic branching itself is unlikely to explain the acquisition of the skills necessary for self-knowledge. The branching of the dendrites is most pronounced during the first 6 months of life, and continues well beyond the age of 24 months (Goldman-Rakic et al., 1983). To argue that self-knowledge is a consequence of dendritic branching is to claim that some (apparently arbitrary) degree of branching occurring well after the end of the most rapid period of dendritic branching development but before dendritic branching is completed is the determining factor in the emergence of important cognitive skills.

Nor has myelinization been shown to be related to the development of any specific functions, even though the degree of myelinization is a rough index of overall neurological development (Parmelee & Sigman, 1983). For instance, Humphrey (1964) reports that in some cases functions may precede myelinization of the neurons involved in the functions, whereas in others myelinization "has appeared in late developing tracts such as the cortical spinal long before there is any evidence of function" (p. 113). At this point, there is little persuasive evidence that neurological myelinization is prerequisite for the development of any specific skills.

Finally, Kagan's claim that adult neuronal density is necessary for the development of mental representations and the maintenance in active memory of those mental representations is subject to similar criticisms. Reviewers have concluded that the number of neurons in the brain at any particular point in neurological development has unknown consequences for behavior (Parmelee & Sigman, 1983) and that synaptic density is not linearly related to functional capacity (Goldman-Rakic et al., 1983). Again, the current state of knowledge regarding the relationship between specific cognitive achievements and specific neurological developments is too limited to permit a persuasive claim in favor of the neurological underpinnings of self-knowledge.

Kagan's argument that self-knowledge directly depends upon particular neurological developments must be characterized as speculative at this point. Too little is known about how age-related changes in the brain are related to the acquisition of specific skills and abilities. Nonetheless, Kagan's biological-deterministic theory may be useful in counterpoint to theories (like Mahler's) that tend to neglect maturation entirely. No doubt certain deficits in self-awareness during early infancy eventually will be linked to neurological immaturity, although we remain skeptical that this will ever suffice as a sole explanation.

Further, Kagan's claim that self-awareness emerges rapidly at 15 months with neuronal maturation seems untenable in light of other research on infant cognition. Studies of infant bodily self-recognition, for example, have painted quite a different picture. Research within the Gibsonian tradition has found multiple evidence of self-discovery far earlier than 15 months. One review concludes that "infants' discovery of their bodily self is not a single unified process. Nor is there any magic moment when self-awareness suddenly emerges" (Harris, 1983, p. 747). When the many other aspects of self-understanding are considered with bodily self-awareness, an even more pluralistic and elongated process emerges.

Finally, Kagan explicitly concerns himself only with the *capacity* for self-awareness and not with the form or substance of self-knowledge as it actually functions during the various periods of development. Even if we granted Kagan's biological view of this capacity's emergence – which we do not – we would still have much to learn about how infants, children, adolescents, and adults understand themselves. Clearly the nature of one's self-concept is deeply influenced by social feedback. Whatever the contribution of maturation to the human self-knowing capacity, when we analyze the individual's self-knowledge we are confronted with a system that evolves throughout life in accord with the individual's continual interaction with the social environment. This analysis requires something more complex than a one-step biological model.

Social-cognitive approaches

Social-cognitive theory began with the writings of James Mark Baldwin (1902). His account of infant self-discovery influenced a host of later theorists and researchers who shared Balwin's assumption that knowledge of oneself can only be constructed through social interaction.

In his own theorizing, Baldwin chose imitation as the key social process in self-development, a choice that created a problematic legacy. Most troublesome to us is its implication that self-knowledge follows directly from knowledge of others, and thus that it is formed and shaped in much the same way. We believe that this implication has misguided much subsequent social-cognitive research on self-understanding. In our Chapter 9 discussion of contrasts between self- and other-understanding, we shall take up in detail this matter as well as Baldwin's particular theoretical legacy.

For now we focus on research that has, directly or indirectly, come out of the social-cognitive tradition that Baldwin originated. Our purpose here is to present a chronology of self-understanding development as portrayed by social-cognitive research, which we organize in three sections: infancy, childhood, and adolescence.

In this chronology, we wish to provide an overview of the field's current state of knowledge to reveal the ongoing confusions and controversies concerning how self-understanding develops. By providing this background, we can clarify the rationale behind our own conceptual and methodological choices. It also will help us, in the end, to identify where we have made progress and where we have not.

Infancy

Infants cannot verbally express their views on the nature of self, nor can they understand the complex instructions required for engagement in most psychologist's tasks. Because of these and other methodological constraints, studies of infant self-understanding have been narrower in scope than studies of later age periods. In fact, there has been only one experimental paradigm that has yielded reliable data on self-understanding during infancy: testing for visual self-recognition by showing infants images of themselves through pictures, mirrors, and other visual media.

The hegemony of this paradigm has constrained our knowledge of infant self-understanding. For one thing, we do not know whether other nonvisual modes of self-recognition (such as through touch, hearing, and smell) might provide better indexes of infant self-understanding. We do not know whether self-recognition is itself an accurate representation of infant self-understanding in general. Nor do we know whether this one constraining experimental choice is an inevitable result of infants' limited communication abilities, or whether it is an artifact of currently available experimental techniques.

Its constraints aside, the visual self-recognition paradigm has been used successfully by investigators and has produced several mutually supporting accounts of developmental trends. The most common, and the oldest, technique for studying visual self-recognition is observing subjects' reactions to their own mirror images. The scientific use of this technique with infants dates back to Charles Darwin, who noted in his diary descriptions of his 9-month-old son that the boy would look at a mirror and exclaim "Ah!" when his name was spoken (Darwin, 1877). Darwin concluded that this act signified his son's first act of conscious self-recognition. In a nineteenth-century observation of an infant looking in the mirror, Preyer reported a similar "conscious" self-recognition first appearing at 14 months in his infant subject (Preyer, 1893).

Modern investigators have also turned to the mirror as a tool for exploring infants' self-recognition. In a study of five infants followed longitudinally from ages 4 to 12 months, Dixon (1957) recorded the infants' reactions to mirrors placed at one end of their cribs, focusing particularly on "behavioral sequences" like smiling at the image, talking to it, trying to touch it, and so on. In addition, Dixon rigged an experimental setup of one- and two-way mirrors and special lighting that presented to the infants images of self, another infant, and the mother, sometimes simultaneously and sometimes alternately.

On the basis of his observations, Dixon reported a developmental sequence of self-recognition that remained constant for all five subjects. The sequence consisted of four stages, the order of which did not vary across infants, although the ages associated with each stage did. The first stage, which Dixon observed in infants' behavior at 4 months, he called "Mother." The infant shows no sustained interest in its own reflection, but does show immediate recognition of its mother's reflection: The infant smiles, looks, and vocalizes at the mother's image as soon as it is presented. At Stage 2, called "Playmate" by Dixon, the infant becomes interested in its own reflection; but "his behavior toward his mirror image is indistinguishable from that when placed before another infant" (p. 253). Stage 2 lasts until about 6 months. Beginning at around 7 months, the infant "relates the mirror image to himself" by repeating simple actions (opening the mouth) while gazing in the mirror. This phase is Stage 3, which Dixon called "Who dat do dat when I do dat?" The infant is now capable of distinguishing between its own mirror image and that of another infant and prefers to interact with the image of the other rather than that of the self. At Stage 4, beginning at 12 months, the infant may even cry or turn away from its own reflection, supposedly for this same reason. The infant now unambiguously demonstrates recognition of self and other, shifting its gaze appropriately when asked, "Where is (X)? Where are you?"

Although Dixon's study established the fact of self-recognition in young infants and offered some preliminary indications of developmental trends, it left a number of unanswered questions concerning the basis of self-recognition at this early age. From Dixon's observational procedure, it is impossible to determine what the young infant recognizes in its own reflection. As Lewis and Brooks-Gunn (1979) later point out, mirror images contain at least two kinds of clues for self-recognition: contingency clues and feature clues. In the case of the former, a person looking in a mirror sees an image that moves immediately in tandem to the person's own physiological sensations of movement. In the case of the latter, a person looking in a mirror can observe images of particular facial and bodily features, some of which may become familiar to the person through repeated observation. Dixon's experimental design offered no means of isolating or disconfounding these two types of self-recognition clues. In addition, Dixon's study is weakened by its small sample size, lack of reliability, and other psychometric shortcomings.

Using an ingenious technique similar to one introduced by Gallup (1977) in chimpanzee research, Amsterdam (1972) was able to isolate a type of facial feature that young infants can use in self-recognition. In Amsterdam's experiment, infants' noses were surreptitiously dabbed with rouge, and the infants were placed in front of mirrors and asked "See?" and "Who's that?" Amsterdam recorded responses similar to those noted by Dixon (smiling, vocalizing, gazing, touching), although in more systematic fashion, with traditional reliability checks. Also, Amsterdam's study had a full sample size of 88 infants ages 3 through 24 months, including 2 infants followed longitudinally from 12 to 24 months. Amsterdam defined full self-recognition as self-directed behavior indicating awareness of the red spot on the nose. Her assumption was that "the child's ability to locate a red spot on the face shows that he associates his own face with the face in the mirror" (p. 304). In addition, of course, special attention to the red spot indicates an awareness that the self has stable facial features that do not include a reddened nose. Amsterdam reported that this type of "full" self-recognition was found only at 20 to 24 months. In addition, not until this age did Amsterdam's infants show other conscious signs of self-recognition, such as "self-admiring" behavior (strutting, preening) and embarrassed behavior (blushing, coyness).

Amsterdam's conclusion, contrary to those of Darwin, Preyer, and Dixon before her, was that fully conscious self-recognition, based on stable features of self, does not normally occur until the end of the second year of life. Prior to this, Amsterdam did find two of the phases described by Dixon: the "playmate" phase (6–12 months), in which the child treats the image as an interacting peer; and a "withdrawal" phase (13–24 months), in which the child expresses weariness of the mirror image. But, unlike Dixon, Amsterdam doubted that during either of these phases the infant "relates the mirror image to the self." Amsterdam suggested that Dixon wrongly inferred self-recognition from the infant's particular concern with the contingency aspects of its own mirror image. She believed that, despite this contingency awareness, the infant younger than 20 months sees only the image of a strange peer in the mirror.

Amsterdam's focus on feature recognition provides a methodologically valuable means of distinguishing components of self-recognition, but one wonders whether she has dismissed the significance of early contingency awareness too lightly. Missing from her design is a means of determining whether contingency awareness, either independent from or in combination with feature recognition, is an index of self-recognition. But she does demonstrate that by 20 months the infant has knowledge of some constituents of the bodily "me," as well as a sense that these are continuous over time.

In a systematic series of studies, Lewis and Brooks-Gunn (1979) were able to present both contingency and feature cues to infants in an orderly and disconfounded way. They separated the two types of cues by using a variety of mediums to present the child with the self's image, such as mirrors, photographs, and videotapes. Mirror images always move contingently with the self, photographed images never do, and videotape images can be either contingent or noncontingent.

In one of their studies using a mirror to present infants with their images, Lewis and Brooks-Gunn followed the same procedure used by Amsterdam with infants from 9 to 24 months of age. Most of their results parallel Amsterdam's, although they found that infants as young as 15 months, 5 months younger than Amsterdam's subject, responded to their reddened noses.

Lewis and Brooks-Gunn designed further videotape studies to separate contingency from feature cues in the development of self-recognition. Infants' responses to three types of television images were compared: "live" images of themselves; images of themselves shot 1 week earlier; and images of another infant. In assessing their subjects' responses to the television images, Lewis and Brooks-Gunn recorded tendency to imitate and play with the image on the screen. In addition, the infants' facial and vocal expressions were recorded as well as their movements toward and away from the image.

Subjects in the television studies were the same ages as those in the mirror study (9 months and older), and these results nicely supplement the mirror-study findings. Infants as young as 9 months distinguished the live television image of self from the other images presented, playing more with it and generally responding more positively to it than to the other images. These results confirm Dixon's tentative findings and indicate that initial visual self-recognition is present at least as early as 9 months and is based on the principle of contingency: When an image moves along with the self, it is possible at a very early age to recognize the self in that image. (Papousek and Papousek [1974] found signs of such self-recognition even prior to 9 months, although their techniques do not confirm this as convincingly as do Lewis and Brooks-Gunn's. Further, Lewis and Brooks-Gunn found a steady increase in infants' awareness of contingency through the second year of life.)

But the most striking developmental advance was not in the infants' use of contingency but in their use of physical appearance in recognizing the self. To uncover this developmental advance, Lewis and Brooks-Gunn compared their subjects' responses to the noncontingent televised self-image (shot the prior week) with their subjects' responses to the televised image of another baby. Not until 15 months of age did infants distinguish their own pretaped images from images of another child on the television. When they were able to make this distinction, they smiled at and moved toward the other baby's image more than toward their own image, and they imitated and played with their own image more than with the other baby's image. These differences in behavior, which began at about 15 months, increased as the infants grew older. Lewis and Brooks-Gunn speculate that the infants of 15 months and older were able to distinguish their own images from the images of other babies by referring to differences in the facial features of the two, meaning that at about 15 months infants begin to know what their faces look like.

This developmental progression is confirmed further by the findings of Lewis and Brooks-Gunn's picture study. By showing infants pictures of themselves and other babies, the researchers found the first clear feature recognition of self in infants aged 15 to 18 months. Signs of this recognition included smiling, gazing, and pointing to one's picture when one's name was called, as opposed to ignoring or frowning at the picture of peers. (In one small pilot sample the researchers found the smiling sign in infants as young as 9 months, but only occasionally and sporadically.) Because pictorial images are noncontingent on a subject's actions but do reveal facial and other physical cues, age trends from the picture study coincide with the age trends from Lewis and Brooks-Gunn's television and mirror studies.

Further findings from the picture study suggest the basic categories that infants, beginning at 15 months or so, use to identify themselves – namely, gender and age. When infants of 15 months begin distinguishing themselves from others on the basis of noncontingent cues, they are particularly attuned to physical features associated with their gender and their age. They find it especially easy to tell themselves apart from opposite-sex babies and from older persons. The researchers believe that infants are able to discern the distinctive facial features that accompany gender and age: females have different-shaped faces (as well as different hair styles) from males, and babies have faces and heads that are shaped differently from those of older people. In their initial constructions of the self-as-object (the "me"), infants focus particularly on facial features as the Lewis and Brooks-Gunn studies indicate. Of all facial features, those associated with gender and age are particularly apparent to infants as they begin constructing "categorical" knowledge of themselves.

Based on their literature survey and the results of their own studies, Lewis and Brooks-Gunn postulate that there are four major advances in infants' self-knowledge during the first 2 years of life. Because the infants in Lewis and Brooks-Gunn's studies were all 6 months or older, the authors' description of the first self-knowledge advance is conjectural, based on informal observation and outside sources in the psychological literature. From birth to 3 months of age, the first sign of self-knowledge is an unlearned attraction to the images of other people and especially to the images of young babies. This attraction shows up in a young infant's fascination with mirror images, drawings, and pictures of faces, especially when the face is that of the self or of another young infant. Next, between 3 and 8 months of age, infants begin to recognize the self through contingency cues. The third advance, between the ages of 8 and 12 months, is the association of certain stable categorical features with the self. The infant now can go beyond recognizing the self merely as the origin of paired causes and effects in the world and can begin constructing the self as a permanent object with enduring qualities. In this manner, the permanence of the self is realized and becomes an important organizing principle for the infant's knowledge of both self-as-subject and self-as-object. Finally, the fourth infancy advance, occurring throughout the second year of life, is the defining of the self through categorical features alone, independent of any contingency knowledge that the subject may have.

Although Lewis and Brooks-Gunn are referring to the physical constituents of the "me" when they write of the development of knowledge of the categorical features of self, there is evidence indicating that the child is aware of other characteristics of the "me." One finding of the Kagan's research described previously was that children begin making frequent verbal self-descriptive statements ("I play"; "I can do this") late in the second year of life. Self-descriptive statements reflect self-awareness because a child could not make meaningful statements about the self if the child were not aware of the self's qualities.

Kagan's findings reveal that, in addition to knowledge about the self's physical constituents, the child is aware of the self's actions and capabilities, or "active constituents" in Jamesian terms. Active constituents of the "me" (e.g., "I play"; "I can tie my shoe") are qualitatively different from the physical constituents of the "me" (e.g., "I have red hair"; "I have a big bicycle") and must be treated as such in an accurate depiction of self-understanding development. We shall return to this point in the next section.

Column 1 in Table 2.1 summarizes the trends revealed by infant research to this date. The remaining two columns summarize trends from the childhood and adolescent studies that we shall review in the following two sections.

Childhood

Because children can communicate their ideas verbally, the study of childhood self-knowledge is not limited to the study of visual self-recognition, as it was during infancy. Through the use of interview and other verbal procedures, researchers have been able to probe children's conceptions of many psychological issues related to self. These issues include the nature of the self's components (including mind and body), self in comparison to others, self in relation to others, and points of pride and shame in self. From these diverse efforts, we can piece together a rough chronology of self-knowledge as it develops in the childhood years.

In a broad-based study of children's "naive epistemologies" (i.e., their spontaneous philosophical analyses of the world), Broughton asked children open-ended questions about the self, focusing particularly on "I" conceptions such as volition and distinctness from others (Broughton 1978a). Broughton's questions were direct interrogations: "What is the self?" "What is the mind?" "What is the difference between the mind and the body?" These queries were then followed by probe questions. From subjects' answers, Broughton derived a developmental progression of naive epistemologies that covers the period from childhood through middle adulthood. We shall consider only the aspects of Broughton's outline that concern self-knowledge. In this section, we describe Broughton's two childhood levels; in the next section, his two adolescent levels.

In early childhood, according to Broughton, the self is conceived strictly in physical terms. The self is believed to be part of the body. Usually this means the head, although other body parts are also cited, including the whole body. Accordingly, the child confuses self, mind, and body. Because of this type of reasoning, young children typically express a number of peculiar opinions unique to this early level. For example, because young children believe that self and mind are simply parts of the body, they often

Table 2.1. *Summary of research findings*

Aspect of self-understanding	Infancy	Childhood	Adolescence
The "me"			
Physical	Knowledge of physical features and name (Dixon, 1957; Amsterdam, 1972; Lewis & Brooks-Gunn, 1979)	Physical aspects of self more important in early childhood (Selman, 1980) and are more frequently incorporated in self-understanding if they distinguish between self and others (McGuire & Padawer-Singer, 1976)	
Active	Awareness of self's action capabilities (Kagan, 1981)	Self's actions are salient (Keller, Ford, & Meacham, 1978); comparative ability becomes important (Secord & Peevers, 1974; Mohr, 1978; Ruble, 1983); self acts as a result of surrounding physical and emotional environs (Bernstein, 1980)	
Social		Membership in group and familial relationships (Livesly & Bromley, 1973)	Social personality traits are important (Rosenberg, 1979) and are of self's actions (Bernstein, 1980)
Psychological		Self's subjective, psychological experience is distinguished from material experience (Broughton, 1978; Selman, 1980; Johnson & Wellman, 1982; Wellman, 1986)	Belief systems characterize self (Secord & Peevers, 1974); beliefs are rooted in self's conscious or unconscious (Selman, 1980); mental world has own system of internal regulations (Broughton, 1980)

Table 2.1. (*cont.*)

Aspect of self-understanding	Infancy	Childhood	Adolescence
The "I"			
Continuity	Continuity based on physical features (Amsterdam, 1972; Lewis & Brooks-Gunn, 1979)	Continuity asserted on basis of bodily and psychological attributes (Guardo & Bohan, 1971; Aboud & Skerry, 1983); these attributes are believed to be unchanging (Chandler, Boyes, Ball, & Hale, in press)	Past and future of self becomes increasingly important (Secord & Peevers, 1974)
Distinctness	Contingent action and physical features distinguish self from others (Mahler, Pine, & Bergman, 1975; Lewis & Brooke-Gunn, 1979)	Psychological attributes provide criterion of distinctness (Guardo & Bohan, 1971; Broughton, 1978)	Distinctness from others is increasingly mentioned in self-definition (Montemayor & Eisen, 1977); the privacy and immediacy of self-knowledge, as opposed to the difficulty of knowing others, distinguishes self from others (Broughton, 1978)

Volition		Mind as active processor of conscious experience can affect behavior (Selman, 1980); self judges self's actions (Secord & Peevers, 1974; Broughton, 1978a); feeling of self-direction connected with a sense of pride (Rosenberg, 1979)
Self-reflection	Self can manipulate correspondence between external behavior and internal feelings, and therefore can deceive others (Selman, 1980)	Emergence of both an awareness of self-awareness and a belief in unconscious experience (Selman, 1980); belief in real and phony selves (Broughton, 1980)
Organization and integration of disparate self components	Statements about self are segregated from one another (Bernstein, 1980)	Self-statements are organized into self-system (Bernstein, 1980); awareness of potential conflicts among aspects of self-system (Harter, 1986)

say that any body, including animals, plants, and dead people, may have a self and a mind. Further, because self is a body part, it can be described in terms of material dimensions such as size, shape, or color. Children at this level distinguish themselves from others through a variety of physical and material attributes: I am different from Jimmy because I have blond hair, different from that tree because I am smaller, different from my sister because I have a bike. Even the volitional aspects of self – that is, one's motivations and "free will" – are attributed to physical body parts. The child might say, for example that the self is the brain, and the brain tells you what to do.

Broughton's second level of self-knowledge emerges at about 8 years of age. The mental and volitional aspects of self are now understood on their own terms, removed from their direct links to any particular body parts. In other words, children now begin to distinguish between mind and body, although this distinction is not as finely articulated as it will be in the adolescent years. This initial distinction between mental and physical enables children to appreciate the subjective nature of self. One is distinct from others not simply because one looks different or has different material possessions but because one has different thoughts and feelings. The self's essential nature is therefore defined internally rather than externally and becomes a matter of psychological rather than physical attributes. Broughton quotes from a 10-year-old at this level: "I am one of a kind. . . . There could be a person who looks like me or talks like me, but no one who has every single detail I have. Never a person who thinks exactly like me" (p. 86).

A series of studies by Johnson and Wellman (1982; Wellman, 1986) suggest that Broughton's characterization of young children's sense of self may underestimate their understanding of the relationships among mind, self, and body. Rather than rely on children's responses to open-ended epistemological questions, as Broughton did, Johnson and Wellman asked children between the ages of 5 and 11 to make judgments about whether the mind or brain was necessary for various mental (thinking, knowing, dreaming) and behavioral (walking, kicking, drawing) tasks. Johnson and Wellman found that even 5-year-old children distinguish between psychological and physical realities, as evidenced by their claims that the mind and brain are necessary for the mental acts but not for the behavioral ones. This finding suggests that even young children are aware of the unique features of psychological and mental states, a capability not elicited by Broughton's methodology.

Yet some of Johnson and Wellman's findings confirm Broughton's analysis. Like Broughton, Johnson and Wellman found that the older children have a more volitional conception of mental processes. This was indicated by the tendency of older children to claim that the mind or brain was involved in walking, seeing, drawing, and other behavioral tasks. Unlike younger children who believe that the mind is the repository of mental states and psychological characteristics, older children posit a controlling function for the mind that interacts with all of the person's activities.

Using his own interview procedures, Selman (1980) replicated much of Broughton's developmental progression. Rather than asking children direct questions, Selman presented story dilemmas that posed problems in self-awareness. From children's responses to these dilemmas, Selman has outlined three childhood levels and two adolescent ones (which we shall consider in the next section).

Selman's first childhood level, which he calls "physicalistic conceptions of self," is almost identical with Broughton's first level. At this level the child makes no distinction between inner psychological experience and outer material experience. Children at this level typically will deny that a person's statements and behavior can be distinguished from the person's feelings. The self's volitional tendencies are tied to specific body parts and derive strictly from the functioning of these parts; for instance, "I am the boss of myself . . . [because] my mouth tells me what to do" (p. 95).

Later in childhood, according to Selman, children recognize differences between inner and outer states, and define the "true self" in terms of subjective inner states rather than material outer states. Unlike Broughton, Selman believes that this developmental transformation in children's self-knowledge occurs in two levels rather than in one. First, writes Selman, children by age 6 or so realize that psychological experience is not the same as physical experience, but they still believe that the two types of experience are consistent with one another. Then, by age 8 or so, the child realizes the discrepancy between one's inner experience and one's outer appearance. At this point, conscious deception becomes a possibility, because the child is able to manipulate the relation between internal and external reality. The child now sees that the self can monitor its own thoughts in a more direct way than others can. This means that one can put on a facade that others may not be able to penetrate. It also means that one has better access to one's own psychological experience than do others. This appreciation of the private, subjective nature of self, according to Selman, leads the child to "a reflective understanding that the self is capable of gaining inner strength by having confidence in its own abilities" (p. 100).

Although Selman's description adds some intricacies to Broughton's, the two agree on the basic childhood shift from physicalistic to psychological conceptions of self. Research by Guardo and Bohan (1971) on the cognitive bases for self-identity in children ages 6 through 9 provides further evidence of this shift. Guardo and Bohan focused specifically on children's knowledge of four dimensions of self: humanity (the sense that one has human qualities distinct from other life forms); sexuality (the awareness of one's own gender and sex role); individuality (the sense that one is unique in the world); and continuity (one's belief that one is connected with one's past and future self). Somewhat like the Jamesian view discussed in Chapter 1, Guardo and Bohan assert that, taken together, these dimensions provide the individual with a sense that he or she "is one being with a unique identity who has been, is, and will be a male (or female) human person separate from and entirely like no other" (1971, p. 1915).

To test for children's sense of self, Guardo and Bohan asked their subjects if they believed that they could assume the identity of another being. Three types of being were specifically mentioned by the interviewer: a pet (testing for humanity), an opposite-sex peer (testing for sexuality), and a same-sex peer (testing for individuality). The researchers' assumption was that, if children claimed that they could assume the identity of another being, they lacked the dimension of self on which the question focused. In addition to these identity tests, the researchers tested for continuity by asking subjects whether they were the same persons in the past and future. Follow-up questions for all items for children's understanding of the four dimensions were asked. For example, a typical probe question was "Why do you think you could never become a dog?" In this manner the researchers could determine not only whether the child had a sense of humanity but also the cognitive basis of that sense.

Guardo and Bohan found that all children in the 6-to-9 age range had a definite sense of all four self-dimensions. That is, virtually all subjects expressed belief in their own immutable humanity, sexuality, individuality, and continuity. This should come as no surprise to us, considering that Lewis and Brooks-Gunn found some awareness of at least the last three of these dimensions in infants younger than 2 years old. More revealing from a developmental point of view was Guardo and Bohan's finding that the conceptual basis for children's belief in these dimensions changes with age. The beliefs of 6- and 7-year-old children are based on their physical and behavioral characteristics. For example, a 7-year-old might say that it would be impossible to become just like a particular peer because that peer is shorter and not as good at basketball. Or the child might say that he will be the same as an adult because he will have the same name. Children who are 8 and 9 years old use many similarly physicalistic notions but also add to their explanations some psychological ones as well. For example, a 9-year-old might say that it would be impossible to assume a friend's identity because the friend has different likes and dislikes.

More recent research by Aboud and Skerry (1983) confirms the trends reported by Guardo and Bohan. Aboud and Skerry also focused their research on how children provide a sense of their own identity through beliefs in continuous self-characteristics. Aboud and Skerry asked children and adults to name characteristics that describe the self. Each characteristic was assigned to one of three categories: physical (appearance, possessions), social (friend, religion), or psychological (preferences, personality traits). After the elicitation of the five characteristics, the interviewer asked the child if he or she would still be the same person without each of the characteristics offered in the first part of the interview. For instance, if the child responded with "girl, small, smart, friendly, nice" in the first part of the interview, the interviewer would ask, "If you were a boy instead of a girl (or big instead of small, etc.), could you still be yourself?" (p. 18). Those characteristics that were judged by the child to be necessary for continued identity were deemed to be "essential" characteristics.

Several noteworthy findings emerged from Aboud and Skerry's study. First, children by the second grade were much more likely than younger children to name psychological characteristics and less likely to name fewer physical characteristics (e.g., eye color). This trend toward increasing use of psychological characteristics was further confirmed by the experimental manipulation that tested for the "essentialness" of various characteristics. Only 13% of the psychological characteristics offered by the kindergarten children were judged essential to maintaining the sense of self, whereas 24% of the psychological characteristics offered by the second graders, and 74% of those offered by adults were deemed to be essential. There was also with age an increased use of social characteristics for maintaining identity. Conversely, between childhood and adulthood there was a decline in the percentage of physical characteristics judged essential.

One unexpected finding to emerge from Aboud and Skerry's study is that the kindergarten children judge characteristics of all three types to be less essential to selfhood than do children in second grade. This suggests that the younger age group had made less progress than the older age group in articulating for themselves the features of self that serve to establish identity. Self-understanding development may result not only in a broader awareness of what features define the self, but a growing commitment to particular self-qualities.

Chandler, Boyes, Ball, and Hala (1987) even more directly examined the theories that children and adolescents construct in order to perceive continuity in one's personality. To elicit children's understanding of personal continuity, Chandler and his colleagues asked children and adolescents to consider the continuities that may persist in famous fictional characters such as Ebenezer Scrooge from Charles Dickens's *Christmas Carol*. As every child knows, Scrooge was a selfish penny pincher until Christmas Eve, when his nightmares about his past, present, and future made him change his ways. In what ways, Chandler asked his subjects, is Scrooge the same person before and after his revelation?

Chandler and his colleagues found in their subject's answers two developmental levels during the childhood years. At the first level, mainly expressed by children ages 4 to 7, personal continuity is ascribed to the unchanging nature of any personal attribute. Scrooge is the same person, a child might argue, because his hair, face, and house are still the same on Christmas day. At the second level, children develop an "essentialist" theory of identity. Now personal continuity is established by a few central characteristics of self that persist unchanged. Scrooge is the same, say, because he is still self-centered and performs even generous acts out of ultimately selfish motives. Chandler's research does not tell us which types of self-characteristic children are likely to judge as central in this regard.

A line of research by McGuire and his colleagues (McGuire & Padawer-Singer, 1976) provides some further answers. Like us, McGuire argues that one function of the self-concept is to provide a person with a sense of individuality, or personal distinctiveness. In one test of this hypothesis, McGuire and Padawer-Singer asked 250 children in sixth grade to complete two self-concept forms. The first was to assess what the investigators called the spontaneous self-concept. The children received a booklet and were asked to write down as many things about themselves as they could in a 7-minute interval. Next the children were given a second booklet and asked to write a description of their physical appearance. A week later, they were asked to write down their height, weight, hair color, birthdate, birthplace, and household composition.

The investigators found that subjects most frequently chose characteristics of self that were uncommon in relation to other children. For instance, children who were 6 or more months older or younger than the model age for their class were more likely to mention their ages on the spontaneous self-concept measure than age-typical children. Similarly, almost half of the foreign born children mentioned their birthplace in their spontaneous descriptions of self. Children reported their hair color, eye color, and weight much more frequently if their own versions of these were distinct from their classmates. Most dramatically, McGuire and Padawer-Singer found that 26% of the children in a classroom in which they are of the minority gender listed their gender on the spontaneous self-interview, but only 11% of the children of the more common gender did so. This is especially surprising given the slight discrepancies in the distribution of boys and girls. In none of the classes included in the study did the number of students of one gender exceed the number of students of the other by more than a few. Apparently, then, older children are very sensitive to even small quantitative differences in the commonness of particular characteristics.

The McGuire research, therefore, suggests that children often define the self by characteristics that they sense will distinguish them clearly from others. If we are to believe the analyses offered by Broughton, Selman, Guardo and Bohan, and Aboud and Skeely, we would conclude that young children tend to choose physical or material characteristics for this purpose, whereas older children tend to choose social and psychological ones.

But some other studies have given us reason to modify the latter conclusion. In one study, Keller, Ford, and Meacham (1978) showed that very young children (ages 3-to-5) think of the self more in terms of activities than in terms of body parts or material attributes. The researchers used several techniques to arrive at this conclusion.

First, children were asked to say up to 10 things about themselves spontaneously. Second, they were asked to complete sentences like "I am a boy/girl who. . . ." On these items, children responded most frequently with action statements, such as "I play baseball" or "I walk to school." Body image answers ("I am big"; "I have blue eyes") were far less common. In fact, other than action statements, which constituted more than 50% of children's responses, no other category of response occurred more than 10% of the time (although it is also interesting to note that about 5% of even the youngest children's responses referred to their likes and dislikes, a psychological aspect of self).

In a further confirmation of the importance of activity in young children's self-definitions, the researchers gave children direct choices between action and body image statements. To do this, the researchers asked subjects which of the following types of statements subjects would rather have written about them: "Johnny has a nice face"; "Johnny can brush his teeth." Children overwhelmingly chose the latter type of statement.

A study by Mohr (1978) suggests that both physical and active attributes play a key role in children's self-definitions, although in Mohr's study the physical did seem to precede the active developmentally. Mohr's procedure was similar to that of Guardo and Bohan. Children in first, third, and sixth grades were asked three questions: "What would you have to change about yourself for you to become just like your best friend?" "What will (not) change about yourself when you grow up?" "What has (not) changed about yourself since you were a baby?" These questions tap the child's sense of personal distinctness and continuity over time. Mohr assigned subjects' responses to one of three categories: external or physical (age, appearance), behavioral (typical activities), and internal or psychological (feelings, thoughts). Mohr found that children in first grade responded most frequently with physical characteristics, that those in the third grade offered many more behavioral characteristics, and that only the sixth graders offered psychological characteristics.

The results of Keller, Ford, and Meachum's and Mohr's studies add the active dimension as a central constituent of self in early childhood. If, of course, the notion physicalistic is conceived broadly enough to include physical actions as well as body image and material possessions, activity can be incorporated into the physicalistic level proposed by the researchers we have cited. In fact, this conception is in line with Selman's use of the word physicalistic: Selman's illustrative examples of his first self-awareness level include instances of children speaking about their actions.

But for the sake of precise developmental description, we prefer to separate the notion of active self-constituents from the notion of physical self-constituents. Dynamic actions are, after all, both logically and phenomenologically quite distinct from static physical objects. Keller, Ford, and Meachum's study shows that young children operationally can distinguish the two without difficulty.

If Keller, Ford, and Meachum are correct, the active self predominates in the preschool years. This conclusion also accords with earlier research by Secord and Peevers (1974), who claimed, on the basis of free-response data, that kindergarten children describe themselves almost exclusively in terms of activities like play. If Mohr is correct, the active self predominates soon after the heyday of the physical self. Either way, it is helpful to distinguish the two, and both clearly play a central role in early self-understanding.

Further, even if action does dominate self-knowledge at early developmental levels, it is often used along with physical notions like body image and material possessions. Because many young children have been found to use both active and physical qualities to identify themselves, self may be conceived in multiple dimensions even in the early phases of development.

There is also reason to believe that action continues to be an important element in self-knowledge later in childhood, only in a somewhat different way. In their study of children's free responses to self-questions, Secord and Peevers report that, even by third grade, children describe the self primarily in terms of activities. But there is a new quality in the third-graders' active self-statements. Unlike preschoolers, who describe self in terms of its typical activities ("I ride a bike"), older children describe themselves in terms of their active abilities relative to others ("I can ride a bike better than my brother").

Secord and Peevers describe this as a shift from a focus on the self's *habitual* action to a focus on the self's action *competencies*. It indicates that children are now distinguishing themselves from others in comparative rather than absolute terms. That is, the issue is no longer what I do (or do not do) but what I can do well in comparison with others. This developmental shift better serves the differentiating function of self, because it provides a sharper means of establishing one's differences as an individual from others.

A recent set of findings in social psychological research confirms the developmental shift noted by Secord and Peevers. In a programmatic series of studies, Ruble (1983) has investigated children's use of social comparisons in their self-evaluations. The basic design of these studies was to give children a difficult task and then to offer them feedback on their own performances as well as information about the performances of other children their age. Subjects were then asked for self-evaluations. Ruble found that children younger than 7 made almost no reference to the information about other children's performances. However, children older than 7 did base their self-evaluations on such social comparisons. Interestingly, Livesly and Bromley (1973) report remarkably similar quantitative results in their study of self-descriptions. At around age 7, children's use of comparative competence notions in their descriptions of self and other triples in frequency.

We can see from the combined results of studies reviewed in this section the early use of both active and physical notions of self. We also see the later transformation of active self-statements to a comparative mode. In addition, we know that psychological self-notions emerge with some frequency by the end of childhood. Indeed, Keller, Ford, and Meachum found a glimmer of such notions in very young children's statements.

Finally, in addition to the use of action attributes in a social-comparative mode, there is also some evidence that the social self makes an appearance during the childhood years. Livesly and Bromley (1973) found that children sometimes refer to social group memberships in their self-descriptions. A child on occasion might say, for example, that he is a Boy Scout or a Catholic. This suggests that, although the social self does not seem to be as predominant during childhood as either the active or the physical self, it is occasionally present in the self-awareness of children even at young ages. Together with the trends already cited, this finding gives us yet another indication of self-understanding's multiple bases during childhood (see column 2, Table 2.1).

Adolescence

There is noteworthy convergence in findings from several independently conducted studies of adolescent self-understanding. Virtually all researchers have found that, with development, adolescent self-understanding shows in increasing use of psychological and social relational concepts for describing the "me," a more prominent belief in the "I" 's agency and volitional power, and a tendency toward integration of the disparate aspects of self into an internally consistent construct system.

In addition, some researchers have reported features of adolescent thinking that are not always apparent in every study because of methodological considerations. One prominent example is the adolescent's growing awareness of self-reflection (another "I" conception). Accordingly, despite a wide overall consensus concerning general developmental trends, there are some important differences among studies in their emphasis on the particular qualities that characterize adolescent self-understanding. In this section we first review studies that investigate childhood as well as adolescent development and that, therefore, have been summarized in part in the previous section. Then we review studies that primarily focus on adolescence itself.

Selman's fourth level (his first in adolescence) implies that the young adolescent knows that one can consciously monitor one's own self-experience. Not only does this new awareness explain the increased self-consciousness of young adolescents commonly observed in the personality-development literature (e.g., White, 1972), but it also accounts for the increased sense of personal agency that most researchers have found during this age period. Because the adolescent now knows the possibility of self-reflection, the adolescent conceives of the mind as an active processor of experience and ultimately as a potential manipulator of one's experience. This conception establishes a new mode of control generated by one's mental powers of self-reflective awareness. Selman offers the following example: In response to a question about one's reactions to the loss of a puppy, a young adolescent might say, "I can fool myself into not wanting to see another puppy if I keep on saying to myself, 'I don't want a puppy; I don't ever want to see another puppy.' "

Although the adolescent at Selman's fourth level generally believes that one has control over one's thoughts and emotions, there is also some awareness that certain mental experience is beyond one's volitional reach. For example, Selman quotes one young adolescent who said "If I did something wrong, I really can't forget about it because of time. I really can't make myself forget; I will always remember it" (p. 103). But this apparent incongruity with the notion of self-reflective self-control poses an unresolvable contradiction to the young adolescent, who simply segregates the two irreconcilable notions of self in disparate, unrelated statements. Only at Level 5, according to Selman, does the adolescent resolve this problem by constructing the notion of conscious and nonconscious levels of experience (or some parallel version of this notion); the solution is that there are mental experiences that can influence one's actions but that are not available for conscious inspection.

According to Selman, therefore, self-understanding in adolescence begins with global notion of the "I" as a self-reflective, active controller of one's experience, with some uncoordinated recognition that there are limits to this awareness and control. Later in adolescence one develops the notion of two different levels of mental experience, one conscious and one nonconscious, both of which can influence one's thoughts and actions. In this manner, the adolescent conceptually constructs a unified self-system while still preserving the notion that self-awareness and conscious self-control have their boundaries.

Selman's self-awareness research is limited by his exclusive focus on perspective taking as the single "underlying" explanation for development. This choice has many unfortunate consequences. Among these are the inability to distinguish self-understanding from other-understanding and the neglect of many aspects of conceptual development that are specific to knowledge of the self. Broughton's research, more broadly based and more directly aimed at self-specific issues, reveals some further trends in adolescent self-understanding development.

Broughton, like Selman, proposes two levels of self-knowledge in adolescence (Levels 3 and 4 in Broughton's scheme). During early adolescence, an initial distinction is made between mental and physical reality. According to Broughton, this Level 3 distinction has several important implications, particularly for the adolescent's understanding of the "I." First, the mind is now seen as an entity in its own right, taking on volitional characteristics independent of the self's physical activity. For example, the "I" is seen as capable of evaluating the self's actions, as in this example: "With our minds we can make our own judgments and do what we feel is right" (p. 87). Second, the young adolescent sees the self as a stable way of mentally processing information, a characteristic mode of knowing the world. One of Broughton's subjects replied that the self is "the way your thoughts go" (p. 88). Third, because the mental functions of self are recognized, the self is seen as having complete and private access to its own inner processes. The "I" knows itself, and this knowledge neither is shared by anyone else nor extends to others. One young adolescent told Broughton, "I know what I feel about things, and I don't know someone else" (p. 88).

Although the young adolescent recognizes the distinction between mental and physical, basing a new understanding of the self-as-subject on this recognition, there is still little appreciation of the mental self's unique qualities. Broughton believes that such an appreciation develops late in adolescence, at Level 4. The adolescent at this level has some understanding of the mental world's internal system of relations and regulations. This enables the adolescent to conceive of the mental self as a system of distinct elements, sometimes operating concordantly and sometimes "divided." For example, Broughton quotes one adolescent who speaks of two inner mental selves, one of which is "natural" and one of which "imitates" its ideal (Broughton, 1980). This example, writes Broughton, is typical of this reasoning level, because it represents an attempt to understand both the complexity and the unity of the "I." Other examples include adolescents who are introspective about the logical mechanisms that characterize their thought processes or who posit real and phony mental activities, logical and irrational ones, and so on.

Broughton's analysis of adolescent self-understanding converges with Selman's on the following points. First, both agree that the young adolescent views the self primarily in mental terms, as an active processor of experience. Both also agree that this conception is associated with the adolescent's new respect for the self's volitional powers, either in the sense of monitoring and manipulating its own thoughts and actions (Selman) or in the sense of evaluating itself (Broughton). Thus, both connect the adolescent tendency toward self-reflection to a stronger sense of personal agency.

Finally, both agree that in late adolescence the uneven and sometimes divided workings of mental life are understood. Selman stresses the adolescent's construction of conscious and nonconscious levels of mental experience, whereas Broughton stresses the adolescent's construction of such notions as the real mental self versus the imitative (or "phony") mental self. But despite this difference, both authors portray the effects of the change similarly – as a move away from the notion of a global mental self with mysterious workings to a view of a mental self with disparate elements with multiple, though systematic, rules of operation.

Secord and Peever's (1974) study of self-understanding in children and adolescents found similar developmental patterns. The authors used a free-response method of questioning subjects and analyzed responses intuitively rather than with the aid of a formal coding scheme; but their impressionistic account not only dovetails with Selman's and Broughton's findings but also suggests some further features of adolescent self-understanding.

The first developmental shift noted by Secord and Peevers occurs at the beginning of adolescence. At this age, the self is described in terms of abstractions and general evaluations, rather than simply in terms of specific acts and qualities (as, they write, during childhood). Also, Secord and Peevers report that young adolescents are likely to describe themselves in terms of their past and future selves, whereas younger children almost invariably describe themselves in terms of the immediate present. This attitude, of course, offers the young adolescent a stronger basis for constructing a sense of personal continuity.

The next shift noted by Secord and Peevers occurs in middle adolescence. Here we see many of the qualities reported by Selman and Broughton, though at a somewhat earlier age (during the first of the other two researchers' adolescent levels). This discrepancy could result from either differences in research populations or the relative informality and open-endedness of the Secord–Peevers testing procedure when compared with the more intensively probed interviews of Selman and Broughton. In any event, Secord and Peevers found that their adolescent subjects developed notions of self-reflectivity, volition, and self-evaluation as critical components of their self-understanding. For example, one typical self-reflective statement quoted by the authors was "I saw myself back in high school – just like I could sit back and watch myself go to school" (Secord & Peevers, 1974, p. 136). As an example of the awakened sense of adolescent volition, another subject said "If I don't like a subject, I won't do anything in the subject . . . and, on the other hand, the subjects I do like – my science and mathematics – I really work" (p. 139). This attitude, the authors write, demonstrates a recognition that inner processes like motivation determine the course of one's life events. Thus, the self is seen as active and self-generating: "There is a kind of projection of activities – self as agent enacting various scenes, rather than as a being with qualities" (p. 138).

Finally, in another manifestation of self-reflection and agency, the self is seen as its own evaluator. This, according to Secord and Peevers, takes place mostly on moral grounds, as in the following example: "But I still think that I consider popularity too important above other things, more than I should. . . . I don't like people who talk about other people behind their backs because it's – they wouldn't like it if they were talked about, and I don't think it's right" (p. 138).

A study by Bernstein (1980) elaborates some of the trends noted by

Secord and Peevers, particularly the early adolescent trends not mentioned by Selman or Broughton. Bernstein asked 10-, 15-, and 20-year-olds three types of questions designed to reveal their conceptions of the "self-system." The first type of question was directed at differentiation in self-system conceptions. A typical question was, "Everyone behaves differently in different situations with different people. List all the ways that you act." The second type of question, directed at abstractness in self-system conceptions, was of the following sort: "You have listed a number of different ways that you act. What does each of these tell you about yourself?" The third type of question was aimed at integration and asked the subject to "Put all of this together in a statement about yourself."

Bernstein expected that older subjects would demonstrate greater differentiation in their self-system conceptions than younger subjects by making statements from a larger number of self categories. This expectation was not confirmed. But Bernstein did find an age-related difference in the types of categories that subjects used. Children at age 10 were likely to refer to situational, behavioral, and emotional aspects of self (e.g., "I play at the playground"; "I hit my brother"; "I get mad at my mother") as respective examples of statements from situational, behavioral, and emotional categories. Adolescents at ages 15 and 20 were likely to refer to their social personality characteristics, their beliefs, and their acceptance of social rules, respectively ("I am really friendly, so I can make new friends easily"; "I think being a good sport is important, so if we lose a game, I am never a spoilsport"; "My mother thinks that it is wrong to cheat, so I don't").

As for abstraction, Bernstein reports that his youngest subjects generally were quite concrete, linking the self to direct action in most of their statements (e.g., "I mow the lawn at home"). Subjects in mid-adolescence linked together a variety of self-actions according to one common theme, thus demonstrating an initial abstraction. In older subjects, Bernstein found abstraction on the basis of "an underlying dimension which provides internal consistency for behaviors which appear discrepant" (p. 237).

Like Bernstein, Harter and her colleagues have demonstrated increased differentiation in adolescents' sense of self (Harter, 1986). In her prior research on children's understanding of multiple emotions, Harter had found that children and young adolescents had great difficulty in understanding that a person can experience both positive and negative emotions simultaneously. Extended to the self-concept, this finding led Harter to predict that only older adolescents are capable of acknowledging that the self can be characterized by traits and qualities that are opposites – for instance, that one can be "smart" and "dumb" at different times.

To test this hypothesis, Harter asked students in grades 7, 9, and 11 to describe themselves in four social contexts: with family, with friends, in school, and in romantic relationships. Each quality provided in these self-descriptions was written onto a label. Students were asked to place similar qualities together, as well as to place these qualities in one of three concentric circles representing qualities that are most important, of medium importance, or of little importance as descriptions of self. Next students were asked to indicate, by drawing lines, which of the qualities depicted in these "self-diagrams" were opposites. For instance, an adolescent might draw a line between "shy" and "outgoing" because these two qualities of self are polar extremes of the same dimension. Finally, Harter asked students to indicate whether any of their paired oppositions "clashed" to produce distress. Students were asked to draw arrowheads on the lines connecting the opposite characteristics that "clashed" with each other.

Harter found that there was a dramatic increase between 7th and 9th grade in the number of paired oppositions and clashes identified by adolescents. But these numbers declined by 11th grade, though still remaining higher than in 7th grade. This suggests that conflicting traits are recognized in early adolescence and later integrated into the same system.

Bernstein found a similar developmental trend toward conceptual integration of the self-system. Integrating statements of 10-year-old children were generally confined to a simple reiteration of previous self-definitions, without recognition of possible contradiction in diverse definitions. By mid-adolescence, diversity of self-definition is recognized, but no coordinating principle between discrepant elements is yet constructed. For example, one such response might be, "Well, when I am around my friends, I am really talkative and animated, but just around my family I sort of keep to myself. It's sort of like I am two different people; I don't know why." By the end of adolescence, according to Bernstein, integrating principles that recognize diversity yet maintain the coherence of the self-system are found. An example of an amended version of the previous statement might be, "When I am around my friends, I am really talkative because I feel like they are treating me like a person who has something interesting and important to say. My family doesn't listen to what I say, so I just don't feel like talking to hear myself speak." The principle here that coordinates between the two contradictory self-statements (talkativeness and silence) is the self's desire to engage in meaningful communication when talking.

Like the other research summarized in this chapter, Bernstein's work shows an adolescent transition from action-based conceptions of self to conceptions based on psychological characteristics, such as beliefs. Bernstein's research also taps into the divided self of adolescence as portrayed by Broughton and, like Broughton and Selman, shows how older adolescents resolve the contradictions of this division by constructing conceptual principles that coordinate the various features of self into a coherent system. Like Secord and Peevers, Bernstein stresses the adolescent tendency toward abstraction around stable, unifying qualities of self.

One such stabilizing quality emerging as primary in Bernstein's findings is the social-personality aspect of self. Bernstein shows how the young adolescent moves from a definition of the "me" in terms of transient actions and emotions to a definition revolving around stable personality traits with social implications. When, in later adolescence, one's personality becomes reformulated as reflecting one's enduring belief systems, the adolescent understands self primarily in abstract and psychological terms.

A study by Montemayor and Eisen (1977) asking children and adolescents for their free descriptions of themselves uncovered many of the same trends. Montemayor and Eisen used Gordon's self-concept coding system (Gordon, 1968) to analyze the free self-descriptions of subjects ages 9 to 18. The researchers found that, with age, adolescents more frequently used the following categories from Gordon's system (the proportional use of the categories with increasing age follows in parentheses): ideological beliefs (4%–39%), interpersonal style (42%–91%), psychic style (27%–72%), existential individuating (0%–54%), sense of self-determination (5%–49%), and sense of unity (0%–21%). Although the nominal labels of Gordon's categories differ somewhat from the language other authors have used, the concordance of results becomes apparent when we translate "existential" into "self-reflective"; "sense of self-determination" into "sense of volition" (or "personal agency"); "interpersonal style" into "social-personality characteristics"; and "psychic style" into "manner of mentally processing experience." Montemayor and Eisen also found that with age adolescents use the following categories less frequently: territoriality or citizenship (11%–8%), possessions (50%–8%), and body image (87%–16%).

Finally, it is noteworthy that even some studies that have focused primarily on self-esteem have tapped some of these developmental patterns. Rosenberg's broad-based series of studies into self-concept includes three components relevant to the issues in this review (Rosenberg, 1979). In one study Rosenberg asked subjects aged 8 through 18 about the following issues: points of pride and shame in self ("Could you tell me what things are really best about you?"; "Do you have any weak points, that is, any things not as good about you?"), sense of distinctiveness and commonality ("In what ways are you different from most other kids you know? In what ways are you the same?"), and ideal self ("What kind of person would you like to be when you grow up?"). Rosenberg found that, in response to these questions, children generally describe the self in terms of physical and active qualities whereas adolescents refer to psychological aspects. In addition, Rosenberg reports the rising importance of the self's social-personality characteristics during adolescence. When questioned about points of pride, 9% of the 8-year-olds' responses were interpersonal traits. When asked about the person the subject would like to become, 36% of the 8-year-olds' responses were interpersonal traits, whereas 69% of the 14- to 16-year-olds' responses were interpersonal traits. Finally, Rosenberg found that the self's ability to control itself becomes much more prominent during adolescence. When questioned about points of shame, only 14% of the 8-year-olds' responses were general traits reflecting self-control, whereas 32% of the 14- to 16-year-olds' responses were these kinds of general traits.

In a second part of his study, Rosenberg investigated the locus of self-knowledge – that is, who knows the self the best. Rosenberg reports that, with age, the perceived locus of self-knowledge shifts from the other (especially the parent) to the self. This finding, combined with reported increased use of psychological dimensions in adolescents' self-definitions, supports Broughton's position on the consequences for the adolescent of distinguishing the mental from the physical self. Once the mental self is understood on its own terms, according to Broughton, the self quickly becomes seen as the privileged and omniscient processor of one's experience. This leads to an awareness that no one can ever understand one's experience as fully as can oneself.

We have seen considerable congruence in research findings on adolescent self-understanding. Several researchers working independently have documented similar developmental trends, with regard to "me" (increased use of social-personality and psychological categories and declines in active and physical or material ones) as well as the "I" (increased awareness of personal agency, continuity, distinctness, and self-reflectivity). There are, of course, different emphases in the various investigations, and different speculations as to the conceptual roots of these changes. Column 3 in Table 2.1 summarizes the developmental trends uncovered thus far by research on adolescent self-knowledge.

When all the studies reviewed in this section are considered together, we have an approximate chronology of self-understanding development from infancy to adolescence. There are, however, many blank spaces, unresolved questions, and even contradictions in this chronology. We do not know, for example, the developmental relation between physical and active aspects of the "me" during childhood. Nor do we understand exactly how social and psychological considerations supplement (or do they replace?) physical and active ones during late childhood and early adolescence. Or is this really a developmental progression in the first place? A seeming contradiction here is that research has found evidence of active, social, and psychological self-conceptions in early childhood; and we also know that there is a continued later prevalence of physical self-conceptions during adolescence. What, then, is the nature of the developmental trend in self-understanding?

Further, we know that there is increasing awareness of the "I" throughout this age span, but we do not know how this development is related to developments in the "me" (although we do have a number of disparate and piecemeal speculations about this from many of the studies that have been done). In short, at this point we have a very rough chronology of self-understanding in childhood and adolescence; but this chronology is not nearly systematic enough to comprise a developmental model. In addition, the chronology as it now stands may be riddled with inaccuracies. The first purpose of this book is to try to improve this situation. In Chapter 3 we shall propose our own developmental model of self-understanding in childhood and adolescence, drawing from the existing rough chronology where it proves helpful.

3   A developmental model of self-understanding

In this chapter we present our theoretical model of self-understanding development during the years spanning childhood through late adolescence. The model derives from our literature review (presented in Chapter 2) and from the new interview responses that we collected in our current investigation. In the literature review, we found many working hypotheses but also a number of contradictions and significant gaps. We used our new data to confirm or reject various working hypotheses, resolve the most glaring contradictions, and fill the gaps wherever possible.

The new data that helped us formulate our developmental model were drawn from pilot work and from the early phases of studies described in Chapters 5 and 6. In preparation for these studies we designed a clinical interview procedure that drew extended verbal statements about self from our child and adolescent subjects. We discuss the interview procedure and the logic of the questioning that elicited these self-statements in Chapter 4. In the present chapter we quote some of the statements elicited by this interview in order to illustrate the substance of our model.

Also discussed in Chapter 4 is the scoring manual on which most data analyses throughout this book are based. Implicit in the scoring manual are the conceptual principles comprising our developmental model. In fact, the scoring manual is no more than an operational manifestation of the model, along with procedures guiding its application to actual verbal protocols. Therefore, before describing our methods of data collection and analysis, we present in the current chapter the theoretical distinctions that generated these methods.

As noted, the self-understanding model that we propose here derives in part from our literature review. In these reports of previous social and developmental studies, we found some widely replicated ontogenetic patterns. In our reading of these studies, the most important patterns of change in self-understanding during childhood and adolescence were the following:

53

1. An early awareness of self based on one's own activity and contingencies arising from such activity
2. An early awareness of physical categories of self like gender and size
3. An age-related shift from defining oneself through external characteristics (physical, material, and active categories) to defining oneself through internal qualities (psychological and "spiritual" categories)
4. An age-related tendency to integrate the diverse aspects of self into a seemingly coherent system

The trend toward internal categories (number 3) has been replicated so frequently that it has tempted many developmentalists to reduce self-concept development to unilateral dimensions like "surface to depth" (Flavell, 1977). Other researchers similarly have proposed dimensions like levels of abstraction (Fischer, 1980; Harter, 1983) and hierarchization (Montemayor & Eisen, 1977) to capture other aspects of these trends.

Nevertheless, in our opinion the ontogenetic data elude such unidimensional attempts. In both the prior literature and in the interview responses of our own subjects we found a far more complex and multidimensional pattern of development.

From a number of studies, including our own, it is clear that "surface to depth" (or, alternatively, physical to psychological) cannot be taken literally as the criterial index of a genuine developmental shift. First, there is much evidence that early self-understanding extends far beyond an awareness of external, physical qualities. Very young children readily express self-statements that are active and social in nature (e.g., their group activities and memberships); and they are also cognizant of aspects of their psychological selves (e.g., their emotional states). Further, advanced self-understanding continues to draw heavily on external categories. Physical and material characteristics of self remain important in many individuals' self-understanding throughout life. In fact, psychologists long have noted that the physical self, after a period of relative neglect, once again waxes in significance in a person's self-concept by late adolescence (Freud, 1922; Kohlberg & Gilligan, 1971).

We do not doubt that there are age-related phenomena that have led several researchers to analyze self-concept development in terms of a "surface to depth" or "physical to psychological" dimension. But we believe that these particular chosen labels do not capture the essence of these phenomena, and that they in fact misplace the locus of the actual developmental shift.

We would make a similar argument about the dimension of "abstractness." There is nothing necessarily more or less abstract about self-understanding as it develops: examples of highly concrete and highly abstract self-statements can be found all through the ontogenetic data. There may be some truth in the notion of developing abstraction as it is formulated in terms of systematic hierarchization: In this sense, although self-statements do not simply become more abstract with age, there is an increasing ability to move back and forth between the various possible levels of abstraction. But, again, the developmental shift that this notion tries to capture is most accurately represented by a multidimensional model that respects distinctness in the various components of self-understanding.

Figure 3.1 depicts the multidimensional developmental model that we shall be working with throughout this book. We explain below the features, assumptions, and implications of the model.

Organization of the self-understanding model

The model is organized horizontally along two major dimensions, represented by the front and side faces of the cube depicted in Figure 3.1. The front-face dimension corresponds to the Jamesian "me," the side-face dimension to subject's conceptual awareness of the Jamesian "I." The model also provides subdimensions. The "me" along the cube's front face is broken down into four constituent "self-schemes": the physical, active, social, and psychological schemes. The "I" along the side face is broken down into three subjective processes of awareness: the sense of continuity, the sense of distinctness, and the sense of agency.

The vertical dimension of the model represents the progressions through which the various components of self-understanding develop during the period from childhood to late adolescence. These developmental progressions play themselves out somewhat differently across the model's horizontal dimensions and subdimensions. Strictly speaking, each subdimension of both "me" and "I" develops in the direction of its own concerns: hence, the particular contents of each of the model's 28 boxes.

But apart from the specific nature of each developing subdimension, there are varying degrees of commonality across the horizontal components. Most notably, the developmental progressions in the model's front-face "me" schemes have enough in common that they can be described as a general "me" sequence. In Figure 3.1, this general "me" sequence is given numbers and labels to the left of the cube's front face. As for the "I" components, there is also some degree of commonality in developmental direction, especially between the senses of continuity and distinctness. Such commonalities, however, do not extend so far as to constitute a general "I" sequence.

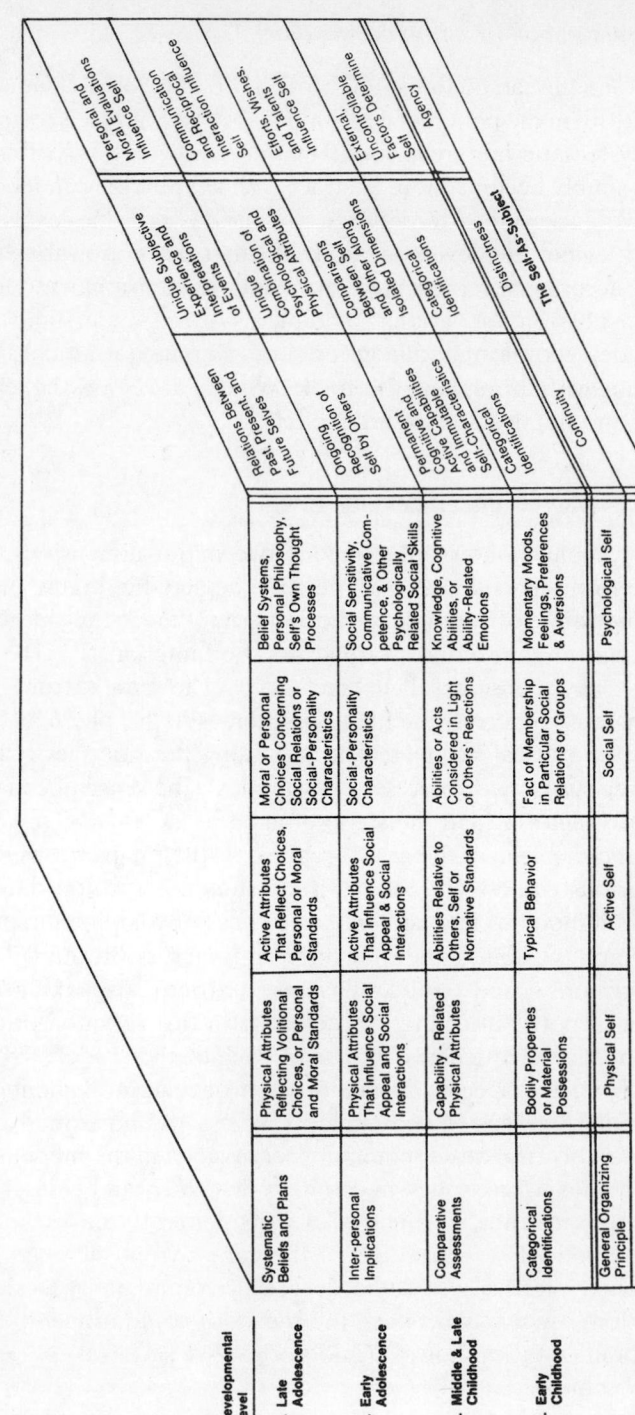

Fig. 3.1. The developmental model of self-understanding.

The front-face progressions: understanding the self-as-object

The front-face progressions, as noted previously, represent developments in the self-as-object, or Jamesian "me." We have chosen to subdivide the self-as-object into four basic schemes, the physical, active, social, and psychological. This choice follows, we believe, the natural contours of the "me"'s domain, and reflects distinctions made by James in his outline of the objective self's constituents.

The choice to represent the four self-as-object schemes as horizontal rather than vertical dimensions of the model indicates one of our fundamental assumptions about self-understanding development. Unlike previous researchers, we do not believe that a true developmental shift is expressed in children's movement from physical to active, social, and psychological conceptions of self. Rather, as the model suggests, we believe that each of the physical, active, social, and psychological modes of construing self undergoes developmental change throughout the entire period from early childhood to late adolescence (and no doubt beyond, though that is not the subject of this book). At all ages, children have some understanding of their physical, active, social, and psychological selves. Knowledge of each scheme changes with development, but never to the extent that one scheme disappears or turns into another scheme, as a developmental shift from (say) the physical to the psychological might imply.

The developmental progression common to the four self-as-object schemes is hierarchical in nature. It signifies a conceptual reorganization as opposed to a mere preferential shift or some other empirical tendency. We admit to the possibility that there *may* be age-related trends along the horizontal dimension, as for example the oft-posited trend toward construing the self in social or psychological terms. But we maintain that, if such trends indeed exist, they do not consist of developmental reorganizations in which one mode of self-understanding becomes transformed into another. The developmental transitions in our model, therefore, take place along the vertical dimension alone. Whether there are additional age-related movements from one scheme to the next along the horizontal front face is an empirical question unrelated to the main developmental reorganizations embodied in this model.

The logic of the general self-as-object sequence is explicated in the following descriptions. It is important to note that, in a hierarchical model such as this one, the earlier levels become part of the later ones, though in a somewhat new form. Thus, for example, self-understanding of the "me" is always categorical, as at Level 1; but later levels employ the categorical mode for new purposes. Thus, earlier forms of self-understanding neither disappear nor are retained per se. Rather they continue to function in transformed state as part of later forms.

We also note here that when we write of hierarchical levels we refer to forms of self-understanding and not to subjects. In the model that we present, each level incorporates the preceding one; but this does not mean that children as they grow move neatly from one level to the next by reorganizing all their self-notions of a piece. Our claim that earlier forms of self-understanding are incorporated into later forms bears no implication for the unity of a child's reasoning about self. In describing herself, a 10-year-old could well make many statements representing multiple developmental levels. To say that the higher-level statements that she makes incorporate lower forms does not mean that everything this child says can be analyzed at the higher levels. Simply put, the developmental sequence presented below is intended to analyze self-statements. How a particular self-statement made by a particular child relates to other self-statements by that child, and what the aggregate of the child's self-statements on a given occasion say about the child's functional capacities for self-understanding, are separate questions not addressed by the developmental sequence itself.

Although the following progression is logical and hierarchical, we do not see it as inevitable. With different social-contextual conditions, alternate sequences are possible, even likely. This is not to say that Level 1 could ever follow from Level 2, or 3 from 4; such inversions would defy the logic of developmental reorganization. But a variant form of Level 2 could probably grow out of Level 1, and so on for Levels 3 and 4, under cultural conditions where the boundaries of self are drawn differently than in contemporary urban America. We shall explore one such set of conditions in Chapter 8. From repeated documentations in the sociological and anthropological literatures, we are convinced that many other such conditions exist in the world today.

Below we describe each level in the developmental sequence of self-as-object, as depicted along the front face of the cube in Figure 3.1. First we discuss the general features of each level, and then we discuss the actual manifestation of these features in the developmental progressions on the four self schemes (physical, active, social, and psychological). As can be seen from the following descriptions, the intersection of level and scheme in each case defines a unique conception of self-as-object. To illustrate the 16 level-by-scheme descriptions, we offer examples of self-statements drawn from our interview with children and adolescents between the ages of 4 and 18.

Level 1 – Categorical identifications

The self is understood as a number of separate categorical identifications with taxonomic value only. Categories like group memberships, typical activities, and physical characteristics are offered as simple face descriptions without further underlying significance. This is because they are seen as sufficient in themselves. No relational links between the various categorical identifications are expressed, and many of the self-descriptions therefore have a transductive quality.

As noted previously, categorical identifications of self continue to be made throughout the entire self-as-object sequence, because the self-as-object inevitably must be conceived in terms of some set of categories, however organized. Lewis and Brooks-Gunn, recognizing this inevitability, refer to the self-as-object in their own investigation as the "categorical self" (Lewis & Brooks-Gunn, 1979). In our hierarchical developmental model, the higher levels incorporate the categorical mode of Level 1 into new forms of organization. Categories become linked to one another and to various ulterior rationales in different ways at different levels. At Level 1 the categorical identifications are fundamental, as they must be for any construction of the Jamesian "me." But unlike higher-level constructions, there is at Level 1 little else beyond the face categorical description.

Determination of a Level 1 response in an interview relies on proper use of the clinical method, as discussed in Chapter 4. Without probing, it may be impossible to determine whether a subject offers a categorical description as a self-definer in and of itself, or whether the subject has in mind a further rationale or system of relationships underlying the categorical description. Only when a categorical statement is probed by a question like "Why is that important?" and no further meaningful response is offered by the subject can the statement be analyzed as an example of Level 1.

Level 1, physical self-scheme. Physical and material attributes of self, which may include one's size, gender, race, distinctive bodily features, age, dress, possessions, or physical environment, are important in and of themselves.

Examples

WHAT KIND OF PERSON ARE YOU? I have blue eyes. WHY IS THAT IMPORTANT? It just is.

WHAT KIND OF PERSON ARE YOU? I sweat a lot. WHAT DIFFERENCE DOES THAT MAKE? I just do. I sweat a lot.

WHAT COULD YOU NEVER CHANGE ABOUT YOURSELF? That I'm a man, I'm a boy. IS THAT AN IMPORTANT THING ABOUT YOU AS A PERSON? Yes. HOW IS THAT IMPORTANT?

I don't know, but I just like being a man. WHY DO YOU LIKE IT? Because that's just what I am.

WHAT ELSE WOULD YOU LIKE TO CHANGE ABOUT YOURSELF? My arms. If I had floppy arms I would look like Ernie. DO YOU WANT TO LOOK LIKE ERNIE? (Shakes head no.) NO? No, if I had floppy arms like Bert, I would look like Bert. So if I didn't have floppy arms, I would look like myself.

WHAT MAKES YOU DIFFERENT FROM ALL THE OTHER KIDS IN YOUR CLASS? Well, some people are six in my class. WHY IS IT IMPORTANT THAT SOME PEOPLE ARE SIX AND SOME PEOPLE ARE FIVE LIKE YOU? I don't know.

WHAT ELSE COULD YOU SAY ABOUT YOURSELF? I live at 31 Pleasant Avenue. WHY IS THAT IMPORTANT TO YOU? 'Cause that's where I live.

Level 1, active self-scheme. The self is described in terms of typical activities that one performs, or that one is expected, allowed, or not allowed to perform.

Examples

WHAT ARE YOU LIKE? I play baseball. WHY IS THAT IMPORTANT? I'm not sure.

WHAT CAN YOU TELL ME ABOUT THE KIND OF PERSON YOU ARE? Yesterday I went to visit my cousins at their new house. WHY IS THAT IMPORTANT TO SAY ABOUT YOU? 'Cause I never went to their house before.

HOW ARE YOU DIFFERENT FROM YOUR MOTHER? 'Cause I play a lot and I read a lot. IS THAT WHAT MAKES YOU DIFFERENT FROM YOUR MOM? Sure, my Mommy just watches television, cooks, or cleans. AND YOU READ. And I write, and I play with my toys.

Level 1, social self-scheme. The self is defined by the fact of one's association with family, friends, or other social figures, or by one's memberships in defined social groups.

Examples

WHAT CAN YOU TELL ME ABOUT THE KIND OF PERSON YOU ARE? Well, I have a little sister named Samantha, and I'm gonna have a baby (i.e., this child is about to get a new sibling). And I have a mother and a father. WELL, WHY IS IT IMPORTANT TO TELL ME ABOUT ALL THOSE PEOPLE? I don't know, they're just my family.

WOULD YOU BE SARAH IF YOU HAD A DIFFERENT MOMMY OR DADDY? (Shakes head "no.") WHY? Well, 'cause if I had no Daddy and no Mommy and no cat and no dog and no cat and no self, there would be none family.

WHAT WILL BE THE SAME ABOUT YOU IN FIVE YEARS? I'll still be friends with Sean. WHY IS THAT IMPORTANT? 'Cause Sean's gonna be my friend, and he's my friend now.

WHAT KIND OF A PERSON ARE YOU? I'm Catholic. WHAT DOES THAT SAY ABOUT YOU? I'm Catholic, and my mother is, and my father is, and my grandmother, and my grandfather, and I'm Catholic too.

ARE YOU PROUD OF ANYTHING ABOUT YOURSELF? Yeah, I'm proud that I made little league. WHY ARE YOU PROUD OF MAKING LITTLE LEAGUE? 'Cause I didn't make it last year, and this is my last year to be in it, and I'm proud that I made it.

Level 1, psychological self-scheme. Psychological attributes of self are moods, thoughts, feelings, and attitudes that have their own significance, unrelated to permanent dispositions, abilities, or beliefs.

Examples

WHAT KIND OF PERSON ARE YOU? I get funny ideas sometimes. WHAT KIND OF IDEAS? I don't know, they just pop into my head. WHAT DO THESE IDEAS TELL YOU ABOUT YOURSELF? They just make me laugh.

WHAT KIND OF PERSON ARE YOU? I'm a happy person. WHY IS THAT IMPORTANT? I don't want to be a sad person.

WHAT KIND OF A PERSON ARE YOU? I don't like to stay on the porch. WHY IS THAT IMPORTANT? I don't know.

WHAT WOULD BE DIFFERENT ABOUT YOU IF YOU HAD DIFFERENT PARENTS? The difference would be, like, like when I'm five years old and my parents bring me to a store and then as I grow older, like I'm eight and they bring me to another store but it's not the same parents, maybe my excitement or feelings would change in different ways and I wouldn't feel the same.

Level 2 – Comparative assessments

The self is defined in relation to others and to normative physical or social standards. Self-understanding focuses on comparisons between the performances and capabilities of self versus the performances and capabilities of real or imagined others.

Such comparisons can be explicit ("I do . . . better than . . . ") or implicit ("I can't stay in the sun very long"). In either case, categories of self are transformed into relational statements that make a statement about the self's capabilities or quality of performance ("I play baseball better than my sister"; "I am smart for my age"; "I am a good Catholic"). Information about self is used to establish or support such actual or implied comparisons.

The relative capabilities that define the self can be drawn from any of the self schemes. They may include size, strength, looks, talent, intelligence, social behavior, effort, or virtually any other self-characteristic that can be compared against others' personal qualities or against external normative standards. When self is compared against a norm rather than an actual person or people, issues of approval or disapproval by others may enter (e.g., "I know when I am doing as well as I can because my teacher gives me a smile when I am and a glare when I'm not").

Comparative assessments may be one of many possible second-level reorganizations of self-understanding following from Level 1 categories identifications. Certainly it seems the dominant if not the only one found in our culture, judging from our own findings as well as Ruble's data on mid-childhood developments in self-conception (Ruble, 1983). But as noted earlier, we believe that alternative versions of Level 2 may exist in social-cultural circumstances that differ from the urban United States.

Our exploratory study of children and adolescents living in a small Puerto Rican fishing village, described in Chapter 8, bears this out to some extent. The alternative version of Level 2 that we found in this study followed closely the less individually competitive and more socially judgmental cultural ethic of the small fishing community. There was some conceptual overlap between the mainland U.S. and Puerto Rican Level 2 self-statements, but there was also a culturally related emphasis in each that distinguishes the two sets of mid-childhood responses. In even more radically variant cultural circumstances we would expect even less overlap and greater distinctiveness in the sequence of developmental reorganizations following Level 1.

Level 2, physical self-scheme. Physical and material attributes of self reflect or influence one's capabilities.

Examples

WHAT ARE YOU LIKE? I'm bigger than most kids. WHY IS THAT IMPORTANT? I can run faster than everybody.

IS THERE ANYTHING YOU WANT TO BE THAT YOU'RE NOT? Yeah, tall. WHY DO YOU WANT TO BE TALL? So I could play basketball like Dr. J.

WHAT'S MOST IMPORTANT TO SAY ABOUT YOU? Probably that I like sports. WHY IS THAT MOST IMPORTANT? 'Cause, I don't know, that's what most of the boys like and that's what most people like to hear about boys.

WHAT ARE YOU LIKE? I have really light skin because I'm Scandinavian. WHAT DIFFERENCE DOES THAT MAKE? Well, in the summer I can't go to the beach or sit in the sun for long because I get sunburnt.

WHAT ARE YOU PROUD OF ABOUT YOURSELF? I have a good build. Like, I have muscles. WHY DOES THAT MAKE YOU PROUD? Because I'm strong and good at sports.

WHAT IS IMPORTANT ABOUT THE KIND OF PERSON YOU ARE? My brain's important; my legs are important. HOW ARE YOUR BRAIN AND YOUR LEGS IMPORTANT TO THE KIND OF PERSON YOU ARE? I can run fast. I'm smart.

Level 2, active self-scheme. Self is defined in terms of actions and abilities that are implicitly or explicitly compared with actions and abilities of others, of normative standards, or of oneself in different circumstances.

Examples

WHAT ARE YOU LIKE? I'm not very good at school. WHAT DIFFERENCE DOES THAT MAKE? My grades are like C's and D's.

DESCRIBE YOURSELF. I'm good at doing things. WHAT THINGS? In school, like in math and history and reading. But I'm not so good at art or gym.

WHAT KIND OF PERSON ARE YOU? Athletic. WHAT DO YOU MEAN? I play lots of sports, and I play aggressively. WHAT DO YOU MEAN, YOU PLAY AGGRESSIVELY? It means I try to win really hard, and I'll take chances, like in football kicking into a kid who's bigger than me.

WHAT ARE YOU LIKE? Not very active. IN WHAT WAY ARE YOU NOT ACTIVE? I don't do a lot of things. Well, I do things. Usually quiet things, though, like reading or watching TV. But I don't do really active things, like sports.

WHAT WERE YOU LIKE FIVE YEARS AGO? Not as particular as I am now. WHAT DO YOU MEAN? Well, most people, when they do something, like when they clean their room, they just do it a little, like hang up their clothes or something. But I always clean everything really carefully.

Level 2, social self-scheme. One's abilities are considered in light of the reactions of other people. Such reactions may include approval, disapproval, or any affective response.

Examples

WHAT MAKES YOU FEEL PROUD? When my Mom and Dad come and watch a game, and I play really well, like I hit a lot of homers, and I can hear them cheering really loud. WHY DOES THAT MAKE YOU PROUD? 'Cause they're letting me know how I did good.

HOW WAS WHAT YOU TOLD ME DIFFERENT FROM HOW YOU WERE FIVE YEARS AGO? Nothing, really, except I used to cheat a while ago. WHY DO YOU THINK YOU USED TO CHEAT? Because I wasn't sure of myself. I wasn't sure that I would do good on the test, and I wanted to get good marks in school because if I didn't I'd get grounded. AND NOW? Now I know I can do well in school. AND WHAT DIFFERENCE DOES THAT MAKE? Well people, my parents respect me for it and all, I don't have to worry about what they'll think about it if I come home with a bad mark on something.

Level 2, psychological self-scheme. Self is construed in psychological terms reflecting one's cognitive capabilities, relative knowledge, or ability-related emotional states.

Examples

WHAT ARE YOU LIKE? I'm not as smart as most kids. WHY IS THAT IMPORTANT? It takes me longer to do my homework.

HOW DO YOU KNOW YOU'RE THE SAME PERSON? 'Cause through my mind. WHY IS YOUR MIND IMPORTANT? 'Cause if you didn't have a mind, you wouldn't think that good.

WHO ARE YOU MOST LIKE? No one. NO ONE? No. WHY? Because I'm different. HOW DO YOU KNOW YOU'RE DIFFERENT? 'Cause I read and they don't. A few kids don't know how to read. Well, lots of kids don't know how to read in my class. AND THAT MAKES YOU SPECIAL? Well, they can't read hard books, but I can.

HOW WILL YOU BE DIFFERENT IN FIVE YEARS? I'll get more mature. WHEN YOU SAY YOU'LL GET MORE MATURE, WHAT DO YOU MEAN WHEN YOU SAY THAT? Like when you're getting older, like when you're little you don't know stuff, a lot of stuff, and you say the wrong things. When you're getting older you know what to say. Like if you have a child, like they wouldn't know what to do so you could tell 'em.

Level 3 – Interpersonal implications

Self-understanding focuses on characteristics of self that determine the nature of one's interactions with others. Categorical identifications with interpersonal implications are emphasized. These may include personality traits, action propensities, physical attractiveness, material appeal, or states of mind that determine the type or manner of one's interpersonal life.

In Level 3 self-statements, the comparative mode of Level 2 is transformed in the assessment of one's capacities for conducting interpersonal relationships. The main concern is now transformed from drawing relational analogies between self and others to identifying one's manner of interacting with others. Implicit or explicit comparative statements, therefore, assess the quality of one's interactional capacities. Beyond comparisons, there is also a concern at Level 3 for the nature of any stable personality traits that may define one's place and manner of operating in the social network.

The emergence of Level 3 self-understanding in later childhood and early adolescence has led many researchers to conclude that conceptions of the social self develop at this time. We believe that this conclusion is a misrepresentation of the developmental shift that actually occurs – namely, the shift to Level 3 conceptions of self.

Level 3, as we have defined it, does indeed have a strong social component, but we believe that it is nevertheless inaccurate to conflate Level 3 with the social self. As our developmental model suggests, awareness of the social self is always present, from early childhood through late adolescence (and no doubt beyond). At every level in the self-understanding sequence there is a social-scheme conception. The social self, therefore, goes well beyond Level 3, and includes a host of notions that strictly speaking do not focus on the implications of one's characteristics for the nature of one's interpersonal interactions.

Level 3 is a particular mode of using categorical, comparative, and stable personality notions to determine how one gets along in the social world.

It transverses all of the self-schemes, from physical to psychological, drawing interpersonal implications from each where appropriate. Level 3 therefore is neither limited to the social self nor exhausts the domain of the social self. It is an interpersonally oriented mode of construing the self that transforms prior-level notions into a new perspective on all aspects of the self-as-object.

Level 3, physical self-scheme. Self is defined by physical or material attributes that influence one's interpersonal interactions. Such physical or material attributes may reflect one's personal appeal, may affect one's social relations, or may determine one's group memberships and associations.

Examples

WHAT IS THE MOST IMPORTANT THING TO SAY ABOUT YOU? I'm very strong and I'm in terrific shape. WHY IS THAT IMPORTANT? Well everybody I meet respects me for it.

WHAT KIND OF A PERSON ARE YOU? A four-eyed person. WHAT DOES THAT MEAN? I wear glasses. That's what all the kids call me. WHAT DIFFERENCE DOES THAT MAKE? They make fun of me.

WHAT IS THE MOST IMPORTANT THING TO SAY ABOUT YOU? I'm a girl. WHY IS THAT IMPORTANT TO SAY ABOUT YOU? Because girls usually play with girls, and boys play with boys. So if someone wants to be my friend, they would want to know if I was a boy or a girl.

WHAT'S GOOD FOR YOU? To have blond hair. WHY IS THAT GOOD FOR YOU? Because boys like girls with blond hair. THEY DO? Yeah, like all the boys in my class like this blond girl, and she has three boyfriends. I only have one boyfriend. If I had blond hair, maybe I could have more.

WHAT KIND OF A PERSON ARE YOU? Pretty rich. WHAT DIFFERENCE DOES THAT MAKE? Well, my family has a lot of money, so we can belong to the country club.

Level 3, active self-scheme. Self is construed in terms of activities that influence one's interpersonal appeal, social relations, or group memberships.

Examples

WHAT KIND OF A PERSON ARE YOU? I play sports. WHY IS THAT IMPORTANT? Because all the kids like athletes.

WHAT'S GOOD FOR YOU? Getting an education. WHY IS IT GOOD FOR YOU TO GET AN EDUCATION? So you won't be dumb. WHY DON'T YOU WANT TO BE DUMB? 'Cause if you're dumb, no one really wants to be your friend if you're stupid.

WHAT'S IMPORTANT TO SAY ABOUT YOU? That I treat people well, I share whatever I've got with kids I play with, and I don't get into too many fights over stupid things. WHY ARE THOSE THINGS IMPORTANT? Because it means that I'll always have friends when I need them. People notice how you act to them and it counts in the long run. IT COUNTS FOR WHAT? For your friendships, for the way they like you.

WHAT ARE YOU LIKE? I'm not a stiff grind or anything like that. WHAT DO YOU MEAN? Well I don't spend all my time studying or hanging around the teacher. WHY IS THAT IMPORTANT? Well I don't think my guys would appreciate me very much if that's all I did.

Level 3, social self-scheme. Self is understood in terms of social-personality characteristics that reflect or influence one's interactions, interpersonal appeal, or group memberships.

Examples

WHAT KIND OF A PERSON ARE YOU? I'm a nice person. WHAT'S NICE ABOUT YOU? I'm not selfish. Like if somebody says, they go to the teacher and say, "I don't have any ice cream, and I don't have any lunch either, and I can't have any money to buy any fruit. I need that lunch, and the lunch guys won't give me any lunch." I would say, "Here, have my money." I did that to Shannon.

WHAT ARE YOU LIKE? I'm an honest person, and I was raised that way, and people trust me because of it.

WHAT KIND OF A PERSON ARE YOU? I am friendly. WHY IS THAT IMPORTANT? Other kids won't like you if you aren't.

WHAT'S IMPORTANT TO SAY ABOUT YOU? I guess that I'm very, very shy. I was that way ever since I can remember and I still am. WHAT DIFFERENCE DOES THAT MAKE? Well it means that I'm very quiet in public. I don't have a lot of friends, but the ones I have are good ones. WHY DO YOU THINK THAT IS? Well probably because I'm the quiet type and we feel comfortable with each other.

Level 3, psychological self-scheme. Psychological attributes of self reflect social skills or influence social interactions.

Examples

WHAT KIND OF PERSON ARE YOU? I am very smart. WHY IS THAT IMPORTANT? My friends only like smart kids.

WHAT ARE YOU PROUD OF? I'm really good with people. WHAT DO YOU MEAN? Well, I can understand them. Like when they have problems, they come to me to talk about it. My friends, like, do that.

WHAT KIND OF A PERSON ARE YOU? I'm the kind of person who loves being with my friends. WHY DO YOU THINK YOU FEEL THAT WAY ABOUT YOUR FRIENDS? I just feel so good about them. I can really be myself with them. They make me feel good about me.

WHAT MAKES YOU FEEL REALLY PROUD? I guess one thing is that I'm really smart. Like I know a lot about bikes and how to fix them. WHY DOES THAT MAKE YOU PROUD? Well everyone's got a bike and word gets around that I know how to fix them, and I've met a lot of people and made a lot of friends that way.

WHAT ARE YOU LIKE? I know a lot about the world and how it works and I have a great desire to learn more. WHY IS THAT IMPORTANT? My teachers respect it. I've had very good relations with my teachers and I've gotten a lot of things, a lot out of it.

Level 4 – Systematic beliefs and plans

Categories of the self-as-object are organized through systematic beliefs and life plans. Characteristics of self draw their meaning for one's identity through such beliefs and plans, which may include philosophical or moral belief systems, ideological choices, or any variety of personal goals. The priority of the belief or plan creates a new coherence in self-understanding, because self-defining categories are selected and related to one another only in a manner consistent with the belief or plan. At this level, therefore, a consciously systematic conception of self is first achieved.

Because the focus of self-understanding at Level 4 is on one's cognitive constructions (beliefs and plans), there is a danger of conflating Level 4 with the psychological self-scheme. Indeed, studies often have found a purported increase in "psychological" self-conceptions during late adolescence, when Level 4 first emerges. We believe that this conception is similar to the mistaken conflation of Level 3 with the social self-scheme.

Awareness of the psychological self can be found at every developmental level. What emerges at Level 4 is the focus on a particular aspect of the psychological self, one's beliefs and life plans, and a tendency to construct a coherent self-concept system based upon such beliefs and plans. In the process, all aspects of the self, including the physical, active, and social, may be incorporated into the system. Thus, Level 4 goes far beyond the psychological self, while at the same time representing one, relatively advanced, version of psychological self-conception. Previous studies, in concluding that self-conceptions simply become more psychological with age, have misidentified the nature of the late-adolescent developmental transition.

Level 4, physical self-scheme. Physical or material attributes of self reflect one's personal philosophy, moral or ideological beliefs, or life plans and goals.

Examples

WHAT ARE YOU LIKE? I don't have many things. WHY IS THAT IMPORTANT? It's not fair to have a lot of things when some people don't have anything.

WHAT ARE YOU NOT LIKE? Skinny. And I'm not fat. WHAT DOES THAT SAY ABOUT YOU? Well, I don't want to be skinny because it makes me think of all the starving people all over the world, and it's a terrible thing that some people are fat and other people are starving to death.

HOW HAVE YOU CHANGED IN THE PAST FIVE YEARS? My clothes have changed. In my religion, a woman has to be modest in dress. WHAT DO YOU MEAN? Well there's rules, like when you get to be twelve you have to wear dresses that go down to your knees.

WHAT ARE YOU PROUD OF ABOUT YOURSELF? I'm pretty without having to wear makeup. WHY DOES THAT MAKE YOU FEEL PROUD? Because it's like a lie to wear makeup, because that's not what you really are. Everyone should just be themselves. WHY IS IT IMPORTANT THAT YOU'RE PRETTY? Because beauty is the most important thing in the world. Not just in the way you look, but in everything that you do and are, it's good to be beautiful, but only if it's real and not false.

Level 4, active self-scheme. Self is defined by activities that reflect one's personal philosophy, ideology, moral beliefs, or life plans.

Examples

WHAT ARE YOU LIKE? I go to church every Sunday. WHY IS THAT IMPORTANT? Because I want to be a faithful Christian.

WHAT MAKES YOU MOST PROUD OF YOURSELF? Reading well, being a good reader. WHAT MAKES YOU PROUD ABOUT BEING A GOOD READER? Well, it helps you in learning a lot because you have to do a lot of reading in school. WHY DO YOU WANT TO DO WELL IN SCHOOL? Well, 'cause if you get good marks you get into a better college and get a better chance of getting a good education. WHY DO YOU WANT A GOOD EDUCATION? Well, it makes me feel proud of myself for one thing, and also I want to do something that requires a lot of education. It is really important for me to be artistic and expressive, and I want to be a writer or something, and you have to know a lot about literature, and having good grades. If I do well in school I'll have a better chance of doing it.

Level 4, social self-scheme. Social aspects of self reflect one's personal philosophy, ideology, moral beliefs, or life plans.

Examples

WHAT ELSE IS IMPORTANT ABOUT YOU? I'm a Girl Scout. WHY IS THAT IMPORTANT? Because we do good things. We help people and stuff. If more people did what we did, the world would be a better place.

WHAT ARE YOU LIKE? I act really good with my friends. WHY IS HOW YOU ACT AN IMPORTANT THING TO SAY ABOUT WHAT YOU'RE LIKE? Because you want to have a lot of friends. Sometimes kids could care less about friends, but I think that I would want a lot of friends. So the way you act has a big deal, because if you think you're big then people will say don't go near him 'cause he's doing this. Or if you smoke or something kids will just stay away from you. Or kids will join you in what you're doing, and you don't want to be a leader in, like, badness. That's bad. WHAT DO YOU MEAN? Kids will follow the person who they think they'll idolize. RIGHT. And you don't want to idolize bad kids, you want to idolize good. WHY? Because our society will turn into a disgrace.

Level 4, psychological self-scheme. Psychological aspects of self reflect one's personal philosophy, ideology, moral beliefs, or life plans.

Examples

WHAT KIND OF A PERSON ARE YOU? I believe in world peace. WHY IS THAT IMPORTANT? I don't think wars solve anything and I think we should try to keep from fighting.

WHAT'S GOOD FOR YOU? Morals. HOW ARE MORALS GOOD FOR YOU? They control everything. WHAT DO YOU MEAN? Well, I think that people should all stick together and help each other out. So everything I do, I do like that. And I'll always be like that.

WHAT ARE YOU ESPECIALLY PROUD OF ABOUT YOURSELF? I'm always learning and growing. HOW ARE YOU ALWAYS LEARNING AND GROWING? I try to find out as much as I can about things, all different things, and put it all together so I can really know what's going on. And I'm always getting better and better at it. WHY IS THAT IMPORTANT? That's what's going to make me become the kind of person I want to be, a person on top of things.

WHAT KIND OF PERSON ARE YOU? I am someone who believes that everybody is created equal. WHY IS THAT IMPORTANT? Because I want to work for equal rights for everybody. WHAT DO YOU MEAN? I'm going to be a lawyer and take cases and see that everyone gets rights, even if he's very poor or the wrong color or something.

WHAT'S GOOD FOR YOU? To be true to my self, to what I believe in. WHAT DOES THAT MEAN? It means being really honest with yourself and others, and to get something you believe and stick to it. WHAT DIFFERENCE DOES THAT MAKE? Like I believe in health, holistic medicine, that kind of thing. I'm a vegetarian. It helps me figure out what foods to eat, how to live my life, everything. I don't smoke or drink, and I don't spend a lot of time with people who do.

Further examples of the self-as-object levels will be presented in Chapter 5 along with our report of findings from our longitudinal study. There we offer some extended quotes from the interview responses of two subjects as a means of illustrating their transitions from childhood to adolescent modes of understanding self.

The side-face progressions: understanding the self-as-subject

The side face of the model depicted in Figure 3.1 represents developing conceptions of the self-as-subject, or Jamesian "I." We emphasize that the three self-as-subject sequences are progressions in *conceptions* of the self-as-subject and not in the self-as-subject per se. Thus, as noted earlier, we concern ourselves here with children's and adolescent's developing under-standing of the "I" and not with the developing "I" itself. Of course there is likely to be a relation, or a set of relations, between the two. For example, one's conception of one's own agency may well reflect or influence the nature of one's agentic acts. But for the purposes of this investigation we assume no such links, focusing instead on the nature of the conception in and of itself.

The model's three self-as-subject components – agency, continuity, and distinctness – largely cover the domain of the subjective self as explored in philosophical and psychological analyses. The most salient omission is the dimension of reflection, inaccessible to us because of methodological difficulties. Taken together, the model's three self-as-subject dimensions encompass somewhat different visions of the "I." As noted in Chapter 1, traditions that emphasize the subjective self's role in constructing a sense of personal identity have concerned themselves mainly with the components of continuity and distinctness. Strains of philosophy and psychology influenced by the existentialist perspective have focused instead on agency (and reflection, though we have omitted it here). In his diverse and multifaceted writings on the self-as-subject, William James made note of all these components but did not suggest that they comprise a unified system – nor have others following in his path.

For this reason, we do not propose, nor did we find, a general developmental sequence applying to all three components of the self-as-subject. Rather, we describe the three "I" progressions in our model separately, each on its own terms. There certainly are commonalities between some of the three, particularly as regards continuity and distinctness, that are linked both by their personal identity function and their complementary conceptual status. In addition, there are a variety of conceptual links between the three self-as-subject sequences and the general self-as-object sequences already described. These links will be apparent in our description of the self-as-subject progressions. Much of the developmental direction in the three self-as-subject progressions can be attributed to these links, although each of these three sequences is also directed by its own organizing principles that reflect the distinct concern of each particular component.

Agency component, self-as-subject

Level 1: Supernatural, biological, or social forces determine the existence or formation of self.

Examples

HOW DID YOU GET TO BE THE KIND OF PERSON YOU ARE NOW? I eat and sleep and drink, and it helps me grow. IS THAT THE ONLY WAY YOU GOT TO BE THE WAY YOU ARE NOW? I guess.

HOW DID YOU GET TO BE THE WAY YOU ARE? I just grew. WHAT DO YOU MEAN BY THAT? My body just got bigger.

Level 2: One's talents, abilities, wishes, motivation, or efforts influence the existence or formation of self.

Examples

HOW DID YOU GET TO BE LIKE YOU ARE NOW? I tried really hard. WHAT DIFFERENCE DOES THAT MAKE? Well, I tried really hard to be like I am now.

HOW DID YOU GET TO BE THE KIND OF PERSON YOU ARE NOW? From getting good grades in school from studying. HOW DID GOOD GRADES MAKE YOU THE PERSON YOU ARE? HOW DID STUDYING MAKE YOU THE PERSON YOU ARE? Because I used to do all my homework. Once in a while I might have goofed up or something and I forgot it or something like that. I remember one time, there was this teacher named Miss Cowan, and I forgot my homework once and oh, I remember that. I had to write the words five times each. I wrote about 300 words. Like I wrote cat, cat, cat, cat, cat and dog, dog, dog, dog, dog. All the animals and stuff. SO HOW DID STUDYING MAKE YOU THE PERSON YOU ARE THOUGH? If I didn't study I'd kind of be a little bit dumb.

Level 3: Communication with others influences the existence or formation of the self.

Examples

HOW DID YOU GET TO BE THE WAY YOU ARE? By talking with my parents. They help me understand things better, even if I don't always do what they say.

HOW DID YOU GET TO BE THE KIND OF PERSON YOU ARE NOW. I learned from my parents. I even learned from my friends, just listening to 'em and talking to 'em. HOW DOES LISTENING TO THEM AND TALKING TO THEM MAKE YOU THE PERSON YOU ARE? I probably got a lot of my personality from them too 'cause most of my friends are really nice. So when I first moved here, if I started out hanging out with a bunch of bummy kids who hung around the town all night, I'd probably be out on the street or something. DO YOU BECOME THE KIND OF PERSON YOU ARE JUST FROM WHATEVER YOUR FRIENDS SAY AND HOW THEY ARE? Well, you follow your friends' examples a lot of the time.

Level 4: Personal or moral evaluations of life possibilities influence the existence or formation of the self.

Examples

HOW DID YOU GET TO BE THE WAY YOU ARE? Well, I decided to be kind to people because I've seen lots of kids hurt other kids' feelings for no reason, and it's not right or fair. Nobody should try to hurt another person's feelings or be mean to them. ANY OTHER WAYS? No, not really.

Continuity component, self-as-subject

Level 1: The self's continuity over time is defined with reference to simple categorical identifications. These may include the identification of one's name, one's body, one's possessions, one's typical behavior, one's stable preferences, and one's social membership group as the basis for continuity.

Examples

IF YOU CAN CHANGE FROM YEAR TO YEAR, HOW DO YOU KNOW IT'S STILL YOU? WHAT STAYS THE SAME? My name, and then I would know if it was me if someone called me. OKAY, IF YOU HAD A DIFFERENT NAME WOULD YOU STILL KNOW IT WAS YOU? Yeah. HOW WOULD YOU KNOW IT WAS STILL YOU? If I had a different name, I'd still know my name.

IF YOU KEEP CHANGING, HOW DO YOU KNOW IT'S ALWAYS YOU? 'Cause I have red hair. WHY IS THAT IMPORTANT? I don't know.

HOW DO YOU KNOW IT'S STILL YOU IF YOU CHANGE FROM YEAR TO YEAR? I still have my toys. IS THAT IMPORTANT TO KNOW ABOUT YOU? Yes, 'cause they are mine and will always be mine.

WHAT HAS STAYED THE SAME ABOUT YOU SINCE FIVE YEARS AGO? I still play with my toys. IS THAT IMPORTANT TO KNOW ABOUT YOU? I don't know.

HOW DO YOU KNOW IT'S ALWAYS YOU? 'Cause I still like science, and I still like swimming. And I'd still be doing science. SO YOU STILL LIKE THE SAME THINGS, SO YOU KNOW IT'S ALWAYS YOU? Yeah.

IF YOU CHANGE FROM YEAR TO YEAR, HOW DO YOU KNOW IT'S STILL YOU? Well, I still have my family and friends. IS THAT IMPORTANT TO YOU? Well, yeah. 'Cause they're my family.

Level 2: Self-continuity is established through reference to one's permanent cognitive and active capabilities and to immutable, permanent personal characteristics of self. These may include one's stable knowledge, one's memory, or any mental, physical, or personal trait or ability.

Examples

HOW DO YOU KNOW IT'S STILL YOU? I know it's me because I still know the things I knew five years ago. IS THAT IMPORTANT TO YOU? Yeah, because I'll never forget them.

IF YOU CHANGE FROM YEAR TO YEAR, HOW DO YOU KNOW THAT YOU ARE STILL YOU? You look in the mirror and you're still there. WELL, WHAT IF YOU WOKE UP ONE MORNING AND YOU LOOKED IN THE MIRROR AND YOU LOOKED TOTALLY DIFFERENT? WOULD YOU STILL BE THE SAME PERSON AT ALL? Yeah, inside you would be. WHAT ABOUT INSIDE WOULD LET YOU KNOW THAT YOU'RE THE SAME PERSON? Like if you still had a good personality, if you still liked to talk to people, you'd know that it was you. If it was a really mean person that didn't like anybody and just liked to keep to himself, then you'd know it wouldn't be you.

SO IF YOU ACT DIFFERENT AND YOU LOOK DIFFERENT, HOW DO YOU KNOW YOU'RE STILL THE SAME PERSON? Well, I don't know because I think I just look at something and try to remember that I was that small, and I have a good memory. And I can tell I belong to that family because I have so many things that I remember.

HOW DO YOU KNOW IT'S ALWAYS YOU? I've always been good at baseball. YOU'VE ALWAYS BEEN GOOD AT BASEBALL? Yeah, and I always will be.

Level 3: Self-continuity is established with reference to the ongoing recognition of self by others. At Level 3, self-continuity no longer derives from static categories, traits, or abilities. Rather, it derives from one's constant transactions with the social network extending beyond the self. The sense of continuity now depends on the continuing recognition of self over time by family, friends, and the social world in general.

Examples

HOW DO YOU KNOW IT'S STILL YOU OVER ALL THOSE YEARS? Your skin won't change or anything. You won't turn dark or anything. IS THAT AN IMPORTANT THING TO KNOW ABOUT YOU? Well, yeah, because if my mother saw me or something, she wouldn't recognize me, and I couldn't get into the house or something.

HOW DO YOU KNOW YOU'RE ALWAYS YOU? I'll still have my family. WHY DOES THAT MAKE A DIFFERENCE TO YOU? Well, they are the ones who brought me up and taught me right from wrong. They always know I'm me and not someone else.

IF YOU CHANGE FROM YEAR TO YEAR, HOW DO YOU KNOW IT'S ALWAYS YOU? Well, even though you change year to year, you know, people still like you, you change but not drastically. You know, people will say, "That's Melissa." They know. WHY IS THAT IMPORTANT THAT PEOPLE ALWAYS KNOW YOU? Well, 'cause, you know, I want people to say, "She's nice," and stuff like that.

IF YOU CHANGE FROM YEAR TO YEAR, HOW DO YOU KNOW THAT YOU ARE STILL YOU? I know who I am. Every year I know who I am. BUT HOW? HOW DO YOU KNOW YOU'RE THE SAME PERSON? By the way my friends tell me, I hope. SO YOUR FRIENDS TELL YOU YOU'RE THE SAME PERSON? Well, they'll tell me if I start acting strange, or if I start acting weird, or if I start acting too much of a show-off or something.

Level 4: Self-continuity is established with reference to the relation between one's earlier and present characteristics of the self. At Level 4 the self is no longer viewed as having characteristics that remain unchanged over the lifespan. Instead, the self's characteristics are believed to evolve from earlier ones. Thus, later properties of self are seen to be directly related to, although not identical with, the self's earlier ones. The relation between the self's past and present is often expressed in terms of one's personal feelings and special knowledge of oneself. This may include identification of one's personal feelings and one's self-knowledge in relation to one's continuity across time or identification of one's orientation toward the world in relation to one's continuity across time.

Examples

IF YOU CHANGE FROM YEAR TO YEAR, HOW DO YOU KNOW THAT YOU ARE THE SAME YOU? Well, nothing about me always stays the same, but I am always kind of like I was a while ago, and there is always some connection.

HOW DO YOU KNOW IT'S ALWAYS YOU? By the way I feel inside, I think, yeah. WHAT DO YOU MEAN "BY THE WAY YOU FEEL INSIDE?" You just know that you're the same person. You know yourself.

HOW DO YOU KNOW IT'S ALWAYS YOU? Well, I've always believed that everyone should be equal. WHAT DO YOU MEAN "EVERYONE SHOULD BE EQUAL"? Well, it's just that I think it's so terrible that just because someone has a different skin color that they aren't treated the same or given the same opportunities. It just isn't fair. I think everyone regardless of where they came from should have the same opportunities.

Distinctness component, self-as-subject

Level 1: The self's distinctness over time is defined with reference to simple categorical identifications. These may include the identification of one's name, one's body, one's possessions, one's typical behavior, one's stable preferences, and one's social membership group as the basis for distinctness.

Examples

WHAT MAKES YOU DIFFERENT FROM EVERYBODY ELSE IN THE WORLD? 'Cause there's only one person with my name. HOW DOES THAT MAKE YOU DIFFERENT? I don't know.

WHAT MAKES YOU A DIFFERENT PERSON FROM CHERYL? Well, I think she has brown eyes, and I have grayish bluish.

WHAT MAKES YOU DIFFERENT FROM EVERYBODY ELSE IN THE WORLD? My fingerprints. ANYTHING ELSE? My voice. 'Cause nobody has the same voice.

HOW ARE YOU DIFFERENT FROM YOUR FRIEND CATHLEEN? WHAT MAKES YOU A DIFFERENT PERSON? Well, she has an umbrella, and I don't; and she has different shoes. They don't have shoelaces. HOW DOES THAT MAKE YOU DIFFERENT? I don't know.

HOW ARE YOU DIFFERENT FROM ALL THE KIDS IN YOUR CLASS? I have a different Mommy and Daddy. WHY IS THAT IMPORTANT? 'Cause it is. . . . I don't know.

Level 2: Self-distinctness is established through comparisons between self and other along isolated personality, behavioral, or cognitive dimensions. These may include one's mental or physical abilities as compared with the abilities of others, one's activities as compared with the activities of others, or one's personality characteristics as compared with personality characteristics of others.

Examples

WHAT MAKES YOU SPECIAL FROM ALL THE KIDS IN YOUR CLASS? I got more home runs than everybody else.

WHAT MAKES YOU DIFFERENT FROM EVERYBODY ELSE IN THE WORLD? Well, no one could know just what I know, or they couldn't do just what I could do. They are either a little smarter or a little worse.

WHAT MAKES YOU SPECIAL? Some of the things I like to do. HOW DO THEY MAKE YOU SPECIAL? I don't know.

WHAT MAKES YOU SPECIAL COMPARED TO ALL THE KIDS IN YOUR CLASS? Well, I think I'm friendlier than most kids I know. HOW DOES THAT MAKE YOU SPECIAL? I don't know; it just does.

Level 3: Self-distinctness is derived from one's unique combination of psychological and physical characteristics.

Examples

WELL, IS THERE SOMETHING ABOUT YOU THAT JUST SETS YOU APART FROM ANYBODY ELSE? The way I act. THE WAY YOU ACT? To some things, some people. One thing else, I worry a lot. YOU WORRY A LOT? Yeah, I worry too much and a lot of things that a lot of kids don't care about, you know, I'd worry about. OKAY, DOES THAT SET YOU APART FROM OTHER KIDS? In some ways. But there's really a couple of people that are, you know alike in a few ways, but nobody's exactly somebody else.

WHAT MAKES YOU DIFFERENT FROM EVERYBODY YOU KNOW? I like to be unique. I like to wear different clothes sometimes. I'm not afraid to be me. Some people just want to be exactly like the crowd, and do exactly what everyone else does. I don't like that at all. I want to be my own person. WHY IS THAT IMPORTANT? Because people like you for what you really are then. I think people, you know, they know who you really are then and not just a mask. WHAT IS IT ABOUT YOU THAT MAKES YOU TOTALLY DIFFERENT FROM EVERYBODY ELSE, THAT MAKES YOU UNIQUE? Just who I am. I don't know how to explain it. WHAT IS IT ABOUT WHO YOU ARE, THE KIND OF PERSON YOU ARE, THAT'S DIFFERENT? Well, I think in some ways you're like people. You know, certain people, different things you're like. Like one person, you're like them about one thing; and another person, you're like them about another thing. SO A LOT OF YOUR PARTS MIGHT BE THE SAME AS SOME OF THE OTHER PEOPLE, BUT NOBODY HAS THE . . . Yeah, exact same things.

Level 4: Self-distinctiveness is established with reference to one's unique subjective experiences and interpretations of the world. This aspect may include the identification of one's distinctness in relation to one's personal feelings and the identification of one's distinctness in terms of one's orientation toward the world.

Example

WHAT MAKES YOU SPECIAL? I'm like myself. I'm unique. IN WHAT WAYS? Well, I don't feel like other kids. Some things will not make me happy, you know. I have feelings that are unique to me.

DO YOU THINK THERE'S ANYTHING SPECIAL ABOUT YOU COMPARED TO OTHER KIDS YOUR AGE? I think I'm a lot more understanding than most kids. . . . I know, like when I'm gonna hurt someone's feelings, but it's like other kids, they don't care. And it's like I'm sure they know they're being mean. It's just I could never do some of the things they do.

WHAT MAKES YOU DIFFERENT FROM EVERYBODY ELSE YOU KNOW? Nobody else sees things or feels the same way about things as I do.

4 The self-understanding interview and scoring procedures

In this chapter we present the main data collection and analysis procedures that we use in the studies reported throughout this book. The primary data collection method is a clinical interview focusing on issues of self and self-interest. The primary data-analysis method is a scoring manual derived from the theoretical distinctions proposed in our developmental model of self-understanding.

Both the interview procedures and the scoring manual reflect a particular approach to empirical research, an approach that has won some acceptance within developmental psychology but that remains controversial in many other quarters. The hallmarks of this approach are its pursuit of the principles that organize (or "structure") subjects' knowledge; its focus on transformations in these organizing principles over time; and, toward the end of properly defining such organizing principles, its concern for capturing the full meaning, for the subject, of any verbal or active expression that might indicate the subject's knowledge.

Because of its emphasis on knowledge, organization, and meaning, this approach bears with it methodological correlates quite different from those of scientific approaches that focus on the discrete behavioral act. Many years ago, Kurt Lewin described this opposition as a contrast between Gallilean and Aristotelian modes of scientific inquiry. The Gallilean mode, according to Lewin, gave birth to a structural-developmental search for evolving principles of thought, whereas the Aristotelian mode gave birth to the logical-positivist search for behavioral regularity (Lewin, 1935). Although not always following the identical lines of contrast proposed by Lewin, contemporary social science is full of opposition and debate between advocates of these two positions on psychological science.

We do not wish here to restate the entire contours of this debate; but, in introducing our own empirical procedures, we believe it necessary to make clear certain methodological implications of the structural-developmental approach. These implications have generated a good deal of misunderstanding and unnecessary controversy in the recent developmental literature. A dramatic example of this was the widely quoted but fundamentally misguided review of Kohlberg's moral judgment work by Kurtines and Greif (1974), in which the reviewers attacked the methodological rigor of a structural-developmental research program through a narrow application of logical-positivist standards. Perhaps within a discipline as fragmented as contemporary psychology it may be impossible wholly to prevent such misunderstandings; still, for our current purposes, it seems wise to discuss features of our interview and scoring procedures that may seem controversial when viewed from alternate research paradigms.

For collecting data on subjects' understanding of basic concepts like self, the clinical interview method is an indispensable tool, particularly when there is a wide range of age and verbal sophistication in the subject sample. The appeal of the clinical method lies in its flexibility. Although the interview always contains core issues and questions that must be covered, the wording of these questions can (and must) be varied if required by the subject's comprehension needs, and new probe questions can (and must) be added when needed to explicate fully a subject's line of reasoning. Thus, some subjects will be asked different questions than other subjects. This useful and necessary feature of the clinical method, however, opens the procedure to the criticism that it is unstandardized and therefore unscientific.

Fortunately there are already in print several spirited defenses of the clinical method's scientific credibility. We quote here from three statements that, taken together, explain the various ways in which clinical interview procedures provide a truer scientific account of children's developing understanding than do standardized questionnaires or tests. The first statement comes from Piaget's original introduction of "la méthode clinique" in 1929. In this statement, Piaget rejects the use of standardized "test methods" (such as the Binet IQ test, with which Piaget was intimately familiar) for the purposes of exploring children's "natural mental inclinations":

The essential failure of the test method in the researches with which we are concerned is that it falsifies the natural mental inclination of the subject or at least risks so doing. For example, in trying to find out how a child conceives the movement of the sun and moon, the question may be asked, "What makes the sun move?" The child perhaps answers, "God makes it move," or "The wind blows it," etc. Such answers are not to be neglected, even if they be only the result of "romancing," that is of the peculiar tendency of children to invent when embarrassed by a given question. However, even had this test been applied to children of all ages, no real advance would have been made, since it may well be that a child would never put the question to himself in such a form, or even that he never would have asked the question at all. The child might quite possibly imagine the sun to be a living being moving of its own accord. . . . The only way to avoid such difficulties is to vary the questions, making countersuggestions, in short, to give up the idea of a fixed questionnaire (Piaget, 1969/1929, pp. 3–4)

The second statement comes from Broughton's (1978b) extensive rebuttal of Kurtines and Greif's critique. Broughton points out the importance of flexibility for an inquiry into structural (or "formal") properties of knowledge:

Thus the usefulness of the moral judgment interview does not depend on the "standardization" which Kurtines and Greif (p. 455) see lacking. . . . What Kohlberg's critics often appear to ignore is the fact that the instrument measures the *form* of moral reasoning (the *way* in which ethical issues are approached) not the specific content of the subject's response. As a result, variations in the content of administration and the effect that they have on the content of answers are much less important. The use of Piaget's "clinical method" of questioning, where the interviewer encourages subjects to explain their original responses, is indispensable for elucidating the structural composition of stages, and therefore "standardization" of the interview would have prevented the development of the theory. (Broughton, 1978b, p. 90)

Broughton then expands this point into a general claim about false rigor in the social sciences:

This is not the humanist's plea for "freedom" or "spontaneity." It is the structuralist's plea against the logical positivism that exalts measurement and the strict methods of the natural sciences at the expense of a concern for *meaning*. Rigid standardization of questioning ignores the fact that meanings develop through interpersonal understanding in the test situation and leads to a spurious "objectivity" and trivial results. It also leaves us with the possible problem that regularities in our results are entirely a function of specific factors associated with superficial factors of question form. (Broughton, 1978b, p. 90)

Finally, we quote from an earlier statement in our own research program, a statement that further explicates Broughton's implicit distinction between scientific rigidity and scientific rigor. In this statement, Damon (1977) asserts that true scientific control in a child interview derives from well-guided flexibility rather than from an arbitrary standardization of procedure:

In what way, it must be asked, does such a procedure [varying questions in response to the communication needs of individual subjects] control for the evident differences in stimulus materials presented to children? Devotees of *la méthode clinique* will claim that it is the only means of controlling for the one variable that might actually confound an investigation: the child's understanding and interpretation of the stimulus materials. The assumption underlying the clinical method is that the child plays an active role in creating and structuring his own stimulation. How the materials are understood very much affects the child's performance on the interview; thus the flexibility inherent in the clinical interview actually functions as a control for this important unknown variable. The interviewer's task is to ensure that all children have a comparable understanding of the questions that are being asked of them. To establish this understanding, it may be necessary to alter the verbal presentation from subject to subject. For example, some children may never have heard a certain word, or may not be familiar with some information incorporated in a question, and yet may have a rich understanding of the concept under investigation. This understanding may be accessible only if the investigator substitutes a different word for the unknown one, or changes the specific question to incorporate new information. In such cases, the loss in identical verbal standardization of the interview is more than compensated for by a gain in comparability of the child's understanding of the task. This is a crucial gain, and many would argue that in accomplishing it the clinical method has substituted an essential control for a trivial one. (Damon, 1977, p. 57)

The flexibility of questioning in a clinical interview enables the interviewer to guide subjects through explorations of their own knowledge. Such explorations, however, cannot be random expressions of just any idea that arises in the subject's consciousness, but rather must be focused on the topic of inquiry. Further, they must be structured in a way that allows comparability between subjects in the study sample. To accomplish this, the interview must establish balance between overdetermining the direction of the subject's reasoning on the one hand and allowing the subject to discourse aimlessly on the other. The interviewer must have a working hypothesis about the issues under study without imposing this hypothesis on the subject's responses.

Needless to say, this kind of balance is not easy to achieve during the usually fast-paced interviews, particularly when subjects are children with short and sometimes fragile attention spans. The process combines the art of clinical interviewing with the goals of science. Mastering this art can be time consuming: Piaget wrote that it took at least "a year of daily practice" before his own research assistants were adept at interviewing children (Piaget, 1969/1929, pp. 8–9). Realistic contingencies of modern-day research funding have forced us to shorten this training period considerably, but we have often regretted the imposed haste. Because the clinical method is among the least accessible of research techniques for uninitiated workers, there is naturally resistance to using it widely in large-scale research projects. Still, for the reasons noted, we believe it essential for the kind of basic developmental spadework called for in the present investigation.

The self-understanding interview

The self-understanding interview has seven core items. Four of these core items explore aspects of the self-as-object and three explore aspects of the self-as-subject. Each item consists of a question or set of questions followed by various probe questions, all of which are administered according to the tenets of the clinical method (Piaget, 1969/1929; Damon, 1977).

We will present the seven items in the order in which they are normally given to subjects. The ordering of the items, however, is somewhat arbitrary, and can be varied to maintain the flow of the interview. If, for example, a subject spontaneously raises an issue related to a certain item at an earlier point in the interview than the item would be normally introduced, it is good practice to probe the subject's statements at that point.

In our presentation of the seven items, we offer some sample probe questions that we typically use to follow up each core question. But other probes, "warm-up" questions, and so on are used whenever needed to encourage subjects to expand upon their reasoning about self. The general principle in probing an interview on the concept of self is to continue with follow-up questions until subjects repeat themselves, give an "I don't know" response, or show marked signs of waning attention.

The first four items are intended to explore the self-as-object in some of its most common manifestations: self-definition, self-evaluation, self projected in past and future, and self-interest. As reported in Chapter 5, these different query sets yielded similar results with respect to subject's understanding of self, both in terms of the subject's use of self-scheme (physical, active, social, or psychological) and in terms of the subject's developmental level of self-understanding. These four items, therefore, can be considered alternate but conceptually parallel means of tapping the subject's general knowledge of the self-as-object.

The last three items are each intended to explore one component of the self-as-subject. Item 5 focuses on continuity, Item 6 on agency, and Item 7 on distinctness. As noted in previous chapters, we were also interested in the self-as-subject component of self-reflection, but we were unable to design a satisfactory query set on this issue for the age range of children in our investigation. Some initial steps in this direction, however, are described at the end of Chapter 6. Other than this one preliminary attempt, the studies in this book operationalize the self-as-subject as continuity, distinctness, and agency. Accordingly, the three self-as-subject items included in the interview presented in this chapter correspond to these three self-as-subject components.

Item 1: Self-definition. What are you like? What kind of person are you? What are you not like? *Probes*: What does that say about you? Why is that important? What difference does that (characteristic) make? What would be the difference if you were (were not) like that?

Item 2: Self-evaluation. What are you especially proud of about yourself? What do you like most about yourself? What are you not proud of? What do you like least about yourself? *Probes*: What does that say about you? Why is that important? What difference does that make?

Item 3: Self in past and future. Do you think you'll be the same or different five years from now? How about when you're an adult? How about five years ago? How about when you were a baby? *Probes*: What will be the same? What will be different? Why is that important?

Item 4: Self-interest. What do you want to be like? What kind of person do you want to be? What do you hope for in life? If you could have three wishes, what would they be? What do you think is good for you? *Probes*: Why do you want to (be that way, have those things you hope for, have those wishes)? What else do you (hope for, wish for, believe is good for you)? Why is that good for you?

Item 5: Continuity. Do you change at all from year to year? How (how not)? If you do change from year to year, how do you know it's still always you? *Probes*: In what ways do you stay the same? Is that an important thing to say about you? Why?

Item 6: Agency. How did you get to be the way you are? How did that make you the kind of person you are? How could you become different? *Probes*: What difference did that make? Is that the only reason you turned out like you did? Is that the only reason? What else could make you different? How would that work?

Item 7: Distinctness. Do you think there is anyone who is exactly like you? What makes you different from anyone you know? *Probes*: Why is that important? What difference does that make? In what other ways are you different? Are you completely different or just partly different? How do you know? Are you different from everybody or just from some people? How can you be sure that you're different from everybody else even when there are many people in the world that you don't know?

The interview presented above, when properly probed, takes from 35 to 60 minutes to administer. It can be given to subjects representing a very broad age-range: In the current investigation, we obtained responses that can be coded from children as young as 4 and from adolescents as old as 18. Certainly the age range could be extended upward in future studies, although the verbal limitations of young children probably prevent its extension downward by more than a few months. In the following section we discuss the procedure by which we score protocols obtained through use of the self-interview.

The self-understanding scoring manual

After our initial phase of interviewing was complete (see Chapter 5), we constructed a scoring manual to code subjects' interview responses.[1] The scoring manual was based conceptually on the developmental model described in Chapter 3. It drew its items and examples from the first-round interview data. We randomly selected one-fourth of the first round protocols for the purposes of manual construction. In this way, we left the remaining three-fourths of the first-round protocols uncontaminated in the sense that they could be coded by a manual not developed out of their own material.

The manual has several characteristics compatible with the clinical interview procedure that we used to elicit subjects' self-understanding. Its unit of scoring is defined as a "chunk" of reasoning composed of one self-characteristic mentioned by the subject during the interview; and all the subject's statements, whether spontaneous or in response to the interviewer's probe questions, that explicate the meaning or importance of that characteristic. The following quotes are examples of, respectively, one and two scoring chunks.

Example of one chunk

WHAT ELSE ARE YOU? A boy. WHY IS BEING A BOY IMPORTANT? Because it makes me strong. WHY IS IT IMPORTANT THAT YOU'RE STRONG? I don't know.

Example of two chunks

WHAT KIND OF PERSON ARE YOU? Kind and athletic. WHY IS BEING KIND IMPORTANT? Because then I get along good with my friends. ANY OTHER REASONS? No, not really. IS ATHLETIC SOMETHING IMPORTANT TO KNOW ABOUT YOU AS A PERSON? Yeah. WHY? Because all my friends are athletic and wouldn't be as friendly with me if I couldn't play sports and didn't like to be active.

The manual is divided into seven sections, corresponding to the subdivisions along the front and side faces of the Figure 3.1 model in Chapter 3. As will be seen, these are, respectively, the four self-as-object schemes (physical, active, social, and psychological) and the three self-as-subject components (agency, continuity, and distinctness). Each of these seven sections has a sequence of developmental levels along with prototypical statements illustrating each level. Scoring proceeds by first determining which section of the manual the chunk belongs within and then matching the chunk to a developmental level within that section.

Thus, for the self-as-object, statements concerned with the physical body or material possessions ("I am really tall"; "I have a car") are coded within the *physical self-scheme*, Statements concerned with activities or abilities ("I play baseball every day"; "I can run real fast") are coded within the *active self-scheme*. Statements concerned with social-personality characteristics, social interactions, or social relations ("I am really shy"; "I fight a lot with my friend"; "I have a nice mother and father") are coded within the *social self-scheme*. Statements concerned with emotions, thoughts, or cognitive processes ("I am real cranky in the morning"; "I think really clearly") are coded within the *psychological self-scheme*. For the self-as-subject, statements concerned with the formation, existence, or control of self ("I got to be the way I am now because my parents taught me"; "I tried hard to be like this"; "Everything I do I do because I want to") are coded within *agency*. Statements that defend or explain the sense of self-continuity over time are coded within *continuity*. Statements that defend or explain the sense of distinctness from others are coded within *distinctness*.

In the manual, consistent with the "testing-the-limits" approach behind the clinical interview method, only those chunks that contain fully explicated reasoning may be scored. That is, in the chain of questioning, a subject must be allowed and encouraged to express the meaning of the initial self-statement to the extent that the subject is willing and able to do so. The probe question must be asked, even if it only results in an "I don't know" response; at this point, the subject at least has been given a chance to expand upon the initial statement. If such probe questions or other functional equivalents (e.g., spontaneous probes that subjects may implicitly or explicitly ask themselves) are omitted, the chunk is considered unscorable.

The manual, therefore, allows scoring only for those chunks in which the subject has been given a full chance to explicate his or her reasoning or meaning, if he or she chooses to do so.

Examples

1. TELL ME WHAT KIND OF PERSON YOU ARE. Big.

This is *not scorable* by itself because there is no probing as to why "big" is important for the subject in describing the self.

2. TELL ME WHAT KIND OF PERSON YOU ARE. Big. WHAT DIFFERENCE DOES THAT MAKE? Well, then I can ride a bike.

This is *scorable* because the subject has explicated the meaning as to why "big" is important to the meaning of self.

Frequently, the subject is given an opportunity to explicate his or her reasoning about a particular statement made about the self in responding to a probe question such as "Why is that important?" or "What does that tell me about you?" For a scorable response, the subject does not have to elaborate upon a statement but must be given an opportunity to do so. For instance:

3. WHAT KIND OF PERSON ARE YOU? Well, I have blue eyes. WHY IS THAT IMPORTANT? I don't know.

The above chunk is scorable because the subject was given a chance to develop a more complex response but simply could not or would not. When a chunk is deemed scorable, it is then matched with a point in the manual.

Some chunks may seem scorable at more than one level within a single scheme (e.g., physical self). Consistent with the testing-the-limits approach of the clinical method, the manual calls for scoring the chunk only for the *highest* applicable level in that scheme. For instance:

WHAT KIND OF PERSON ARE YOU? I don't know, kind of big, I guess. WHY'S THAT IMPORTANT? No real reason, well, if I wasn't big then I couldn't play football as well as my friends and then they wouldn't like me any more.

This example is scored *only* at Level 3 of the physical self scheme, although a Level 2 comparative statement may be detected as well.

Some chunks, however, may be scorable in different schemes. If the chunk is scorable in two or more schemes at the same level, the chunk is given *all* of the applicable scores. Consider the following example:

WHAT KIND OF PERSON ARE YOU? I go camping a lot. WHY DO YOU GO CAMPING A LOT? Because I am a Cub Scout. IS IT IMPORTANT FOR ME TO KNOW THAT YOU ARE A CUB SCOUT? Yes. WHY? Because I go camping and stuff.

In this instance, the chunk is scored *both* for Level 1, active scheme, *and* for Level 1, social scheme. Note that the subject was given an opportunity to express his or her responses in both the active and social schemes.

If, on the other hand, the chunk is scorable in two or more schemes at *different* levels, only the score for the highest level in the various schemes is recorded. For example:

WHAT KIND OF PERSON ARE YOU? I'm Catholic. WHY IS THAT IMPORTANT TO KNOW ABOUT YOU? Well, I'm a Catholic because I believe that the Christian virtues espoused by the Church, such as love, patience, and faith in God, are important values that every person should have.

This chunk contains elements that can be construed at Level 1, social scheme ("I'm Catholic") and Level 4, psychological scheme ("important values"). But it is only scored at Level 4, psychological scheme, because it is not clear that "I'm Catholic" has any other meaning beyond the "important values." In such cases, the scorer is to assume that the higher level of one scheme incorporates the lower level of another scheme, *unless* the interviewer probed in a way demonstrating that the lower-level scheme has independent meaning. For example, a different scoring solution would be called for if in the previous example the subject had answered further questions as follows:

WELL, ARE THERE ANY OTHER REASONS IT'S IMPORTANT TO KNOW THAT YOU ARE CATH-OLIC? Yes, it means that I am a member of the Church. WHY IS IT IMPORTANT TO YOU TO BE A MEMBER OF THE CHURCH? I don't know, it just is.

With the above additional answers, the first example would be seen as two *different* chunks that therefore would be scored separately.

The following two chapters report interjudge and test–retest reliability data for the self-understanding scoring manual. In Chapter 5 we report reliability figures for the self-as-object parts of the manual (the first four sections, corresponding to the self-as-object schemes), and in Chapter 6 we report reliability figures for the self-as-subject parts (the last three sections). The age trends and other empirical findings discussed in Chapters 5 through 9 derive from use of this manual. For the Puerto Rican study in Chapter 8, however, we made some fundamental modifications in the manual. These changes were in recognition of the need to make significant adaptations of our developmental model for other cultural contexts.

Note

1 The complete manual may be requested from either author with a brief statement explicating the proposed use to which it will be put.

5   Understanding the self-as-object

This chapter reports cross-sectional and longitudinal findings from studies designed to test the self-as-object components, or "front face," of the model depicted in Figure 3.1. The studies extended over three years of data collection with three testing points, spaced at 18-month intervals. In addition, for the purposes of a test–retest reliability check, there was one additional testing point for a subset of the subjects.

At the start of the studies, our youngest subjects were 4 and our oldest subjects were 14. By the time of the final testing, the youngest subjects were 7 and the oldest were 17. Therefore the studies as a whole encompassed a broad span of childhood and adolescence. The age difference between the subjects enabled us to examine developmental trends cross-sectionally at each of the testing points, whereas the longitudinal design enabled us to observe actual self-understanding transitions made by individual subjects during the course of the 3-year investigation.

Because cross-sectional data analyses are best suited to answer questions different from those posed by longitudinal studies, we devote a section to each in this chapter. A discussion of age trends and other descriptive statistics drawn from cross-sectional data analysis is followed in a later section of the chapter by a discussion of issues of change and stability that only longitudinal data can address. We find both types of analyses helpful in testing the self-as-object components of our developmental model.

For our cross-sectional analyses, we draw on data from the Time 2 testing, 18 months after the study began. We do so for a number of reasons, the most important of which was that data from the Time 1 testing was used heavily for constructing our model and the accompanying scoring manual. Although we do not believe that this totally invalidates the Time 1 data for further empirical purposes (and we do include these data in the longitudinal analyses), we recognize that scoring data with a manual that was in part derived from that same data is a somewhat contaminated process. Further, as we constructed the model and the manual, we learned more about which probe questions are necessary to test the limits of children's and adolescents' self-understanding. This process led to some enhancements of our interviewing procedures by Time 2.

Consequently, Time 1 came to be viewed as an exploratory phase in which we did not have full methodological confidence. This said, we should note (as will be clear from our longitudinal analyses) that the Time 1 results were not substantially different than results at Times 2 and 3; nor were the Time 1 to Time 2 longitudinal trends disparate from the Time 2 to Time 3 trends. Our choice to derive cross-sectional trends from Time 2 (and place at that point our additional test–retest data collection) was made primarily on methodological rather than substantive grounds.

Cross-sectional findings from the Time 2 testing occasion

Subjects. By the Time 2 data collection, there were 82 boys and girls ages 6 through 16 in the study. The breakdown by gender and school grade was as follows: 4 boys and 3 girls in 1st grade; 5 boys and 3 girls in 2nd grade; 2 boys and 7 girls in 3rd grade; 8 boys and 2 girls in 4th grade; 3 boys and 5 girls in 5th grade; 4 boys and 4 girls in 6th grade; 2 boys and 6 girls in 7th grade; 3 boys and 3 girls in 8th grade; 4 boys and 4 girls in 9th grade; and 6 boys and 4 girls in 10th grade. The children were from a racially mixed, middle-class population in Worcester, Massachusetts.

The *procedure* was the self-understanding interview described in Chapter 4. As noted, the interview had been given to all 82 children on one occasion 18 months prior to the present testing, although some new probes were now added at Time 2.

Results

Interrater reliability. To ensure that the protocols used to assess interrater reliability would be evenly distributed across the age range of the study, the protocol of every other subject, ordered from youngest to oldest, was selected for this purpose. Each of these protocols was scored by two raters familiar with the scoring manual. We first determined the extent of agreement about what constituted a scorable "chunk." Of the 621 chunks scored by the two raters combined, 518, or 83%, of the chunks were scored by both raters.

Interrater reliabilities were calculated for all the chunks scored by both raters across all the protocols. Because our analyses focused on developmental level and self-scheme independently of one another (rather than on the specific level-by-scheme intersections on the front face of our model's 16 cells), we calculated reliabilities for general developmental levels across all schemes and schemes across all levels, rather than for each of their 16 intersections. Along with raw percentage of agreement between raters, we present the more conservative Cohen's Kappa figures that correct for chance agreement (Cohen, 1968). The percentage of agreement for developmental level was 86%, Kappa .79; the percentage of agreement for scheme was 71%, Kappa .62.

For many data-analytic purposes, it is desirable to compute weighted means for subjects' developmental levels across scored chunks. By so doing, subjects' overall average performances may be represented for statistical purposes. Weighted means for each subject are calculated by multiplying the number of chunks scored at each level by the cardinal value of the level and dividing this figure by the total number of scored chunks on the subject's protocol. Although this type of statistic violates some legitimate assumptions concerning the ordinal (rather than interval) properties of developmental sequences, it nevertheless is commonly used in developmental studies as a reasonable and necessary approximation of a subject's overall performance. Similar nonparametric weighted averages have been used for countless developmental measures, from Parten's early social participation scale to Rest's DIT (Parten, 1933; Rest, 1983).

Interrater reliability for weighted averages was calculated by correlating the weighted averages derived from Rater A's scores with those derived from Rater B's scores. The coefficient of interrater agreement of weighted averages for the entire self-understanding protocol was $r_s = .88, p < .001$.

In some instances, it may be preferable to preserve the ordinal nature of the development levels by assigning an overall modal level to represent a subject's typical performance. Percentage of interrater agreement for the modal-level score for the entire self-understanding interview was 84%, Kappa, .75. On the average, 61% of the chunks on an interview were at the modal level. Interrater agreement for modal-scheme score was 85%, Kappa .75. On the average, 44% of chunks on an interview were at the modal scheme.

It is also informative for some empirical purposes to record the highest developmental level expressed by each subject. This "best-level" score is an indication of the limits of the subject's expressed competence in a given area, and has been shown in previous studies to be a particularly sensitive indicator of developmental change (Damon, 1977, 1980; Snyder and Feldman, 1977). Percentage of interrater agreement on subjects' best levels for the entire self-understanding interview was 90%, Kappa .73.

Interrelationships among weighted-average, modal-level, and best-level scores were: best with modal, $r = .52$, $p < .001$; best with weighted average, $r = .68$, $p < .001$; and modal with weighted average, $r = .83$, $p < .001$.

Taken together, the range of interrater reliability results indicates that the self-understanding scoring manual yields good agreement between independent judges.

Internal consistency: We determined the relation between responses to different questions to determine the legitimacy of assigning one overall level score for the entire interview. Weighted averages for chunks elicited by each question taken separately were calculated. These weighted averages were then averaged together to form an overall weighted average, or "summary average," in which scores for all questions were equally reflected. Correlations between the weighted averages for all questions and the summary weighted average ranged between $r = .70$, $p < .001$, and $r = .83$, $p < .001$. These strong intercorrelations, indications of good internal consistency, suggest that the different questions on our self-understanding interview tap the same general construct.

Test–retest reliabilities. For the purpose of calculating test–retest reliability, 42 of the subjects were reinterviewed 1 month after the Time 2 testing occasion. Test–retest reliability coefficients were calculated for the various developmental level and scheme scores and for the interview taken as a whole. The correlation between the weighted averages for the initial and subsequent interviews was $r = 49$, $p < .001$; the corresponding correlations for modal and best levels for the two interviews were $r = .28$, $p < .08$, and $r = .43$, $p < .01$, respectively. Sixty percent of the subjects had the same modal level for the two testing times (Time 2 and the test–retest occasion 1 month later), 26% had a higher modal level at the second testing time, and 14% had a lower modal level at the second testing time. For the best level, 64% were at the same level at the two testing times, 24% had a higher best-level score at the second testing time, and 12% had a lower best-level score at the second testing time.

These test–retest coefficients are reasonable for a developmental measure used with children. Often developmental measures for children do not yield strong test–retest reliability because children are frequently in flux with respect to their developing abilities (Kuhn, 1976).

Correlations between the percentages of chunks in a scheme and the percentage of chunks in the same scheme at the subsequent testing time were also calculated. These correlations were: physical scheme, $r = .60$, $p < .001$; active scheme, $r = .42$, $p < .01$; social scheme,

$r = .41$, $p < .01$; and psychological scheme, $r = .51$, $p < .001$. Fifty-three percent of the subjects had the same modal scheme score for the two testing times.

Age trends for developmental levels. Strongly positive correlations between age and weighted average, age and modal-level score, and age and best-level score were obtained. These correlations were: weighted average, $r = .57$, $p < .001$; modal-level score, $r_s = .47$, $p < .001$; and best-level score, $r_s = .54$, $p < .001$. Table 5.1 reports the actual distribution of modal-level scores, weighted averages, and percentage of chunks in each scheme for each of the ten grades.

Age trends for self-schemes. There were significant correlations between the percentage of chunks in the physical, social, and psychological schemes and age: these correlations were, respectively, $r = -.39$, $p < .001$; $r = .35$, $p < .001$; and $r = .23$, $p < .05$. The percentages of chunks in each scheme for each grade are reported in Table 5.1. The correlation between modal scheme and age, with the schemes considered ordered from physical to psychological, was $r_s = .24$, $p < .05$. These correlations are lower in magnitude than the developmental level correlations reported earlier, and the difference in magnitude can be tested using the t distribution (Ferguson, 1966, p. 188–9). The magnitude of the largest correlation between age and percentage in a scheme (the physical scheme) is significantly lower than the correlation between age and the corresponding index of developmental level (the weighted average), $p < .05$. Similarly, the correlation between age and modal scheme is significantly lower than the correlation between age and modal level, $p < .05$.

Interaction of developmental level and schemes. The model could be taken to predict an interaction between developmental level and scheme such that an individual at Level 1 should focus on the physical aspects of self, at Level 2 on the active aspects of self, at Level 3 on the social aspects of self, and at Level 4 on the psychological aspects of self (see Damon & Hart, 1982, for an earlier presentation of this hypothesis). The data from this study do not support this hypothesized interaction. Figure 5.1 presents the number of individuals at each intersection of modal level and modal scheme (these numbers are in the upper half of each box).

The interaction prediction would require that the boxes along the diagonal should contain most of the cases. The adequacy of this hypothesis can be tested using prediction analysis (Hildebrand, Laing, & Rosenthal, 1977). The index of correspondence between the predicted distribution of

Table 5.1. *Developmental level and scheme scores for each school grade and age at testing Time 2*

Grade	Mean age	No. of subjects at modal level				Weighted average	Percentage of chunks in scheme			
		1	2	3	4		Physical	Active	Social	Psychological
1	6	2	5	0	0	1.61	36	25	11	28
2	7	3	5	0	0	1.66	45	24	13	18
3	8	4	3	2	0	1.82	31	21	20	28
4	9	1	7	2	0	1.87	32	19	22	27
5	10	3	4	1	0	1.98	21	19	28	32
6	11	2	4	2	0	2.18	37	21	22	20
7	12	0	5	3	0	2.56	32	18	13	36
8	13	0	3	3	0	2.32	11	22	34	32
9	14	1	4	2	1	2.51	22	20	24	33
10	15	0	3	6	1	2.84	20	15	33	32
Average						2.04	29	20	22	29

Modal Level	Physical	Active	Social	Psychological
4	0 5	0 17	0 32	0 47
3	3 22	1 15	10 34	7 29
2	14 29	1 21	5 18	23 31
1	9 41	3 23	0 16	4 20

Fig. 5.1. Modal scheme and percentage of chunks in each scheme for each modal level.
Notes: The number in the upper left of each cell indicates the number of subjects with that modal level and modal scheme. The number in the lower half of each cell represents the percentage of chunks in each scheme for each modal level.

cases in a frequency table and the actual distribution is denoted V, which is "an index defined by 1 minus the ratio of the number of observed cases in the error cells to the number of observed cases expected under independence" (Froman & Hubert, 1980, p. 139). With all cells except those along the diagonal designated as error cells, V for the intersection of modal level and modal scheme is .13, not significant (n.s.). Thus, knowing the modal level of an individual does not aid in the prediction of that individual's modal scheme.

At most, some very partial and qualified support for the interaction hypothesis can be garnered through an analysis of the average percentage of chunks in each of the schemes at each modal level. Figure 5.1 also presents, in the lower half of each cell, the average percentage of chunks in each scheme for individuals at each of the four modal levels. With modal level as the grouping variable, ANOVAs revealed significant differences in the percentage of chunks in the physical F (3,78) = 7.28, $p < .001$, social F (3,78) = 8.43, $p < .001$, and psychological schemes F (3,78) = 3.93, $p < .05$. An analysis of the cell means in the physical scheme using the Scheffe test revealed that individuals at modal Level 1 had a higher percentage of statements in this scheme than did individuals at the higher modal levels. In the social scheme, results of the Scheffe test revealed that individuals at modal Level 3 had a higher percentage of statements in this scheme than did subjects at modal Levels 1 and 2. No pair of groups means in the psychological scheme were found to be significantly different from each other.

Gender. The developmental level scores for boys and girls were of essentially the same order on all parts of the interview, regardless of whether weighted average, modal-level score, or best-level score was used as an index. These relations were examined in a MANOVA, with the different developmental level scores as the dependent measures and sex and grade as the factors. Only the main factor of grade was found to have a significant effect. Separate ANOVAs with the percentage of chunks in each scheme as the dependent measures and grade and gender as factors found significant main effects for grade in the physical and social schemes, $F(9,62) = 3.19$, $p < .01$, and $F(9,62) = 2.61$, $p < .05$, respectively. A significant main effect for gender was found only for the percentage of chunks in the active scheme, males ($M = 22\%$), females ($M = 18\%$), $F(1,62) = 4.44$, $p < .05$. No interactions were significant.

Replication data

After the main investigation discussed in this chapter was completed, a further study was conducted to replicate on a different sample of children and adolescents the cross-sectional findings of the main investigation. The subjects in this replication study were 81 middle-class children and adolescents from a small New Jersey town. The grade and gender breakdown of this sample was: 12 boys and 11 girls from grade 5, 10 boys and 9 girls from grade 7, 11 boys and 9 girls from grade 9, and 8 boys and 11 girls from grade 11.

Procedure. Each subject was individually interviewed, and responded to query sets 1 and 2 of the self-understanding interview. Only two query sets were used due to time constraints and because the findings of Study 1 indicated that the different query sets tapped the same issues. All of the interviews were coded by the scoring procedures outlined above.

Results

Age trends for developmental levels. Positive correlations between age and weighted average, age and modal-level score, and age and best-level score were obtained. These correlations were: age and weighted average, $r_s = .48, p < .001$; age and modal level, $r_s = .42, p < .001$; and age with best level, $r_s = .40, p < .001$. Table 5.2 presents, for this replication study, the distribution of weighted averages, modal levels, and percentages of responses in each scheme for each grade.

Age trends for self-schemes. In contrast to Study 1, there were no significant correlations between age and the percentage of chunks in any one of the four self-schemes, nor was there a significant association between modal scheme and age.

Interaction between developmental level and scheme. The findings of the replication study do not support a hypothesized interaction between developmental level and scheme. Using the prediction analysis procedure discussed previously, the hypothesized association between modal level and modal scheme was not confirmed, $V = .10$. Only limited support for the model's predicted diagonal was provided by ANOVAs of the average percentage of chunks in each of the schemes at each modal level. With modal level as the grouping variable, there was a significant difference only for the percentage of chunks in the active scheme $F(3,77) = 2.88, p < .05$, with means of 20%, 26%, 13%, and 29% for developmental Levels 1, 2, 3, and 4, respectively.

Gender. There were no significant developmental level differences between boys and girls, regardless of whether developmental level was indexed by a weighted average, modal level, or best level. These relations were examined in a MANOVA, with the different developmental level scores as the dependent measures and sex and grade as factors. Only the main factor of grade was found to have a significant effect. Separate ANOVAs with the percentage of chunks in each scheme as the dependent measures, and grade and gender as factors, found significant main effects for grade in the social and psychological schemes, $F(3,73) = 2.69$, $p < .053$, and $F(3,73) = 3.25, p < .05$ for the two schemes, respectively. A significant main effect for gender, as in the original study described previously, was found only for the percentage of chunks in the active scheme: for boys $M=26\%$, for girls $M=14\%$, $F(1,73) = 7.72, p < .01$. No interactions were significant.

Cross-sectional conclusions

The main purpose of the original and replication cross-sectional analyses was to test for age and other trends predicted by the front face (or "self-

Table 5.2. *Developmental level and scheme scores for each grade and age in cross-sectional replication study*

Grade	Mean age	No. of subjects at modal level				Weighted average	Percentage of chunks in scheme			
		1	2	3	4		Physical	Active	Social	Psychological
5	10	4	15	4	0	1.99	6	20	18	55
7	12	2	10	7	0	2.39	9	25	36	30
9	14	0	7	13	0	2.56	8	17	34	41
11	16	0	7	11	1	2.58	8	20	29	43

as-object") part of our developmental model. The data reported in these analyses generally provide support for the model's main predictions as regards these front-face relations. Strong correlations were found between age and developmental level as measured by the scoring manual derived from the model. These correlations were consistently obtained for every index of developmental level used in this research.

One of our main underlying claims – that each of the model's four self-as-object schemes (physical, active, social, and psychological) remain important components in self-understanding at all ages – was confirmed. Statements characteristic of each scheme were made at each grade, and these statements were well distributed across the age levels in the sample. There were some positive associations between scheme and age, but these were weak and spotty. Correlations between age and percentage of chunks in each scheme and between age and modal-scheme score were not significant in the replication study and were low in the original study – significantly lower than the correlations between age and developmental level. Further, the data provide little evidence for an age-related, sequential shifting of modal scheme from physical to active to social to psychological. Nor was there an empirical interaction between modal scheme and modal level around the model's diagonal cell, as might be predicted if indeed the schemes represented a related developmental dimension.

The data suggest that development transformations in self-understanding are best captured by developmental levels and not by shifts in self-scheme use. The levels, as we have discussed, focus on the manner in which self is construed rather than on the aspect of self cited. It is the meaning and importance of the characteristic, and the organizational relationship between multiple characteristics, that changes with development, and not the type of characteristic itself – hence, the pattern of findings regarding level and scheme in our original and replication studies.

Our predicted findings that all four self schemes are used at all ages and development levels places us in opposition to most previous writings on self-concept development. For example, as discussed in Chapter 2, many investigators have asserted that self-knowledge in early childhood is limited to a dim awareness of the self's typical activities and physical characteristics (e.g., Secord & Peevers, 1974). Our cross-sectional data show that even young children frequently describe themselves psychologically. The most plausible explanations for this apparent opposition presented by our findings is our use of probing clinical interview techniques to draw out children's full meaning for their self-statements. The likely failure of previous self-concept research to document psychological self-knowledge in early childhood reflects data collection techniques that inhibit young children's expression of psychological aspects of self. The great advantage of the clinical interview method is its capacity to explore the depths and limits of children's knowledge. This explanation is buttressed by recent "everyday-speech" analyses that clearly show young children talking about many different psychological qualities of themselves and others (Bretherton, McNew, & Beeghly-Smith, 1981).

Although scheme use does not seem to have developmental implications, we believe that it can reveal other important tendencies beyond ontogenetic ones. For example, the relatively low usage of modal active and social schemes in our sample may suggest that children and adolescents in the United States are more oriented toward the physical and psychological qualities of self. We shall discuss this possibility further in light of our data on Puerto Rican children, reported in Chapter 8. In addition, we shall discuss some personality implications of scheme use related to abnormal adolescent adjustment patterns in Chapter 7.

One main purpose of this research was to establish a new measure to assess the developmental state of self-understanding in children and adolescents. As noted in Chapter 1, most existing self-concept measures focus on self-esteem rather than on the nature or developmental status of the child's self-conception. As a consequence, self-esteem measures attempt to assess how children feel about themselves without taking into account what children believe the self to be in the first place. Clearly these attempts lie on shaky conceptual grounds, and empirical efforts based on such attempts have suffered accordingly (Rosenberg, 1979; Wylie, 1979; Damon & Hart, 1982). At this point, establishing a developmental measure of children's self-conceptions is essential. Clearly, the positive findings regarding reliability as well as age trends are noteworthy results. In addition, the lack of gender differences suggests that the instrument can be used equally well for boys and girls.

Longitudinal findings

Longitudinal data are essential to any complete test of a developmental model. Only through observations of individual progress across time can cohort effects and other extrinsic influences be separated from true developmental patterns. In addition, longitudinal data enable us to inspect the nature of transitions between specified developmental landmarks. Periodic assessments of individual subjects can help us determine whether their achievements come abruptly or gradually – with sudden transforming insights or with tentative, emerging hunches – and whether such achievements can be predicted by precursory ideas, acts, or experiences.

In this section we shall address these developmental issues through a report of findings from our longitudinal sample. Our primary purpose is to provide a further empirical test of our self-understanding model's front face. In addition, the longitudinal data will enable us to examine features of the transitional process governing how subjects acquire higher-level conceptions of self-as-object. Finally, we shall use our longitudinal findings to address a basic self-concept issue that has concerned social psychologists more than developmentalists – the core empirical stability of the construct itself. We believe that our developmental approach, bolstered by our longitudinal findings, can help resolve this troublesome problem that has posed a formidable obstacle for the social-psychological study of self-concept.

Subjects. The longitudinal sample consisted of 52 boys and girls who participated in three self-understanding interview sessions over a 3-year period. In the first year of testing (Time 1) there were 120 students divided evenly by sex and distributed equally across nursery school through grade 8. In the second year of testing (Time 2), 82 of these children continued participating in the study. It was Time 2, as noted above, that provided the sample for the initial cross-sectional analyses reported in the previous section. By the final year of testing (Time 3), subject attrition had further reduced the sample size to 52 boys and girls. For the purpose of our longitudinal analyses, we composed a data set of these 52 subjects' self-interviews across the three testing occasions.

By the final testing occasions, the 52 longitudinal subjects were distributed as follows: 4 boys and 3 girls in grade 2, 4 boys and 2 girls in grade 3, 2 boys and 5 girls in grade 4, 4 boys and 2 girls in grade 5, 2 boys and 3 girls in grade 6, 2 boys and 1 girl in grade 7, 4 boys and 1 girl in grade 8, 1 boy and 2 girls in grade 9, 3 boys and 2 girls in grade 10, and 3 boys and 2 girls in grade 11. Of course, all subjects were 3 years younger in Time 1: the grade 2 children were in nursery school, and so on up to the grade 11 adolescents, who were in junior high school at the outset of the investigation.

Subject attrition during the study's 3 years reduced the original sample by more than half, an amount that was greater than expected or desired. This considerable attrition was due mostly to parents moving to a school district that was inaccessible to us for geographical or other reasons. In addition, a few children declined to participate in either the Time 2 or 3 testings, for reasons ranging from lack of interest to temporary health problems. We compared modal self-understanding scores of subjects who left the study after Time 1 with those who continued to participate in the study through Time 2 through ANOVAs, with each subject's Time 1 the dependent variable. No significant difference was found between subjects who did not participate and those who did. A similar analysis found no difference between those who withdrew after Year 2 and those who participated at Year 3.

Procedure. Each subject was interviewed on three separate occasions, with 18 months between each testing occasion. The basic query set remained the same, but new probes were added as called for by the clinical method approach.

Results

For the 52 longitudinal subjects (as for the larger samples in our previous cross-sectional analyses), there were strong positive associations between age and modal developmental level at each of the three testing times. The correlations were: $r_s = .48$, $p < .001$, $r_s = .48$, $p < .001$, and $r_s = .67$, $p < .001$ for Times 1, 2, and 3, respectively. From year to year, our longitudinal subjects tended to rank in the same position relative to other subjects with regard to their modal levels of self-understanding. Correlations between Time 1 and Time 2 modal levels was $r_s = .33$, $p < .01$; between Time 2 and Time 3, $r_s = .49$, $p < .001$; and between Time 1 and Time 3, $r_s = .41$, $p < .001$.

The pattern of transitions from one year to the next reveals a gradual and orderly process of self-understanding change. Combining both sets of transitions occurring between the three testing periods (Time 1 to Time 2, and Time 2 to Time 3), there were 29 transitions to the next highest adjacent level, 8 transitions to a nonadjacent higher level, 8 transitions to a lower level, and 59 with no change. Thus, when change took place, it tended to be in a positive direction. A nonparametric sign test (one-tailed) revealed that this tendency to change positively rather than negatively from one time to the next was significant at the $p < .001$ level. In the sample as a whole, there was considerable regularity to this progressive pattern. Only in two instances were subjects' modal-level scores higher in Time 1 than in Time 3; only in one instance did an individual move to a higher level in both Time 2 and Time 3; and only in 14 instances did subjects remain at the same modal levels from Time 1 to Time 3. Table 5.3 shows the modal-level scores of the 52 longitudinal subjects across the three testing times.

An examination of the patterns of transition also revealed that movement from one level to the next was gradual. As Table 5.3 demonstrates, modal-level change tended to be to the next higher level rather than to a non-adjacent one. Only in 5 of 36 positive transitions were there deviations from this pattern.

Further, developmental change in modal level was presaged by partial reasoning advances in prior years. One indication of this was that at both Time 1 and Time 2, the percentage of chunks scored above the then-current modal level predicted advancement to a higher modal level at the next testing occasion, with correlations of $r = .34$, $p < .01$, for the transition from Time 1 to Time 2, and $r = .56$, $p < .001$, for the transition from Time 2 to Time 3. In a further discussion on alternative models of social-cognitive change, we shall offer another empirical indication of this predictive relation between partial reasoning advances and later modal change.

These findings indicate that developmental changes in self-understanding follow a regular and predictable course. Transitions from 1 year to the next tend to be positive and gradual along an orderly sequence of self-understanding levels; and they are forecast by an earlier increase in the reasoning characteristic of the next higher levels in that sequence. Further, subjects' levels of performance, both relative to others and in an absolute sense, are strongly determined by their prior levels of performance.

As for self-as-object scheme use (the subject's selective focus on the physical, active, social, or psychological aspects of self), there was only limited stability from one testing occasion to the next, and little predictability in movement patterns. There were 24 instances of subjects remaining at the same model scheme at Times 1 and 2, and 23 instances of subjects remaining at the same modal scheme at Times 2 and 3. Eleven of these subjects remained at the same modal scheme for all three testing times. Movement, when it occurred, took place fairly evenly to both adjacent and nonadjacent schemes in the model's front face, indicating no particular ontogenetic ordering principle. The only exception was an increase in psychological scheme scores from Time 2 to Time 3. This finding could be attributable to a testing effect that inclined subjects, after repeated interviewing, to think more about the inner self; or to some factor associated with fluctuations in the longitudinal sample. Because we were not able to identify such factors, we prefer the former explanation.

Correlations for modal schemes between Time 1 and Time 2, Time 2 and Time 3, and Time 1 and Time 3 were, respectively, $r_s = .29$, $p < .05$, $r_s = .24$, n.s., and $r_s = .09$. All of these data suggest very limited stability in the self-scheme scores.

In general, we draw the following conclusions from the longitudinal data reported thus far in this section: (1) During the period from early

Table 5.3. *Age and modal level for longitudinal subjects*
at each testing time

Subject number	Age, Time 1	Modal level, Time 1	Age, Time 2	Modal level, Time 2	Age, Time 3	Modal level, Time 3
1	4.75	2	6.25	2	7.75	2
2	4.08	1	5.58	2	7.08	1
3	5.17	1	6.67	1	8.17	2
5	5.17	1	6.67	2	8.17	2
6	4.58	1	6.08	2	7.58	2
7	4.92	1	6.42	2	7.92	2
11	4.67	1	6.17	1	7.67	2
14	5.50	1	7.00	1	8.50	2
15	5.83	1	7.33	1	8.83	1
19	5.33	2	6.83	2	8.33	2
20	5.50	1	7.00	1	8.50	2
22	5.75	1	7.25	2	8.75	2
24	5.92	2	7.42	2	8.92	2
30	7.00	1	8.50	1	10.00	1
36	7.08	1	8.58	3	10.08	3
38	7.42	2	8.92	2	10.42	3
41	8.17	1	9.67	2	11.17	2
42	8.08	2	9.58	2	11.08	2
44	7.83	2	9.33	2	10.83	2
47	7.50	1	9.00	2	10.50	2
48	8.00	2	9.50	2	11.00	1
49	8.83	1	10.33	1	11.83	2
51	8.75	3	10.25	2	11.75	2
54	8.50	2	10.00	3	11.50	2
57	9.08	2	10.58	2	12.08	2
60	8.75	2	10.25	2	11.75	2
63	10.00	2	11.50	1	13.00	3
68	9.42	3	10.92	2	12.42	3
70	9.67	2	11.17	3	12.67	3
73	10.50	1	12.00	3	13.50	3
75	11.00	2	12.50	2	14.00	3
76	11.75	2	13.25	3	14.75	3
81	11.17	2	12.67	2	14.17	2
83	10.92	2	12.42	2	13.92	2
89	11.92	3	13.42	2	14.92	3
92	11.83	3	13.33	3	14.83	3
95	12.17	2	13.67	3	15.17	3
98	12.50	2	14.00	1	15.50	3
100	13.33	2	14.83	2	16.33	3
101	12.83	1	14.33	2	15.83	2
105	13.08	2	14.58	2	16.08	3
107	12.50	2	14.00	2	15.50	3
108	12.67	2	14.17	4	15.67	4
109	13.58	1	15.08	3	16.58	3

Table 5.3. (*cont.*)

Subject number	Age, Time 1	Modal level, Time 1	Age, Time 2	Modal level, Time 2	Age, Time 3	Modal level, Time 3
110	13.50	1	15.00	3	16.50	3
112	13.83	2	15.33	2	16.83	3
116	13.50	2	15.00	3	16.50	2
118	13.92	2	15.42	2	16.92	3

childhood to late adolescence, knowledge of the self-as-other develops in an orderly sequence of levels as defined by the front face of our self-understanding model and operationalized by the scoring manual derived from that model. (2) Transitions from one level to the next are gradual but relentless, with change occurring in small regular increments taking many months to register. (3) Large-scale (i.e., modal) changes are forecast by earlier small-scale increases in higher-level reasoning. (4) A child's progress in understanding self at any given time is predictive of the child's later progress. (5) The major focus of a child's self-statements, whether it be physical, active, social, or psychological, is neither particularly stable over time nor changes in any orderly, sequential manner. Thus "self-scheme use," as we have called it, appears to have none of the developmental implications asserted by previous social-science writings on self-concept.

Longitudinal findings and theoretical models of development change

In recent years there has been a great deal of debate and attendant confusion in the developmental literature about the use of stage models to describe conceptual growth. We do not wish to expand upon the various issues here but can unequivocally state our position that conceptual growth implies progressive reorganizations; and such reorganizations can only be captured through a sequence of qualitatively distinct structures – that is, some sort of stage model.

A large part of the confusion surrounding the stage issue has been the mistaken belief that all proposed developmental sequences carry with them identical assumptions (see, e.g., Brainerd, 1978). But careful overviews of the literature reveal wide variation in how sequential-stage notions have been used (see Flavell, 1977).

We rely heavily on sequential-stage-like descriptions in our writings on social-cognitive development; but this does not mean that we endorse just any use of the sequential-stage approach. We find many stage models in the developmental literature to be far too global, amorphous, and loosely defined (e.g., Kegan, 1983, as just one example). As noted in our introductory chapter, we do not accept unlimited holism or sudden radical transformations as implicit in the notion of qualitative conceptual reorganization. Like some other contemporary developmentalists, we find a more limited use of stage-structural notions to be valuable, even necessary, for capturing the essence of long-term change (Fischer, 1980, 1983; Feldman, 1980; Gardner, 1983; Turiel, 1983; Snyder & Feldman, 1984).

With these more limited uses of sequential-stage models has come a special interest in properties of transition implicit in conceptual growth. The original claims implicit in global-stage models have been challenged. The result has been some interesting speculation, debate, and empirical studies on the twin issues of how conceptual reorganization actually occurs and how it can be predicted from earlier precursors.

As in a previous longitudinal study of social-cognitive change (Damon, 1980), we find our longitudinal data on self-understanding to be revealing in this regard. In this section we shall present our conclusions with regard to issues of developmental transition and shall contrast our approach with two others: first, one of the global-stage approaches, the moral stage theory of Lawrence Kohlberg; and second, a partial approach to developmental sequence like ours, but one that has come to different conclusions about the nature of transition.

Kohlberg's approach

One of the more extensive claims about patterns of change in social development is made by Kohlberg and his colleagues (e.g., Kohlberg & Armon, 1984). Although Kohlberg's own assertions about his stages are based on his work on moral judgment, he and others often have suggested that the same model has applications in numerous domains of social development (e.g., Snarey, Kohlberg, & Noam, 1983).

Kohlberg's claim is that the development of moral judgment proceeds through a sequence of so-called hard stages (Kohlberg & Armon, 1984). Most important for the current discussion is the claim that each emergent pattern of thought, or stage, constitutes a "structured whole." As a structured whole, each stage consists of an inner logic "that organize[s] and govern[s] reasoning operations" (Kohlberg & Armon, 1984, p. 388). This powerful inner logic pervades the reasoning of the individual and determines the individual's reasoning about tasks that "are not manifestly similar" (p. 387). Empirically, stages of this type would be manifested by patterns of data indicating that a person uses only one stage of reasoning, and that there are rapid transitions between stages because each emergent logic quickly replaces the now clearly inferior patterns of thinking of the previous stage (Fischer, 1983).

Of the three models that we shall consider in this section, the "hard"-stage model is least sensitive to the social and task-related contexts of reasoning, because it claims that the same organization governs thinking about different tasks and makes the strongest claims about consolidation (each logic constitutes such a powerful instrument of thinking, that an individual will only evidence thinking characteristic of the highest stage the individual is capable of using).

Generally, reviewers have concluded that the structured wholeness postulate in Kohlberg's theory is at best weakly supported by the data presented in its defense (e.g., Fischer, 1983; Saltzstein, 1983). This is because Kohlberg's data indicate that individuals often reason at several different stages at any one point in development, suggesting that there is not one set of interiorized actions that is consistently applied in different moral contexts. The lack of evidence for structured wholeness in moral judgment is consistent with the absence of support for claims of structured wholeness in the domain of cognitive development (Fischer & Bullock, 1981).

Snyder and Feldman

The consistent finding that emergent patterns of thought do not form structured wholes has led to the development of new stage models more sensitive to evident unevenness in development. One of the most promising of these models is the consolidation–transition model proposed by Snyder and Feldman (1984, 1980). Theoretically, the stages in this model differ from the stages of Kohlberg in two ways. First, a stage in Snyder and Feldman's model is more closely tied to the context in which the reasoning is used. Stages are jointly determined by the consistencies in the individual and by the internal consistencies of the domain of knowledge the subject interacts with. Consequently, development in each domain of knowledge requires its own articulation. Further, even within a domain, certain aspects of the context tend to elicit reasoning that is characteristic of a higher stage, whereas other aspects may tend to elicit reasoning characteristic of developmental stages beyond which the subject had seemingly grown.

A second difference between the two models is that Snyder and Feldman claim development is a very gradual process, with periods of protracted transition between stages. It should be expected, then, that a subject will respond to a series of tasks using reasoning characteristic of several developmental stages, although overall performance will be well represented by the subject's modal stage. Although lengthy, the process of transition is not continuous; Snyder and Feldman predict that periods of consolidation alternate with periods of transition. During these periods of consolidation, the tendency to respond to tasks using several developmental stages diminishes, the likelihood of using the modal stage increases, and the probability of developmental movement to the next modal stage is low. Finally, Snyder and Feldman believe that the distribution of responses characteristic of the modal stage and stages above and below the modal stage can be used to determine whether a person is in the process of consolidation or transition.

The consolidation–transition model allows several important predictions about both changes in the distribution of responses characteristic of non-modal stages and developmental movement to the next higher stage. First, the total percentage of responses above and below the modal stage should be inversely related with changes in the percentage of responses not at the modal stage at a later testing time, because periods of low percentages of responses above and below the mode (periods of consolidation) should alternate with periods with high percentages of responses above and below the mode (periods of transition). A shift of modal developmental stage can also be predicted by this model, utilizing the distinction between those in the process of transition and those whose reasoning is consolidating.

The process of transition to the next highest stage is indicated empirically by more responses characteristic of stages above the modal stage than below it, or "positive bias," whereas the process of consolidation at the present modal stage is identified by more responses characteristic of stages below the modal stage, or "negative bias." Persons in the process of transition are gradually elaborating the reasoning characteristic of the next higher stage, with this next higher stage eventually displacing the current stage as the modal stage. As a result, there should be a strong positive relationship between the percentage of responses characteristic of stages above the modal stage and modal-stage advance. Persons in the process of consolidation at the current modal stage, however, are unlikely to shift to a higher stage in the near future. Thus there should be no relationship between modal-stage advance and percentage of responses characteristic of stages above the current modal stage for negative-bias subjects.

The consolidation–transition model has been shown to represent accurately spatial development measured longitudinally (Snyder & Feldman,

1980), spatial development resulting from a training study (Snyder & Feldman, 1984), and moral development occurring from a training study (Snyder & Norcini, 1982). These very promising figures lead Snyder and Feldman to suggest that this model should replace our own gradual-transformation model, which we shall discuss next, because the consolidation–transition model makes "more precise predictions and encompasses a broader, more comprehensive theoretical scope" (1984, p. 988).

Damon and Hart

Our own gradual-transformation model makes the least extensive claims about the holistic nature of stages and links developmental sequences most closely to the social-cultural and task-related conditions in which they are expressed. Even more emphatically than Snyder and Feldman, Damon (1977, 1983) has asserted that each developmental sequence must be located in the interactions between the subject and a particular domain of knowledge. Further, and in decided contrast to Snyder and Feldman, we claim that developmental elaboration of higher stages may be a continuous process, meaning that periods of consolidation are not necessarily present in the course of conceptual development.

Empirically, according to our position, the percentage of responses above the modal stage at one testing time should be a good predictor for developmental movement to the next higher stage for *all* subjects, because all subjects are in the process of transition (Snyder and Feldman argued that the percentage of responses above the modal stage should predict developmental advance only for the transitional, or positive-bias, subjects). Furthermore, our gradual-transformation model would predict only an inverse relationship of low or no significance between the percentage of responses not at the modal stage at one testing time and the percentage of responses not at the modal stage at a later data. This is because we do not claim that periods of transition (which empirically result in a relatively large percentage of responses not at the modal stage) are interrupted by periods of consolidation (empirically resulting in a small percentage of responses not at the modal stage).

Not claiming consolidation makes the gradual-transformation model potentially most sensitive to contextual influences on reasoning, because considerable variability in responding to a task is considered normal. The gradual-transformation model has been shown to be consistent with patterns of data from longitudinal studies of an understanding of authority and distributive justice (Damon, 1980).

Implications of our longitudinal results

At least in the domain of self-understanding, our longitudinal findings do not support Kohlberg's "hard-stage" notions. For one thing, we believe that the moderate degree of response homogeneity that we found in our sample (66% of the subjects' responses were at the modal stage) was too low to support claims of structured wholeness, and others have taken a similar position (Fischer, 1983). Further, the change patterns in our data revealed a far more gradual and tentative (yet still persistent) picture of transition than the theoretical writings of Kohlberg and his colleagues would predict.[1]

Our longitudinal findings were also inconsistent with the predictions of Snyder and Feldman's consolidation–transition model. To examine the value of Snyder and Feldman's model, in which it is necessary to allow the possibility of negative and positive bias, the analyses we will report included only those students who were not at the lowest stage (which prohibits the possibility of negative bias) or at the highest stage (which would not allow for positive bias). This subgroup from our longitudinal sample totaled 31 students for the transition from the first (Time 1) to the second testing time (Time 2), and 39 students for the transition from the second to the third testing time (Time 3).

Contrary to the Snyder and Feldman model, we found percentage of responses above the modal stage to be about as good a predictor of modal developmental stage change by the next testing time for positive- as for negative-bias subjects. For positive-bias subjects, this correlation was r (18) = .39, $p <$ .06 (one-tailed), for the transitions between Time 1 and Time 2 and Time 2 and Time 3 combined. For negative-bias subjects, the corresponding correlation was r (43) = .42, $p <$ .01 (one-tailed).

The Snyder and Feldman model also predicts a strong inverse correlation between the percentage of responses not at the modal stage at one testing time and the percentage of responses not at the modal stage at a later testing time. The correlation between percentage of responses not at the modal stage at one testing time and the percentage of responses not at the modal stage at the next testing time was r (69) = .28, $p <$ .05 (one-tailed) for the transitions from Time 1 to Time 2 to Time 3 combined.

These results indicate that periods of pronounced consolidation do not occur in the development of self-understanding. The strong inverse relationship predicted by the Snyder and Feldman between the percentage of responses not at the modal stage at one point and the percentage of responses not at the modal stage at the next testing time was not apparent in our longitudinal study. In fact, a positive correlation of .28 was obtained, a correlation of a different sign and magnitude than the − .83 or − .67 reported by Snyder and Feldman in their training studies (Snyder & Norcini, 1982; Snyder & Feldman, 1984). Similarly, the findings that for negative-bias students at both transition periods positive correlations were obtained for the relationship between the percentage of responses above the mode and modal advance at the next testing time contrasts with results of training studies of Snyder and Feldman, in which they report correlations of − .05 and .003 for the same relationship (Snyder & Norcini, 1982; Snyder & Feldman, 1984). However, our findings are consistent with the gradual-transformation model, which makes no claims about periods of consolidation occurring in development.

Longitudinal findings and self-concept stability

Self-concept research assumes a construct with some core empirical stability. Yet within social psychology there is a long-standing and unresolved debate about whether the self-conceptions of individuals are indeed stable over time and context. In fact, extreme but currently influential positions have maintained that self-concept is nothing more than an ephemeral epiphenomenon, and social-psychological research has yet to provide a definitive answer to such claims. We argue that conceptual and methodological approaches from the developmental tradition can inform this debate and provide critical data in support of stability. Through the developmental focus on behavioral organization and orderly change, stability may be found in the midst of flux; and developmental research techniques like the clinical interview help sharpen this focus. In this section we shall discuss this fundamental issue in relation to our longitudinal data. As noted, these data show the regular and predictable nature of self-concept transformations during the years 4 through 18. This approach offers self-concept researchers willing to assume a developmental perspective a long-term stability of sorts. Such stability, however, should not be confused with absolute behavioral constancy, which is practically nonexistent over the course of development.

The importance of "core" construct stability in self-concept

The assumption that an individual's sense of self is to some degree stable over time and context lies at the heart of all attempts to measure self-concept. Unmitigated fluidity of identity in any variable would defy reliable scientific measurement. The stability assumption also makes credible the postulation of theoretical links between the sense of self and many other aspects of cognition, affect, and behavior. Unless an individual's self-concept retains some fundamental identity across occasions, it hardly could be expected to coordinate with other mental or behavioral systems in systematic or regular ways, and consequently would be of little interest to psychologists. This point must be as true for self-concept as for all psychological constructs.

The social-psychological debate

Despite the fundamental importance of core stability for any psychological construct, there has been within social psychology a lively challenge to the existence of stability in individuals' self-conceptions. At one pole of this debate is Gergen, the most ardent contemporary proponent of flux in self-concept (Gergen, 1977, 1984; Morse & Gergen, 1970). According to Gergen, self-knowledge reflects mostly momentary social comparisons subject to radical change: "What is 'true' about self depends on those available for comparison. In the presence of the devout, we may discover that we are ideologically shallow; in the midst of dedicated hedonists, we may gain awareness of our ideological depths" (Gergen, 1977, p. 153).

To test this hypothesis, Morse and Gergen (1970) had people respond to a self-esteem inventory on two occasions: first by themselves, and then in the presence of either disheveled, dirty confederates, or in the presence of well-dressed good-looking confederates. Results indicated significant changes in scores. The direction of the change varied with the context. There was an increase in self-esteem when the second rating was taken in the presence of the disheveled confederate, and a decrease in self-esteem when it was taken with the good-looking accomplice (although it should be noted that only a subset of subjects demonstrated this effect). This finding led Gergen to conclude that "the present analysis suggests that in the case of self-knowledge there is virtually nothing to know" (1977, p. 166). If self-knowledge is susceptible to discontinuous, radical change when the individual is in a different context, temporal stability is impossible.

This position is at least in one way consistent with our opening assertions, in that we and Gergen agree on the necessity of stability to any viable psychological construct. Gergen's view that self-knowledge is infinitely labile leads him to dismiss it altogether as an inconsequential epiphenomenon – a reasonable conclusion given Gergen's belief that self-concept lacks stability. This belief, however, is far from universally accepted.

A more moderate line of social-psychological thought admits to both stability and flux in self-concept (Bem & Allen, 1974; Markus, 1977). It handles the problematic mix of the two by treating it like an individual difference. For some individuals, reason Bem and Allen, dimension x is a stable part of their self-concept (either positively or negatively), whereas others do not consider it important enough to be consistently valued across situations. Bem and Allen's strategy is to remove the latter group of individuals from a study of relations between self-concept dimension x and the variable of interest. (Note that this strategy accepts our assumption, and Gergen's, that stability is essential for establishing predictable relations to other aspects of behavior and thought.)

Consider, for example, Bem and Allen's (1974) study of the relationship between individuals' self-reports and their behavior. The investigators predicted (and found) an association between judgments of the self's friendliness and the degree of friendly behavior demonstrated at a later time in a different social context. But the investigators also found that this association obtained only among individuals who considered friendliness to be one of their central, and stable, personality attributes.

Bem and Allen's approach is founded on their belief that there are at least two types of variation in individual's self-concepts. Individuals may vary not only on the extent to which they define themselves according to certain personality traits, but also on whether the traits are applicable in the first place. Bem and Allen argue that most individuals are "aschematic," or without active self-awareness, with regard to most traits. Consequently, there may not be much interindividual overlap on any particular dimension used to define the self. Bem and Allen attribute the reported lack of empirical correspondence between self-concept and behavior to psychologists' mistaken search for cross-individual dimensions:

Nearly all the research is based on some variant of the nomothetic assumption that a particular trait dimension or set of trait dimensions is universally applicable to all persons and that individual differences are to be identified with different locations on those dimensions. (Bem and Allen, 1974, pp. 508–9)

Bem and Allen's methodological solution, as noted, was to provide subjects with a prepared inventory of traits from which subjects were asked to choose important ones, and to then remove from their sample subjects for whom the target trait (e.g., friendliness) was unimportant. Similarly, Markus (1977) achieved some empirical success by separating subjects whose choices from a self-rating scale included a particular dimension (independence–dependence) from subjects whose choices did not.

The message of this approach is threefold: First, lawful empirical relations surrounding self-concept can only be found when the investigation begins with stable features of self. Second, only features that individuals themselves consider to be important will be stable. Third, there is widespread variation between how individuals choose and define their own central features. Hence, we have the Bem and Allen "idiographic" approach to self-concept assessment.

Of course, we must recognize that even Bem and Allen's own work does not go all the way in the promising direction of having individuals define their own self-concept dimensions. The Bem–Allen solution of fabricating lists of predefined traits for subjects to choose among does not meet the idiographic goal of respecting the totality of subjects' meaning-making capacities: Such a solution cannot distinguish between two subjects who select the same trait word but define it differently, nor can it capture the sense of a subject who thinks of the self in categories that are more ephemeral and less stable than traits. Bem and Allen realize this limitation, calling their own instrument modifications a "token gesture towards more idiographic assessment" (p. 512).

Nor have many social psychologists taken Bem and Allen's message to its logical conclusion by using a genuinely idiographic approach to studying self-concept. Such an approach would mean treating every individual's conceptual framework as a unique system, and devising a methodology allowing individuals to express their own way of formulating self-definitional characteristics. This reluctance is not surprising; social psychology is an experimental discipline not easily oriented toward an idiographic approach. The instruments, as in the Bem and Allen inventory, are designed to elicit easily codible responses from large groups of subjects efficiently and not to capture subtle individual variations in experience or interpretation. The scientific intention of social-psychological research is the nomothetic goal of uncovering group norms of behavior. The recent self-concept work in social psychology falls solidly within this tradition. It has employed none of the methods of the idiographic approach: ethnographies, case histories, or phenomenological interviews. It has shown a concern neither with individuals' total lives nor with their idiosyncratic conceptual systems.

In actuality, therefore, Bem and Allen's "small idiographic commitment" (p. 512) was really a move toward a more valid nomothetic procedure rather than toward an idiographic approach. The challenge raised by their argument is to represent accurately the variation in individuals' self-definitions within a scientific framework of analysis that makes intergroup comparisons possible. Unfortunately, the social-psychological attempts thus far do not wholly accomplish this because they neither capture individual meaning systems nor establish compelling categories for cross-group comparisons. What these studies have done, however, is set the stage for further progress toward an approach that respects individual variation while providing group norms for psychological analysis.

Self-concept stability from a developmental perspective

Developmentalists have a special concern with stability because the phenomena of interest to them inevitably change. Yet developmentalists, like all scientists, search for empirical regularities, and this search requires defining and measuring constructs that themselves have some core stability. Consequently, developmentalists have devised conceptual and methodological strategies for finding stability in the midst of behavioral flux.

The key conceptual strategy is choosing for study the organizational features of the behavioral system in question, rather than the behavioral pattern in and of itself. These organizational features are considered in some approaches to be "structures," in others "processes," and in others both. They tend to change slowly over time, if at all. Further, when organizational change does occur, it is orderly, following a predictable sequence and reversing itself only rarely. This orderly quality in itself yields a critical stability to developmental changes, because it defines lawful regularities that govern the flux.

Hand in hand with this conceptual strategy must go methodological techniques for tapping the organizational features of behavior. One such technique is the clinical method of interviewing that we use in the present investigation. As discussed in Chapter 3, the rationale behind this method has much in common with Bem and Allen's justification for their own "idiographically" oriented assessments. The intention of both is to encourage subjects to express their full understanding on its own terms, without forcing subjects to rely on a set of dimensions prepackaged by the experimenter.

Clinical interviews, however, go further in this direction than do Bem and Allen's procedures. Through an individualized set of questions and challenges, a clinical interview probes for the subject's own way of defining and understanding the topics of investigation. Subjects are required not only to respond to interview items but also to disclose their own interpretations of these items. Developmentalists sensitive to the special features of their subjects' reasoning assume that subjects' interpretations will vary from one another as well as from those of the experimenter. Uncovering these interpretations is a necessary step in any developmental investigation.

Unfortunately not all who study developmental phenomena (e.g., age-related changes in social cognition) use developmentally appropriate techniques like the clinical interview. In the widely studied area of children's self-concept, techniques have ranged from content analyses of various fixed and free-response interview formats to semantic differential and other rating scales. Such techniques fail to tap fully the quality and organization of children's thinking because they do not probe the child's meaning in adequate depth. Further, they differ greatly from one another in procedure, with commensurately varying types of biases. This difference has led to a spectrum of confusing and incompatible findings regarding the fundamental issue of self-concept stability.

Some self-concept studies bring us the message that self-concept changes with age in major and only partially predictable ways. For example, Montemayor and Eisen asked children and adolescents to write 20 answers to the question "Who am I?" These responses were then coded using a content-analysis scheme developed by Gordon (1968), in which each answer is assigned to 1 of 30 categories. There were significant age-related changes in the percentage of responses in 15 of the 30 categories. Further, this study inferred change from cross-sectional data; it is likely that longitudinal testings using the same procedures would yield even more temporal instability, because then test–retest fluctuations would be combined with age-related change. Keller, Ford, and Meachum (1978), Livesly and Bromley (1973), and Secord and Peevers (1974) have obtained similar results using similar procedures.

In contrast, some investigators have concluded that it is stability across age that best characterizes self-concept during childhood and adolescence. These investigators generally have used rating scales of one type or another. For example, Dusek and Flaherty (1981) used a semantic differential technique requiring each student to rate which of a pair of adjectives (e.g., happy–sad, friendly–unfriendly) is most characteristic of the self. Analyses of both cross-sectional and longitudinal samples covering the age range from 11 to 18 years found no significant differences in the factor structures of responses to the semantic differential.

These and similar analyses led the authors to conclude that despite other well-recognized changes in patterns of friendship, cognition, social understanding, and societal demands during the childhood and adolescent years, "the evidence presented in this (monograph) indicates that these events do not cause a restructuring of the self-concept for all or even most adolescents" (Dusek & Flaherty, 1981, pp. 33–4). Other researchers have reached similar conclusions. In a study using the Coopersmith Self-Esteem Inventory for children in grades four through eight, Kokenes (1974) claimed that "on the whole, it must be concluded that in this population there was little factorial difference in expressed self-attitudes from grade level to grade level" (p. 958).

How are such conflicting results to be reconciled? Some variability no doubt arises from conceptual differences in how self-concept is defined and operationalized by investigators. We can only speculate about how such differences translate into conflicting findings. How certain data collection strategies create systematic, though opposing, biases in findings with regard to stability and change is clearer.

As Bromley (1977) has argued, semantic differentials and other rating scales overly constrain subjects' self-expressions. In developmental research, this can have the effect of obscuring emergent aspects of self-awareness (Hill, 1981; Harter, 1982). There is a tendency, then, for rating scales to overestimate the fixity of self-understanding during development, because they are insensitive to new elements in their formative phases.

Content analyses of standardized response data (answers to unprobed questions like "What kid of person am I?") suffer from the opposite problem. This procedure characterizes subjects' self-statements only in terms of their response frequencies across predetermined content categories. In testings over time it is impossible to know which changes in category usage reflect measurement error, test–retest unreliability, or developmental reorganization (and if the latter, reorganization of what – linguistic abilities, cognitive orientation, sense of self?). All of these sources get lumped into the undifferentiated notion of instability, despite the regular and predictable nature of many of the sources. Content analyses, therefore, are likely to underestimate the stability of self-concept.

The development case for "reorganizational stability" in our longitudinal findings

We have made the claim that stability during development must be seen as orderly change rather than as absolute behavioral constancy over time. The results of our longitudinal study demonstrate this kind of orderly change in self-concept during childhood and adolescence. In a strict sense, we found little stability: Only 14 subjects organized their ideas about themselves in the same way at the end as at the beginning of our 3 years of testing. But the observed changes were not random. Indeed, they were quite predictable in light of developmental theory: A change in modal level of self-understanding was almost always to the next higher level, and this change was initially heralded by a gradual increase in the percentage of reasoning characteristic of the higher level. Further, across the study's three testing occasions, most individual children continued to demonstrate the same degree of advancement relative to other subjects. These are all signs of stable relations governed by systematic laws.

These developmental findings contrast sharply with our findings about the four self-schemes. Here, with a focus on which aspects of self subjects emphasized rather than on how subjects organized their thinking about self, we found considerable flux and little stability or regularity in the movements over time. There was much less evidence for developmental progression in the self-schemes: age $\times$ scheme correlations were low, and movements from one modal scheme to another generally were not to the next highest adjacent one, as they were between modal levels. Further, we observed low degrees of either absolute stability (identical scheme scores across testing time) or relative stability (correlations between scheme scores across testing times).

The one exception to the lack of pattern in scheme scores over time was with regard to the psychological scheme: Modal use of the psychological scheme increased significantly across the three testing times. Yet age was not a factor here either. We believe that this longitudinal pattern was due to a testing rather than a developmental effect. It seems likely that the very process of interviewing children and adolescents about the self could trigger a more psychological focus during future interview occasions. An interview experience might well make subjects more reflective about the self during direct questioning (which is, after all, rare in the everyday lives of children and adolescents). This experience could serve to orient subjects more strongly toward the psychological aspects of self in their responses to further interviews.

In a similar vain, Gergen (1965) has demonstrated that an experimentally induced orientation during a self-interview can indeed alter a subject's subsequent self-ratings. Such changes may be nothing more than context-specific responses to the testing situation, without great lasting or general import. Indeed, we would expect that subject's use of self-schemes, in contrast to their use of developmental self-understanding levels, would be susceptible to just this sort of short-term change through environmental manipulation.

Despite their relative lability, the self-schemes offer us access to issues that have long interested social psychologists. This claim is particularly true in relation to subjects' scheme use in interaction with their modal developmental levels of self-understanding. Individual differences in orientation to the social world, in social-cultural background, and in personality itself may be revealed by patterns of self-scheme use in relation to developmental self-understanding level. Such patterns may be hidden to less probing (and less idiographic) self-concept measures. We shall explore such patterns further in Chapter 8. In addition, we shall see that some abnormal populations, such as highly socially oriented males, show significantly less lability long-term in their self-scheme use. Thus even this nondevelopmental aspect of self-concept may have some core empirical stability for some populations, particularly when viewed in context of the developmental aspects of our self-understanding model.

Two cases of longitudinal change

To close this chapter, we offer some quotes from two cases in our longitudinal sample. We do so in order to bring to life the levels and transitional processes that we have been discussing throughout this chapter. In each case we quote from two testing occasions, Times 2 and 3 (spaced, as noted, at 18-month intervals). The first boy ("Paul") was 11 at Time 2 and 13 at Time 3; the second ("Ben") was 14 at Time 2 and 16 at Time 3. In the course of these two testing times, the first boy's scored protocols changed in modal level from one to three and the second boy's scored protocols changed from three to four.

Paul provides us with an example of an unusual shift across two developmental levels in the space of 18 months. When Paul was interviewed at Time 2, he generally relied on physical, active, and material categories to describe himself and his personal aspirations. When asked the first question about how he would describe himself to somebody else, Paul referred to his height. Later in the interview, Paul spoke about his physical strength and about his "looks," including hair and eye color. He talked about changing himself by lifting weights and making himself "tough." As for his wishes and aspirations, the following dialogue gives a sense of Paul's focus on material goods and activities:

WHAT WOULD YOU WISH FOR? A minibike. OK, A MINIBIKE. A new house. And money. AND MONEY? OK WHY WOULD YOU WISH FOR A MINIBIKE? 'Cause they look like fun. I've ridden on one with a friend. They look fun. OK, SO YOU THINK IT WOULD BE A FUN THING TO DO, RIDE A MINIBIKE AROUND? Uh huh. OK, AND WHY WOULD YOU WANT A NEW HOUSE? 'Cause our house is old. OK, YOUR HOUSE IS PRETTY OLD. OK, SO WHY WOULD YOU WANT A NEW ONE? 'Cause new houses are nice. OK, WHAT DO YOU MEAN NICE? We would have more things like there may be a swimming pool in that house that we don't have in our other house. OK, SO YOU'D WANT A HOUSE WITH A SWIMMING POOL? Yeah. AND WHY ELSE WOULD YOU WANT A NEW HOUSE? AND WHY WOULD YOU WANT MONEY? 'Cause you can buy a lot of things with money.

OK, ARE THOSE THE THINGS THAT YOU HOPE FOR MOST IN LIFE: A MINIBIKE, A NEW HOUSE, AND MONEY? Yeah, except I don't want a minibike when I'm older. OK, WHY DON'T YOU THINK YOU'LL WANT A MINIBIKE WHEN YOU'RE OLDER? 'Cause I'd be too big for it. OK, SO YOU'D BE JUST TOO BIG FOR IT TO BE ABLE TO RIDE AROUND ON

IT? Yeah. OK, WHY ARE THOSE THE THINGS THAT YOU HOPE FOR MOST IN LIFE? 'Cause I like 'em the best. O.K., IS THERE ANYTHING ELSE THAT YOU HOPE FOR IN LIFE BESIDES A MINIBIKE, A NEW HOUSE, AND MONEY? My health. YOUR HEALTH? Yeah, I want to move to Florida. OK, YOU WANT TO MOVE TO FLORIDA. And that's all really. OK, WHY DO YOU WANT TO BE HEALTHY? 'Cause I don't want to be sick with a disease or something. OK, WHY NOT? 'Cause you can't do anything if you have a disease that's bad. OK, WHY DO YOU WANT TO MOVE TO FLORIDA? It's nice down there. HAVE YOU BEEN TO FLORIDA? Yeah. AND YOU REALLY LIKE IT? OK, WHAT MAKES IT NICE FOR YOU? The weather. OK, THE WEATHER. And it's just an exciting place to be. OK, WHAT DO YOU FIND EXCITING ABOUT IT? Everything really. I like going in the swimming pool, and the beaches. The water is warm there. There's a lot of sharks though. OK, WHAT DO YOU THINK THE MOST IMPORTANT THINGS ARE THAT ARE GOOD FOR YOU? I can't think of anything. Uh, living a good life. Like going traveling and all instead of just sitting home and growing old. OK, SO LIVING A GOOD LIFE IS IMPORTANT. Having a good time.

At Time 2, Paul also expressed some Level 2 comparative self-descriptions, asserting that he was "fun to be with" and "not dumb." But these occasional comments were overshadowed by his predominant use of simple categorical statements to describe self and thus did not affect the modal Level 1 score of his self-understanding protocol.

By the time of the next interview, Time 3, Paul's interpersonal characteristics had become his main concern. Paul was now 18 months older, and the difference in the quality of his self-understanding is striking:

WHAT ELSE CAN YOU SAY ABOUT YOURSELF, BESIDES THAT YOU'RE A GOOD PERSON? Well, I guess I'm helpful, kind. WHAT DO YOU MEAN BY YOU'RE HELPFUL? Well, I help people if they have problems in school, if they need help in math or whatever. And I help a lot around the house. IS THAT IMPORTANT TO YOU THAT YOU'RE HELPFUL? DOES THAT MATTER TO YOU? It does some. WHY IS THAT IMPORTANT TO YOU THAT YOU'RE HELPFUL? It encourages you. WHAT DO YOU MEAN? It makes you feel good that you can help someone else do something. HOW COME YOU THINK IT MAKES YOU FEEL GOOD THAT YOU CAN HELP SOMEONE? Just knowing that you helped someone with something that they didn't understand or couldn't do. You just feel good. OK, DID YOU SAY "KIND" AFTERWARDS? Yeah. WHAT DO YOU MEAN BY KIND? Well, I'm not mean. I'm not rude to anyone. I don't sass the teachers in school. DOES THAT MATTER TO YOU? IS THAT AN IMPORTANT PART OF YOU? Yeah.

CAN YOU THINK OF ANYTHING ELSE TO SAY ABOUT YOURSELF, WHAT KIND OF PERSON YOU ARE? I'm fun to be with I guess. You can have a good time. WHAT DO YOU MEAN YOU'RE FUN TO BE WITH? Well, you have a good time wherever you go. IS THAT IMPORTANT TO YOU THAT YOU'RE FUN TO BE WITH? Yeah, 'cause I mean you have more friends 'cause you're fun to be with. WHY IS THIS IMPORTANT TO YOU TO HAVE MORE FRIENDS? 'Cause you'll be more popular and all the kids will accept you in the in crowd. WHY IS THAT IMPORTANT? To be in the in crowd? Because if you're not, you're like an outcast. They make fun of you, and they'll do different things. IS THERE ANY OTHER REASON BESIDES THAT THEY MAKE FUN OF YOU? It's just fun to be in with all the other kids.

CAN YOU TELL ME SOMETHING THAT YOU'RE NOT? I'm not mean. IS THERE ANYTHING ELSE THAT YOU DIDN'T SAY BEFORE? I'm not unthankful for anything. I'm glad that I have, you know, but I do want more stuff but I'm not— BUT YOU'RE NOT UN-

THANKFUL? No. WHY IS THAT IMPORTANT? I don't know. WHY DO YOU THINK IT'S AN IMPORTANT THING TO SAY ABOUT YOU? WHY DOES IT MATTER THAT YOU'RE NOT UN-THANKFUL? Because people that aren't thankful, they just take things and they don't care what they do with 'em. Like someone that buys you a car, you really don't care if you get into an accident. But if you buy it yourself, it's your own money and you really care about it. WHY ELSE IS IT IMPORTANT TO BE THANKFUL? I guess when you're thankful, you make someone feel better because they're really happy that you thanked them for what you got. OK, WHY IS IT IMPORTANT FOR YOU TO MAKE PEOPLE FEEL BETTER? It just makes you feel better to have other people feel good, so they'll know that I'm thankful.

In the preceding dialogue, Paul refers to his helpfulness and charity to others, a notion that emerged for the first time on the Time 2 interview. This, of course, is a notion based on one's social interaction with others. Paul also repeats a theme that was present at Time 2, that he is "fun to be with." But now Paul expands this theme in some important ways. He makes note of its implications for social acceptance (he will not be an "outcast"), and for his sense of reciprocity (the need to be thankful so that others will "feel good"). Finally, Paul includes among his wishes and aspirations the desire to be more "good-natured."

In the space of 18 months, therefore, Paul's statements about himself and his aspirations have changed in a consistent direction. These statements increasingly reflect Paul's awareness of his social personality aspects. In particular, Paul acknowledges his kindness, helpfulness, gratitude, and good-naturedness. These characteristics do not constitute a systematic or well-integrated philosophy but do indicate a concern with the interpersonal and moral quality of one's social relations. This concern emerged as a significant part of Paul's self-understanding between the ages of 11 and 13. In our longitudinal sample, we have observed similar changes (though usually taking longer) in the self-understanding of many other young adolescents.

The second case that we shall consider here started out at Time 2 at about the same place that Paul reached in his Time 3 interview. We shall call this second subject "Ben." At Time 2, Ben was 13. The following quotes from Ben's Time 2 interview demonstrate the already-dominant focus on social-personality characteristics in Ben's self-understanding:

WHAT ABOUT YOUR PERSONALITY? WHAT DO YOU MEAN? WHAT DO YOU LIKE ABOUT YOUR PERSONALITY? I think I'm rather friendly. Like I would go up to anyone and just talk to them and, you know, I'd help them. But the kids who don't help me, I don't really feel the obligation to help them. I would ask if they really needed it, but say if someone who never helped me asks me for a pencil, I wouldn't give him the pencil. If I had one I'd like to shove it in my pocket and say "I don't have a pencil." I wouldn't like to tell him that I don't have a pencil at all.

I think I'd still not want to hurt people's feelings. I really feel so bad 'cause, like, it's happened to me so many times – it doesn't happen, like, it's not, like, every day. I don't want to give you the impression that every day I go out and lots of people make fun of me. You're gonna sit down at Clark and listen to this tape and say "That poor kid." That isn't the thing: it's just, like, you know, it's happened to me before and I know the feeling. Like when you go upstairs and you just sit there and you realize that you're not doing things that other kids are doing. And I don't like to do that to other people.

I don't judge people usually, unless it's really something severe. 'Cause, like, I really feel bad for people 'cause it's happened to me before. As a matter of fact we had this project to do in a team and there was this one girl – her name is Beth Smith; she's in my music class – and no one would pick her for the group. And I hate groups anyway 'cause they're so, you know. So I felt so bad for her and I don't judge people like that 'cause she doesn't really have that great a personality and she's kind of shy. So I brought her into our group. You know, I'm like that. I don't like the way people judge people. And, like, I don't like the people, 'cause people do that at my age, you know. They're there if you don't play sports you don't belong like and I don't like that. 'Cause it's happened to me and so I don't like doing it to other people.

In these statements, Ben shows an awareness of the social and moral implications of his behavior. His manner of interacting with others is clearly primary to his sense of self. But, like Paul at Time 3, Ben has not worked out a consistent belief system that he associates with his self-identity. Rather, his self-understanding is based on the specific nature of his social personality and on the social and moral interactions that his personality characteristics foster.

On the occasion of Ben's Time 3 testing, Ben's self-statements had a different quality. He now had worked out a personal belief system based on moral views toward honesty and self-sacrifice. In addition, Ben had integrated these beliefs into his own idiosyncratic attitudes about humor. The result is a unique blend of moral and personal self-statements that Ben can truly call his own. Because this belief system is both coherent and absolutely distinct to Ben, it is well suited for establishing Ben's personality identity. Of course, Ben will need to make further choices and syntheses before he has formed a consolidated identity in the Eriksonian sense, but at the time of our final longitudinal interview, he seemed well along on his way there:

TELL ME WHAT YOU'RE LIKE. I don't know. I think I'm basically, like, honest. I don't like people that aren't honest. Pretty good-natured. I don't know. Maybe non-conformist. I think people that lie or something like that must have something to cover up. Like I've never known anyone that it's compulsive, you know, it's just so compulsive for them to lie. It's like on soap operas or something like that; it's just that unreal, someone that lies like that. You know, a one-sided person that lies like that. I don't know how to explain it. Like someone that cheats and stuff like that. I like being honest like with yourself and with everyone. 'Cause, you know, if you're a bad person, lying, is like – that's how I'd label someone. If they lied, they would be a bad person to me. Like they could be, in the eyes of everyone else, like, the best person in the world, but if I knew, like, they were lying or cheating, in my eyes they wouldn't be. Whereas it would be the opposite; like it could be some criminal who never told a lie, you know, if he was brought on the jury stand and said, "I did it," then I would consider him all the more man or person to say he did it, to admit his fault like that.

OK, COULD YOU SUMMARIZE THAT AND SAY WHAT THAT SAYS ABOUT WHAT KIND OF PERSON YOU ARE? I don't know. I guess, like, I respect people more if they respect themselves. So if you cheat, you're not, like, respecting yourself. You're not giving yourself, you know, yourself a chance. I think if you don't like yourself, then no one else will like you. 'Cause you know, what's there to like about you if you don't even like yourself. So if you like yourself you won't abuse yourself, you won't do things like that and you won't cheat. Because if you like yourself, you like what you're doing without the good or bad mark. It shouldn't shock you that much. Unless there's some pressure to do well, like that. So it all goes back to, like, you have to like what you're doing and everything else from there.

When I'm friendly, it's more like, you know, to tell people that it's all right to be yourself. Not necessarily don't conform, but just whatever you are just, you know, be happy with that. Don't, like, you know, try to prove anything for anybody, just be yourself. So I'm not an overly bubbly person that goes around, "Hi, how are you?" you know like that. That makes me sick. But, you know, just if someone wants to talk to me, you know, sure. I wouldn't like, not talk to someone. Just anybody, you know, I'd say hi to. Like that.

I think the total giving of something to, like, one idea is really – especially a good idea. Like if you're gonna devote yourself to, you know, massacres of people, then that's not too good. But if you're gonna, like, devote yourself to the good of people, totally devote yourself then, you know, I think that's great. I don't know. It's "hard" for me to say. 'Cause it ties into, like, my religion. So I don't know, it's not really my belief; it's just been, like, what I've been brought up with. I would think that would be, like, very good to do that. You know, like that. And people like comedians I like very much, you know, like "Saturday Night Live," like Gilda Radner and them, Chevy Chase because they can really make you laugh and I think laughter is really important.

WHY IS LAUGHTER IMPORTANT? Because people take things too seriously. I think so many times, like, I mean things should be taken seriously. I don't think we should all sit there and laugh at everything, you know, the economy's going downhill, you know, and just laugh about it. But I think laughter is very, like important too, to be a good person. You have to know when to laugh. I think there's a right time to laugh, you know. But I think it's very important at some time to laugh, you know. Especially laugh at yourself. I think you have to be able to, like, look at yourself and see something's funny and, you know, laugh about it. I think that you'd be closer to yourself if you can laugh at yourself and view yourself objectively. I know a lot of people who could never laugh at themselves. They'd get really, you know, mad if you laughed at them. Whereas me, if I did something stupid, I'd, like, always laugh at myself. Sometimes I may seem crazy, but I do. I think it's important. I don't think, like, you should always be laughing, but I think a good sense of humor is needed to get along. I think, you know, if you never had a sense of humor, I don't think you could really survive in a world like this where so much bad news is always cropping up. And then I think it's important to have, like, you know, like, a little time when you can laugh. That's probably what I mean when I say, you know, to affect a lot of people at one time. Just something where you could take them away from the problems of the world for a little while, you know, through whatever medium or whatever. And just, you know, give them time to forget the problems and everything. 'Cause, I think, if you didn't have that time there'd be a lot of insane people going around.

THERE ARE, YES, THERE ARE. But that's, like, probably what I mean. So I guess when I grow up I want to be Mother Theresa and Chevy Chase. OK, THAT'S AN INTERESTING COMBINATION. No, those are the two characteristics from the two. I wouldn't want to be, like, so religious that it would divide me from people. That happens a lot. You get, like, a lot of old priests and stuff who view, if you're not Catholic, you know, that's the old saying, the old joke, if you're not Catholic you don't go to heaven or whatever. But that's, like, so absurd, you know. What is heaven anyway? I don't even know. So I think that's crazy. The only reason why I even have a religion is to, like, pacify me. You know, a time when I can, you know, I don't know, put my troubles into someone else's hands. And just, you know, feel that they're resolved. Or if I do something bad, just to talk to someone and just get them resolved and know that they're forgiven or whatever. That would be my only reason. Like I don't think that, you know, I don't take it as strongly as some people do, so medievally, I guess, so mystic. I don't believe in it in that way. I just think, you know, it's just something that I use to pacify my needs like that.

Note

1 It is important to note that data reported in Kohlberg's own longitudinal study conform less to the neat picture painted by these theoretical writings by Kohlberg and colleagues than to our own gradual-transformation model. In his longitudinal sample, Kohlberg found considerable stage mixture as well as lengthy, slow, somewhat confused periods of transition prior to stage change (Colby et al., 1983). We are taking issue here with the theoretical claims of the Kohlbergian school rather than with the empirical reports of this research program.

6 Understanding the self-as-subject

Along its side face, our developmental model of self-understanding contains three self-as-subject components: continuity, distinctness, and agency.[1] The present chapter reviews our empirical findings concerning these three dimensions and their developmental trajectories from childhood through adolescence. The findings were drawn largely from our longitudinal database; analyses were obtained through the self-as-subject components of our scoring manual. Here we report these empirical findings as a test of our model's side face and of the scoring manual's utility in the area of the subjective self.

Although continuity, distinctness, and volition are all aspects of the "I" component of self-understanding, it is useful to consider continuity and distinctness apart from volition. As noted in Chapter 1, partitioning the "I" in this way follows a classic philosophical distinction in how the subjective self has been conceptualized by different traditions. It also corresponds with our psychological intuitions concerning the distinct personality functions served by the various components of the subjective self.

Continuity and distinctness together form the basis for personal identity. One's sense of oneself as a person derives from the twin experiences of self-sameness over time and of being a unique individual. In Chapters 1 and 2 we considered some of the philosophical and psychological literature that has made this point. In the first part of the present chapter we take up this issue again in order to place our empirical findings on continuity and distinctness in a personality perspective.

The agency aspect of self-understanding corresponds to a different set of philosophical and psychological issues. One's sense of agency over the world and over the self entails an awareness of the self's control of its own destiny. The nature of this awareness determines the extent to which one feels that events are subject to one's volitional intent as opposed to uncontrollable forces beyond or within the self. One's conception of agency, therefore, underlies one's sense of personal freedom and self-determination

(Mead, 1934) or, in some cases, the lack of such a sense. In the second part of this chapter, we shall discuss, in light of findings from our longitudinal study, the genesis of agency awareness through the childhood and adolescent years.

Continuity and distinctness

The function of personal identity

Personal identity is a key construct in both philosophy and psychology. Here we would like to explicate briefly the role of personal identity in both disciplines (a full discussion of these issues is available in Hart, Maloney, & Damon, 1987).

Among philosophers, the concept of personal identity is an essential component of accounts of rational planning and moral responsibility. Consider planning for the future. It is one's plans for the future that stand in the way of continually seeking immediate gratification: Money is saved to purchase a car next year rather than spending it today on a desired object; candy and fattening foods are avoided in order to lose 10 pounds by Christmas, even though the thought of eating them now makes one's mouth water; and so on. These and all similar examples of human behavior are incomprehensible without a belief in personal identity. For instance, if our dieter has no sense of continuity into the future, meaning that there is no feeling of connection between the self of today and the self at Christmastime, the person who would benefit from the dieting would have no clear connection to the person who did the sacrificing. In this case there would be little reason to inhibit one's desire to eat tasty but fattening foods.

Philosophers (Parfit, 1971a, b; Williams, 1970) have also pointed to the relevance of personal identity for understanding our intuitive notions of morality. When people assume moral responsibility for their acts, they assume that they will bear, as individuals, the blame or credit for such acts; they will remain the same individuals who committed the acts in the first place.

Psychologists too have been intrigued with the concept of personal identity, but with a focus on the clinical implications of identity problems. Erikson's well-known work (1950, 1968, 1982) on development across the lifespan has drawn attention to the importance of constructing a sense of identity, as well as illuminating the difficulties that the adolescent faces in this task (see also James, 1961/1892, and Laing, 1968). Building upon Erikson's clinically oriented theorizing, Marcia (1966, 1980) and others (e.g., Josselson, 1973) have attempted to describe the deficits of those adolescents who seem not to "have" an identity. Empirically, Marcia and his colleagues have demonstrated that identity-failure adolescents and young adults lack serious, thoughtful commitments to occupations, ideologies, social relationships, sexual issues, and so on.

Although Marcia's characterization of identity deficits has expanded our understanding of the trials of adolescence, we do not believe that it is the presence or absence of commitments themselves that determines whether a person has developed a sense of identity. If developing an identity means only making occupational, ideological, and sexual commitments, then it is a task that must await late adolescence, when children are sufficiently freed from parental influence to make these choices. This would mean that children and young adolescents would be considered to be without a sense of personal identity, a characterization at odds with the lifespan perspective of Erikson (1968). In addition, there are reasons to believe that the notion of commitment to work and to an ideology as a basis for personal identity is ethnocentric and possibly male centered as well (Geertz, 1975).

Finally, commitment itself must rely on deeper expectations and beliefs. Most important, these include the expectation that one will endure as the same person who made the commitment so that one can, at some future time, make good on it; and the belief that one takes individual responsibility for the commitment, which means that it can be attributed only to oneself and to no other person. For these "root" notions of commitment, we must turn to the subjective self-components of continuity and distinctness.

Personal identity has two conceptual underpinnings that are far more basic than beliefs in one's life commitments: knowledge of the self's continuity and of its distinctness. As we noted in Chapter 1, these two components of identity are common to philosophical and psychological accounts of personal identity.

Although other psychological investigators have commented on the importance of continuity and distinctness in the sense of personal identity (e.g. Aboud, 1979; Harter, 1983; Leahy & Kogan, in press), there has been relatively little developmental research on them. One of our main research goals has been to describe with precision the developmental transformations in the understanding of continuity and distinctness that take place in the period from early childhood to late adolescence.

A second aim of the research described in this section was to examine the relationship between the child's developing understanding of continuity and distinctness on the one hand and the child's developing understanding of the objective self on the other. Personal identity, experientially established by one's beliefs in continuity and distinctness, necessarily incorporates aspects of the objective self. The substance of one's personal identity revolves around the "me." Further, one's beliefs in continuity and distinctness are often supported by reference to one's self-as-object characteristics. For instance, when Guardo and Bohan's (1971) subjects defended their claims to self-continuity, they did so by citing (among others) their physical and psychological characteristics, constituents of the "me."[2] This does not mean that these self-as-subject components are limited to self-as-object considerations, but rather that, as James wrote, the "I" frequently draws upon the "me" in forming its shape and substance. We expect that this is the case ontogenetically as well as moment-by-moment throughout the flux of experience. Because continuity and distinctness both draw, in part, from the self-as-object, we can expect to find some conceptual and developmental affiliations between each of them and the self-as-object. In the next section of this chapter, we review our research on children's understanding of personal continuity and distinctness (preliminary results of which are found in Hart, Maloney, & Damon, 1987).

Empirical findings on children's and adolescents' understanding of continuity and distinctness

Subjects. For the sake of these analyses we draw upon the subjects who were in our longitudinal sample at testing Times 2 and 3. In addition to the self-as-object questions on our self-understanding interview, these subjects at Time 2 were asked questions on continuity; and at Time 3 they were asked questions on both continuity and distinctness. (Both additional questions are described in Chapter 3.) We do not have data on either continuity or distinctness for Time 1 or data on distinctness for Time 2, because we had not yet formulated these additional questions. In general, we had difficulty creating interview questions and probes that consistently elicited developmentally interpretable responses for the self-as-subject components. Although we experimented with a large number of potential interview items in pilot testing prior to the Time 1 interviewing, we were unable to develop questions that fully elicited children's understanding of continuity prior to Time 2 or distinctness prior to Time 3. Thus, in this report we are limited to the subject samples at those testing points.

To repeat briefly the design of the study, at the second round of testing there were 82 children and adolescents from grades 1 to 10; by the third round of testing, 52 of the children and adolescents remained in the study.

Procedure. Each subject responded to the interview questions described

Table 6.1. *Average ages (in years : months) for best levels of self-continuity, distinctness, and the "me"*

Best level	Time 2, self-continuity	Time 3, self-continuity	Time 3, distinctness	Time 2, "me"	Time 3, "me"
1	7:6	7:5	7:6	7:6	7:9
2	9:4	10:6	9:7	9:0	8:9
3	11:0	11:6	13:2	11:2	13:0
4	13:1	14:4	14:2	13:2	14:0

in Chapter 3. Of particular interest in this chapter are the responses to the questions "If you change from year to year, how do you know you are always you?" (continuity) and "What makes you different from everyone else in the world?" (distinctness).

Coding. Responses to the continuity and distinctness questions were scored according to criteria presented in the self-as-subject sections of the manual described in Chapter 4. Because there were far fewer responses to the self-as-subject questions than to the self-as-object ones, we determined that modal level was not a meaningful index of the self-as-subject components. Instead, we settled on highest scored level as the most valid developmental index consistent with the clinical method for short interviews like these (see Damon, 1977, for a further discussion of this assessment strategy). The rater assigned one developmental score to represent the highest level expressed by a subject in response to the question sets concerning continuity and distinctness. Two raters agreed on the highest level of continuity evidenced in an interview in 87% of the instances and the highest level of distinctness for 86% of the interviews.

Results

Table 6.1 presents the average age of subjects attaining each developmental level of continuity and distinctness at the two testing times, as well as the average age of subjects achieving each of the four best developmental levels of the objective self. The pattern of subject distributions in Table 6.1 shows an ontogenetic trend from the lowest to the highest levels in the two self-as-subject sequences. Correlational and longitudinal analyses confirmed the developmental nature of the levels of continuity and distinctness. In our earlier analyses (Hart et al., 1987), we found highly significant correlations between age and developmental level of continuity of $r_s = .60$ and

and $r_s = .54$ for Times 2 and 3 respectively and a similar finding for developmental levels of distinctness, $r_s = .78$ (Time 3). In the longitudinal analysis of continuity levels, we examined scores only for subjects who were at Level 2 or Level 3 at Time 2. Restricting the sample in this way allows an examination of the extent to which subjects advance to a higher level, or regress to a lower one, by Time 3. Among these 34 subjects, 18 moved to a higher level at Time 3 and only 2 moved to a lower one.

The developmental levels of continuity and distinctness were also found to be related to each other as well as to the levels of the self-as-object. These correlations, all statistically significant, for Time 3 were: continuity and distinctness, $r_s = .55$; continuity and the self-as-object $r_s = .59$. Finally, our analyses suggested that the additional introspection and reflection demanded by the self-as-subject questions resulted in a tendency for subjects to be more advanced in reasoning about the self-as-object than about continuity and distinctness (see Hart et al., 1987, for details).

The data described in this section provide empirical support for two of our developmental model's side-face progressions. Thus, we have initial grounds for concluding that understanding the self-as-subject, like understanding the self-as-object, requires a series of conceptual reorganizations in the course of ontogenesis.

During the period from childhood through adolescence, both the sense of continuity and the sense of distinctness develop in the ordered sequence proposed along the model's side face. For each of these sequences, strong positive correlations were found between age and developmental level, as measured by the scoring manual derived from the model. Further, short-term longitudinal trends for the continuity sequence showed predominantly forward movement toward the higher levels over time. Similar longitudinal data were unavailable for the distinctness sequence because of methodological difficulties. But the close conceptual and empirical links between the two sequences, combined with the strong longitudinal support obtaining for the first, suggest that similar longitudinal trends would have been likely for the distinctness progression as well.

As expected, we also found strong associations between each of the two investigated self-as-subject sequences and the general self-as-object sequence. This confirms our belief that the senses of continuity and distinctness draw heavily upon the objective self for their shape and substance. There also was some indication that understandings of the objective self ontogenetically tend to precede parallel understandings of continuity and distinctness (or at least the verbal expression of such), at least for many children. If this is so, the tendency no doubt derives from the greater introspection and reflectiveness demanded by conceptions of the subjective self. The pattern of developmental lags, however, was by no means uniform in our data; we would therefore call this relation a probabilistic tendency rather than a strong developmental priority.

With the exception of Marcia's valuable but narrowly focused research, empirical psychology has paid little attention to the construct of personal identity. Consequently, the one established research perspective on its meaning or development is slanted toward notions (e.g., commitment to work or ideology) that may be culture or gender bound. In this section we have adapted more cognitively based philosophical and psychological approaches into a new starting point for future research on this critical topic in personality development.

The findings reported in this section are also useful for understanding the adolescent identity problems noted by so many theorists. During childhood, the sense of identity – continuity and distinctness – is attributed to unchanging self-characteristics. This is so because of the child's inability to imagine transformations (Piaget, 1983) as well as difficulties in remembering significant changes in the self. However, the rapid cognitive, social, and physical changes that accompany adolescence makes this belief in the absolute stability of self-characteristics untenable. As a consequence, the adolescent turns to the social environment as a source for continuity and distinctness (Hart et al., 1987). This dependence on the network of friends and family for the sense of personal identity may be one reason that adolescents are particularly sensitive to interpersonal difficulties; such problems not only threaten a relationship but the sense of self as well.

Agency

That we have volitional control over our own thoughts and actions is a common belief and a fundamental part of our "folk psychology." We act on this belief and expect others to do so as well. Our societal system of rewards and punishments, ranging from work compensation to criminal justice, is guided by it. Notions of personal agency are communicated early to the young: Children and adolescents are forever beseeched to "try harder" in doing their schoolwork, obeying their parents, performing their household chores, and so on. The belief in agency runs deeper than ideology or specific doctrine. Even persons who are skeptical about the human ability freely to choose and carry out behavioral courses generally still retain a sense that their own perspective on events is self-constructed and in some sense willed.

Yet as many scholars have noted (Secord, 1984), scientific psychology has proceeded as if agency is not an integral part of human behavior.

Howard and Conway (1986) have suggested that the omission of agency from the domain of scientific psychological constructs can be traced to the Baconian revolution in the physical sciences. During this period of scientific history, the formulation of scientific laws underwent a fundamental change. The established Aristotelian tradition of describing natural events in terms of inner motives was replaced by a paradigm in which references to motivation or desires were considered unparsimonious. Howard and Conway illustrate this point with an example drawn from Spragens (1973): "Compared with Galileo's formulation of acceleration as the precise proportion of speed to time squared, the Aristotelian explanation of acceleration as the 'jubilation' of the falling body as it neared its 'proper place' is pitiably inadequate" (p. 1242). The physical sciences abandoned the search for inner motives in favor of causal laws operating on objects as explanations of observed phenomena.

Contemporary scholars note, however, that psychology's emulation of the modern physical-science approach may lead to the exclusion of important facets of human behavior – in particular, volitional action and the attendant sense of personal agency. Personal agency may not be a necessary component of our understanding of gravity, but it is difficult for us to understand our own or others' behavior without reference to it. Howard and Conway (1986) describe several studies in which they purport to show that agency can be studied empirically, and that this construct provides great explanatory power.

Our own work assumes the existence of volitional action as described by Howard and Conway and by Secord, and seeks to describe children's and adolescents' understanding of it. Volitional control over the self is to the individual the most compelling component of the "I." In response to his own question asking what is the most central facet of the experience of self, James answered:

Probably all men would describe it in much the same way up to a certain point. They would call it the *active* element in all consciousness; saying that whatever qualities a man's feelings may possess, or whatever content his thought may include, there is a spiritual something in him which seems to *go out* to meet these qualities and contents, whilst they seem to *come in* to be received by it. It is what welcomes or rejects. It presides over the perception of sensations, and by giving or withholding its assent it influences the movements they tend to arouse. . . . It is the source of effort and attention, and the place from which appear to emanate the fiats of the will. (James, 1890, pp. 297–8)

What makes up this experience of agency? In James's analysis, the experience of agency, or what he calls the "active element in all consciousness," is accompanied by and constituted of the motor movements of the mouth, head, and neck that attend psychological activity. For instance, an individual wishing to remember where in her house she left her keys experiences the unconscious movement of her eyes as an indication of her effort or will. The logical consequence of this biological reductionism is the conclusion that "the 'self of selves,' when carefully examined, is found to consist mainly of the collection of these peculiar motions in the head, or between the head and throat." (p. 301)).

James's outline of the place of agency within the experience of self is insightful and valuable for understanding human behavior research. But his interpretation of the experience of agency in terms of bodily movements clearly limits its potential usefulness for our own research. Although the experience of agency may be associated with feelings of physiological movements, the former need not be identical with the latter. As Blasi (1986) points out, agency is identifiably independent of those biological correlates:

First, the experience of my acts (seeing, attending, writing) is experience of my acting, of my agency, and not of movements within me; second, while the experience of bodily movements changes depending on the nature of my act, the concomitant awareness of self as subject is fundamentally the same in all experience.(p. 14)

Blasi's implicit critique of James suggests that, although James's account of agency and its role in the experience of self is fundamentally correct, James overlooked some of its distinctive qualities.

Mead (1934) accepts James's ascription of centrality of agency to the experience of the "I"; but Mead also rejects the Jamesian reduction of identifying agency to motor movements, preferring instead to emphasize its experiential importance. Rather than following James's path of biologizing the sense of volition, Mead situates the "I" within a social context, along with the objective self.

Mead believed that, in reflecting on the "me," one implicitly assumes the perspective of other persons in one's social group. Thus, when a child describes her psychological qualities – say, for instance, her intelligence – she may be doing so from the perceived perspectives of parents and teachers. As a consequence of considering the self from the perspectives of others, the "me" assumes role obligations and restrictions. To continue with our example, as a smart student the child recognizes others' expectations that she will study hard and do well on examinations. If there were only a "me" component to the self, behavior would become automatic and completely consistent with social expectations. The fact that no person's behavior is absolutely robotic is a reflection of the activity of the "I."

The "I," according to Mead, is one's freely chosen response in any given situation. As Mead puts it, "that movement into the future is the step, so to speak, of the ego, of the 'I'" (p. 177). One may respond with a time-honored action (for our smart girl, this might be studying after school, as she does every day) or unpredictably (e.g., deciding to play with friends instead of preparing for the important test at school the next day). This indeterminacy of actions in any situation, deriving from the "I," gives rise to the experience of choice or freedom. Understanding this experience is an integral part of understanding self.

Research problems

The writings of James and Mead on personal agency communicate both its prominence and its elusiveness in human experience. It may be the least predictable aspect of the subjective self. Unlike self-continuity and distinctness, which to some extent are directly or indirectly read from the "me" constituents of self-understanding, the experience of agency is usually detached from the objective self. It may even stand in opposition: commonly people perceive themselves as struggling, by choice, against the constraints of their physical attributes, material conditions, limited abilities, or current beliefs. Agency means the freedom to select a different path or vision at any time, even if this path represents a radical departure from one's physical, active, social, or psychological self. Thus, the self-as-object is relevant to one's experience of agency only if and when one chooses it to be. Otherwise, the relation between the two may range from orthogonal to antagonistic.

In psychological research, the most prominent research on the sense of agency and its development has been the "locus of control" line of work. On the locus of control dimension, persons can range from internal to external. Those characterized by an internal locus of control believe that their own choices determine the courses of their lives. This reflects a strong belief in the self's agency. Those characterized by an external locus of control feel powerless to affect their own fates, reflecting a lack of faith in their agentic capacities.

A wealth of research has been conducted on locus of control in children and adolescents (see Maccoby, 1980). Generally, these studies report that older children and adolescents have a more internal locus of control than younger children, indicating that with age developing children feel as if the world is more reactive to their own actions. Among children and adolescents of the same age, individual differences in locus of control have been shown to be related to academic achievement, involvement in extracurricular activities, popularity, and self-esteem (Nowicki & Strickland, 1973).

Although the locus of control line of research has proved valuable, for our purposes it shares the shortcomings of self-esteem research, as discussed in Chapter 1. First of all, the locus of control instrument is itself nondevelopmental. The same items are used to test individuals of widely different ages; however, the assumption that the same question is equally relevant across the developmental spectrum cannot be valid.

For an illustration, consider one item from the popular Nowicki and Strickland (1973) locus of control scale: "Most of the time do you feel that getting good grades means a great deal to you? – Answer yes or no." (Nowicki & Strickland, 1973, p. 150). In our research studies on the development of the "me," presented in Chapter 5, we found that the importance of the self's relative abilities, for instance as reflected by grades, follows a predictable developmental trajectory, emerging in middle childhood and peaking, on the average, at the end of the elementary school years. This suggests that the sample locus of control item just presented would be most relevant for children during the middle elementary school years, and far less important to older or younger children. This item and many others in the scale were intended to be age general, whereas in reality they are quite age specific. The result is a skewed picture of self-concept unreflective of major developmental trends.

Even more important, the locus of control literature provides no description of how children and adolescents understand their own sense of agency. As noted in Chapter 1, self-understanding development can be captured only through qualitative descriptions of the organizing principles that constitute the awareness of self in all its aspects, and through all its developmental phases. Simply assigning a locus of control score to a child or adolescent based on his or her endorsement or rejection of experimenter-generated items cannot provide such an account.

In Chapter 2, we reviewed studies by Broughton (1978a) and Selman (1980) in which an interview method was used. By asking children and adolescents to describe themselves or to respond to hypothetical dilemmas, Broughton and Selman were able to elicit from their subjects some information about how the sense of agency develops. Their findings are summarized in Table 2.1. Selman's and Broughton's interview questions, however, were not designed to tap agency, and so their studies provide only the barest outline of its developmental course through the childhood and adolescent years. To paint a fuller picture requires a special effort. An understanding of agency cannot, for example, be elicited simply through questions that are directed towards the individual's understanding of the "me." Instead, a new set of questions must be developed, and the questions must be focused on the issue and yet at the same time be broad based. The experience of agency clearly can be multifaceted, ranging from feelings of volitional body movements (James) to a sense of freedom and self-determination (Mead).

In the research to be described, a special set of questions was designed specifically to elicit an understanding of agency. Our purpose was to construct a more differentiated picture than that available in previous accounts, and to examine the relationship between the development of agency and other aspects of self-understanding. Because agency is a component of self-understanding, we expect its development to be associated with development of other components. But, because of the unique features of agency, these associations should be less strong than the associations reported in our study of continuity and distinctness.

Empirical findings on the sense of agency and its development

Subjects. The subjects in this study were the longitudinal subjects from Time 2 and Time 3 (82 subjects at Time 2 and 52 at Time 3). As in the study reported in the first part of this chapter, we were unable to develop satisfactory interview questions prior to Time 1, so data on agency is available only for Times 2 and 3.

Procedure. As noted in Chapter 4, our basic question set for agency was "How did you get to be the kind of person you are now?" and "How do you change in the present and future?" Further probes in this question set are described in Chapter 3. The question set was intended to elicit children's and adolescents' ideas about the processes controlling self-formation. Self-formation is a key issue in the understanding of agency. We have already discussed Mead's view that agency necessarily projects the self into the future. By probing for theories of self-formation, we hoped to tap children's and adolescent's beliefs about what shapes them now, in the past, and in the future; and, as a consequence, what controls their destinies.

As with the other self-understanding questions, agency questions were given to all children at Time 2 and again, 18 months later, at Time 3. All children were able to make some response to the agency questions that could be coded.

Coding. Responses were scored according to criteria set forth in the agency section of the scoring manual described in Chapter 4. A developmental score for agency was assigned only when a subject's reasoning was fully elicited through the basic question set and follow-up probe questions.

Interrater reliability. Forty-one interviews, one-half of the total interviews

Table 6.2. *Average ages (in years : months) for subjects at the developmental levels of agency and best levels of the "me"*

Level	Time 2, agency	Time 3, agency	Time 2, "me"	Time 3, "me"
1	8:5	8:9	7:6	7:9
2	10:6	10:10	9:0	8:9
3	11:1	13:3	11:2	13:0
4	13:1	15:0	13:2	14:0

from the second testing time, were coded by two raters to assess interrater reliability for agency scores. The two raters assigned the same developmental level score to an interview in 80% of the instances.

Results. The findings from this study support the proposed agency sequence as depicted along the developmental model's side face. The correlation between age and developmental level of agency for the second testing time was $r_s = .48$, $p < .001$, $(df = 71)$, and for the third testing time, the correlation was $r_s = .52$, $p < .001$, $(df = 46)$. Two ANOVAs, with school (grades 1 to 6 versus grades 7 to 11) and sex as factors and volition scores as dependent measures, found significant effects only for school (F [1,72] = 21.8, $p < .01$, and F [1,47] = 16.6, $p < .01$, for Times 2 and 3 respectively). These correlations indicate that developmental levels of agency are strongly associated with age. Table 6.2 presents the average ages for subjects at the four developmental levels of agency for Times 2 and 3. For purposes of comparison, we place these ages alongside the average ages for the developmental levels of the objective self.

Longitudinal trends between Time 2 and Time 3 confirm that the proposed levels of agency constitute a developmental sequence. Over the 18-month interval, 17 subjects (39% of the subjects with agency scores for both Time 2 and Time 3) moved to a higher level of agency. Only 7 subjects, 16% of the sample with agency scores at both times, had a lower agency score at Time 3 than at Time 2 (the remaining 19 subjects had the same score for agency at the two interview times).

Table 6.3 presents intercorrelations among developmental level scores for agency, self-continuity, distinctness, and the "me." Only the correlations for Time 3 are presented, because developmental level of distinctness was assessed only at this time.

These correlations indicate that, in general, the sense of agency understanding develops in accord with the other components of self-understanding in our model. But the correlations between agency and the

Table 6.3. *Correlations among age and developmental levels of agency, self-continuity, distinctness, and the "me" at the third testing time*

	Age	Agency	Self-continuity	Distinctness
Agency	.51(46)**			
Self-continuity	.54(37)**	.24(34)		
Distinctness	.78(38)**	.52(35)**	.55(33)**	
The "me"	.67(50)**	.42(46)*	.57(36)*	.59(37)**

$^*p < .01$;
$^{**}p < .001$.

other components were lower than the intercorrelations among self-continuity, distinctness, and the self-as-object. In particular, the development of agency is not significantly associated with the development of continuity.

Conclusions

Our findings indicate that a key aspect of agency, self-formation, develops through four developmental levels. At the first of these levels, children experience the process of self-development as essentially nonvolitional. Changes in the self reflect the intercession of external biological, social, or supernatural forces. In mid-childhood, the understanding of self-formation undergoes a rather dramatic change. The belief in the external shaping of self is replaced by an understanding of self-formation in which the self's own wishes and desires are by themselves sufficient to control the evolution of self. In late childhood and early adolescence, self-formation is conceived as a process that occurs within a social matrix of communication. The self develops as a consequence of an interchange with others. Finally, in mid-adolescence, one's volitional control of self-formation derives from deeply held personal values or philosophies.

The development of agency understanding, as characterized in our research, can help explain the few clear patterns of results from the locus of control literature. For example, in Nowicki and Strickland's (1973) study of over 1,000 children and adolescents from grades 3 through 12, mean locus of control scores ranged from approximately 18 in grade 3 (external) to 12 in grade 12 (internal). Most of the age-related change in locus of control occurred between grades 5 and 6, dropping approximately 4 points between those two grades. Our interpretation of this striking finding is that it reflects the developmental reorganization in the understanding of agency that occurs in the transition from our Level 1 of agency to Level 2, between the ages of 10 and 11. As the child abandons the lower level of understanding of agency in which external forces control the self in favor of the Level 2 belief in the self's abilities to direct its future, an increasing confidence in self-determination is reflected in a more internal locus of control.

We believe that in other instances where developmental patterns have been robust enough to register on locus of control measures, they can be best explained by conceptual changes in agency understanding. But we also believe that instruments like ours will be sensitive to developmental processes in agency that locus of control procedures fail to capture.

The development of an understanding of agency as described in our model seems also to confirm some recent theoretical work by Blasi (1986). Blasi reinterpreted responses to some of the sentence stems on the Loevinger, Wessler, and Redmore (1970) Sentence Completion Test in terms of the understanding of agency implicit in them. This reinterpretation was especially difficult because these sentence stems do not directly elicit the individual's understanding of agency, requiring Blasi to infer the underlying logic that generated the different types of responses. In addition, Blasi did not have the opportunity to probe deeply into the meaning of subjects' statements, as in a clinical interview. Nonetheless, there are some interesting parallels between Blasi's conclusions and the early agency levels observed in our study.

Based on his reinterpretations of the Loevinger data, Blasi posits an agency awareness sequence. At the first level in Blasi's sequence, "the person seems to feel almost causally dependent on others and on situations" (p. 46). This of course is similar to our agency Level 1. At Blasi's Level 2, the individual seeks to gain autonomy, a desire that may be reflected in "exasperated independence, counterdependent and counterphobic autonomy" (p. 50). A similar notion emerges in our model's Level 2, when subjects emphasize that self-formation is determined by the self's own choices and abilities, a claim for personal autonomy that exceeds the reality of late childhood and early adolescence. Not surprisingly, given the restrictions on Blasi's database, Blasi's later levels bear less resemblance to Levels 3 and 4 in our own agency progression. In-depth probing is particularly important for drawing out the full extension of self-as-subject understanding at the higher levels.

As for relations between the sense of agency and other aspects of the objective and subjective self, we found positive but not strong associations, with the exception that the development of agency was unrelated to the development of continuity. The associations between agency and the objective self (at Time 2, $r_s = .40$, $p < .001$; and at Time 3, $r_s = .42$, $p < .001$) are lower than those between continuity, distinctness, and the objective self, reported earlier in this chapter.

This mixed pattern of correlations reflects the partial similarity and partial dissimilarity between the personal identity components of the "I" (self-continuity and distinctness) and the agentic component. As discussed earlier in this chapter, both continuity and distinctness necessarily incorporate features of the objective self and therefore are conceptually related to the development of the "me." But the understanding of agency does not "borrow" from the objective self in the same manner or to as great an extent. For this reason, the relatively lower associations between agency and the objective self are consistent with our expectations about this special feature of the subjective self. Further, these findings highlight once again the separate social-cognitive and personal functions served by the multiple components of self-understanding.

Notes

1 A fourth possible component, reflection, was omitted from the model because of methodological difficulties in studying children's understanding of self-reflection. As a side study, Hart and Damon (1984) took a small exploratory look at this meta-cognitive problem, but the results were difficult to interpret. Neither the somewhat murky results from that small study nor any ancillary findings from our main database have encouraged us to include a reflection sequence in our model's side face of self-as-subject progressions. Should further research show self-reflection to be a developing component of the subjective self, we believe that it also will show self-reflection to have many properties differing from those of the other components.

2 We have no argument with this conclusion. In our view, Guardo and Bohan's mistake – and a common one at that – was in treating physical and psychological self-conceptions as opposite poles of a developmental dimension rather than as nondeveloping self-as-object constituents (or "schemes," as we have called them).

7 Self-understanding and adolescent mental health

With MIRA ZAMANSKY LEVITT

In this chapter we take up the relation between self-understanding development and mental health during one period of the lifespan, adolescence. It is not an easy relation to define, and the two studies that we shall discuss in this chapter are only first steps toward this attempt. Yet a book about self-understanding development would seem incomplete without some consideration of psychological adjustment. As Vallacher, Wegner, and Hoine (1980) note: "Self theories *should* have something to say about person problems. After all, if self principles are implicated in much of our daily living, then surely the difficulties in living should be explainable with reference to those principles as well" (p. 252). We believe that self-understanding is influential in the children's and adolescents' lives, and for this reason we subscribe to the general notion that self-understanding is related to psychological adaptation and maladaptation.

Of course, self-understanding, like any conceptual system, serves certain psychological functions and not others. For this reason, it is unlikely to be of central importance in every realm of mental health. We would not claim, for example, that self-understanding is a "master trait" that alone controls behavior and that underlies every problem of adaptation. A child who has great difficulty establishing friendships may have more problems in understanding the skills and nature of friendship than in understanding self. In this chapter, we will explore the importance of self-understanding for two adjustment problems, anorexia and conduct disorder, that we believe to be particularly linked to developmental difficulties in understanding self during the adolescent years.

Adolescence is an appropriate age to examine the relations between mental health and self-understanding because it is an age during which adjustment disorders arising from self-concept problems are relatively common. In a study of adolescence and adulthood, Lowenthal, Thurner, and Chiriboga (1975) found that during adolescence, self-criticism is highest, and that throughout adulthood people are most likely to identify adolescence as the worst period in life. Rosenberg, in fact, has written that adolescence is the age at which there are most likely to be disturbances and conflicts in self-concept (Rosenberg, 1985).

What challenges of adolescence are responsible for this emotional turmoil and self-criticism? In the studies considered in this chapter, two tasks appear related to the mental health problems that are under investigation: conducting family relationships and forming an identity. First, as the child grows into adolescence, various changes occur in the family system's patterns of interaction (Hill, 1980). Primarily these changes occur to accommodate the maturing capabilities of the adolescent, but other life changes in the adolescent's parents also may contribute to the reconstruction of typical patterns of family interaction. Second, as Erikson has convinced many of us, the most formidable intrapersonal task of adolescence is constructing a coherent psychosocial identity. In this chapter, we shall discuss some connections between self-understanding, family interaction, and identity, in the context of adaptive and maladaptive patterns of adolescent psychological development.

In other studies in this book, we focus on the nature of ontogenetic changes and cultural differences in self-understanding. One purpose of these studies is to describe similarities in the understanding of self between members of particular age or cultural groups. A focus on mental health, however, shifts the focus from the similarities among members of an age cohort to individual differences (Rutter & Garmezey, 1983). This is because differences in psychological adjustment patterns may be related to differences in self-understanding: In focusing on an individual difference, one seeks to identify contrasts in self-understanding between, for instance, a 13-year-old anorexic and a normal-weight adolescent of the same age.

Because our model of self-understanding is primarily a developmental one, individual differences are most likely to emerge in terms of the model's developmental levels. Relating mental health difficulties to an adolescent's failure to reason about the self at an age-normal developmental level raises several issues. One issue concerns causation. We do believe that self-understanding problems contribute to mental health difficulties and shall attempt to illustrate this in later sections. But self-understanding likely serves primarily as a proximal contributor to mental health problems. Distortions of self-understanding are an outgrowth of pathological conditions that in turn exacerbate mental health problems. A current mental health problem, then, may be in part a consequence of self-understanding developmental problems, the genesis of which can be traced to still other sources.

A second issue raised by the consideration of development and mental health difficulties concerns description versus prescription. In our previous chapters, we have described the changes that occur in self-understanding as children and adolescents grow older. To the extent that mental health difficulties are associated with developmental delays in self-understanding, one goal of educational or therapeutic intervention could seem to be fostering progress to higher levels of development. But the possibility that older children and adolescents are usually at higher developmental levels of self-understanding does not by itself demonstrate that the higher levels constitute a goal for intervention. After all, older is not always better: There are a number of adolescent characteristics that are mercifully absent in children. Further, one could argue that fostering change in self-concept (to the extent that this indeed could be accomplished) does no more than encourage a troubled adolescent to think about the self "just like everyone else does." Why would we consider such an achievement advantageous?

Our response to this sort of argument is twofold. First, as we have described, developmental delays are likely to be a consequence of other pathological influences. Development to higher levels of self-understanding therefore can serve as an index of therapeutic success, as the underlying pathological influences are addressed. Second, and more to the point, we refer to our articulation of the developmental model in Chapter 3. There we defined self-understanding levels as hierarchical in the sense that each higher developmental level incorporates the understanding of self characteristic of the adjacent lower one, but also infuses the lower-level understanding with new meaning. This means that each higher developmental level results in richer, more variegated self-understanding. If these characteristics of the higher developmental levels are seen as adaptive for the individual (certainly a reasonable assumption), developmental progress can then be considered a legitimate and demonstrably valuable intervention goal.

We believe that a developmental model of self-understanding can provide an interpretative framework for analyzing certain mental health problems. One of the primary contributions of a developmental perspective to an understanding of mental health is an awareness of the transformation of behavior over time (Cicchetti, 1984). As Broughton (1980) demonstrated in his reanalysis of a clinician's case history of an adolescent, the failure to situate mental health problems within a developmental context leads to a failure to disentangle age-typical problems from pathological ones. Further, as Leahy (1985) notes, without an understanding of the fundamental ways in which self-understanding of children and adolescents differs from that of adults, it is difficult for a clinician, teacher, or parent to find a common ground on which a therapeutic dialogue with a younger person can take place.

The study of relations between self-understanding and mental health can also be useful for model validation (Selman, 1980). To the extent that the model of self-understanding development and its associated coding system are sensitive to mental health difficulties during adolescence, the model's correspondence to the reality of self-understanding during this age is further demonstrated. But clinical research can do more than simply validate a model; it can offer a new perspective on development. In Cicchetti's (1984) overview of the emerging field of developmental psychopathology, he points out that theorists beginning with Freud have claimed that basic developmental processes are revealed in the study of pathology. Certainly it might be dangerous to assume, as Freud sometimes did, that the study of pathology can by itself yield a veridical account of human development. But as a complement to normative research strategies as employed in previous chapters, clinical research can enrich our account of self-understanding as well as suggest future directions for research.

Contributions of a self-understanding model for interpreting mental health problems

We are not the first to suggest that there is a relationship between self-concept and mental health. However, we believe that in comparison to other self, self-esteem, or self-concept models, a developmental model of self-understanding offers some advantages. To identify these advantages, we shall briefly present an overview of dominant trends in the self-concept approach to mental health difficulties.

One dominant theme in traditional theory linking self-concept and psychological adaptation is the concern with "self-esteem." The assumption underlying this orientation is that children's and adolescents' successes in negotiating the challenges of interpersonal relationships, schoolwork, and intrapersonal crises derive from the degree to which they like themselves. The adolescent with low self-esteem is considered most likely to develop adjustment problems in virtually every area of life. For instance, Coopersmith, one of the most articulate advocates of the importance of self-esteem for mental health, has written about children with high self-esteem:

They approach tasks and persons with the expectation that they will be well received and successful. They have confidence in their perceptions and judgments and believe that they can bring their efforts to a favorable resolution. Their favorable self-attitudes lead them to accept their own opinions and place credence and trust in their own judgments when there is a difference of opinion and also permits them to consider novel ideas. (1967, pp. 70–1)

As we discussed in Chapter 1, theories and research focusing on self-esteem have suffered from various conceptual and empirical problems, some of which are especially important when one considers adolescent mental health. One troubling problem is that a low self-esteem score by itself does not provide any insight into which aspects of self a person finds undesirable, or into whether those aspects are likely to change. For this reason, it makes less sense to treat self-esteem as a factor predicting psychological adjustment (because so little is known about the substance or stability of this "factor") than as a simple outcome or indicator of adjustment.

The link between self-esteem and mental health is further clouded by the possibility of a nonlinear relationship. The common intuition is that it is "good" for adolescents to think well of themselves. But it seems at least possible that extremely high self-esteem might reflect maladaptive megalomaniacal fantasies. Crucial for normal adjustment is an awareness of the mistakes and limitations of the self. In his comprehensive review of peer relations, Hartup (1983) reports that both extremes of low and high self-esteem are associated with friendship difficulties. Even young children, it seems, find it difficult to maintain relationships with those who hold an inflated view of the self.

A final and most telling criticism of the self-esteem approach to mental health is its lack of empirical success. Self-esteem is not usually strongly associated with mental health; the majority of studies examining the relationship between self-esteem and social, academic, and emotional functioning have yielded weak or null results (Wylie, 1979).

Our belief in the centrality of the underlying understanding of self, rather than on self-esteem, is shared by clinicians who employ a cognitive-therapy approach. For instance, a common complaint to a cognitive therapist might be feelings of unhappiness with the self or unworthiness (low self-esteem). The therapist does not view these feelings as themselves revealing of the underlying problem, and for this reason does not attempt to improve the person's life by directly raising self-esteem. Instead, the cognitive therapist's goal is to reveal to an individual the underlying self-attributions that result in the negative affect (Leahy, 1985).

A second dominant theme among traditional self-concept theories is to posit a monolithic self-concept that is related to mental health. This conception of the self is inherent in most self-esteem studies, in which global self-esteem scores are presumed to represent a person's self-concept (e.g., Coopersmith, 1967; for exceptions, see Harter, 1983, and Rosenberg, 1985).

Other types of self theories also make the same sorts of claims. In one example – Kegan's (1982, 1985) theory of the "evolving self" – the self is a construct that includes self-understanding but that is also considerably broader, covering the diversity of phenomena that might be subsumed within Erikson's construct of identity or Loevinger's model of ego development.

According to Kegan, the development of self consists of successive restructurings of the subject–object distinction. This restructuring occurs through a series of stages, each of which composes an underlying logic that guides behavior. Each stage constitutes a particular type of self that permeates all facets of an individual's world. For instance, Kegan proposes that the following types of measurements would all be meaningfully correlated, because of the underlying self logic:

(1) Piagetian physical-cognitive conservation; (2) Selman-type social perspective; (3) Kohlberg-type moral judgment; (4) reality-oriented or fantasy-oriented fantasy, play, drawing; (5) ability to narrate in the retelling of a heard story or seen film; (6) ability to "conserve the self" in a "Describe Yourself" interview; (7) class-oriented or action-oriented word association; color-oriented or form-oriented three-way comparisons; (8) impulsivity versus impulse control; (9) involvement with parents versus involvement with own projects; (10) open- or closed-boundary orientation in the home. (1985, p. 201)

One immediate problem with Kegan's claim, and others like it, is that research in developmental psychology has demonstrated time and time again that cognitive development does not occur simultaneously in different domains (see, e.g., Fischer, 1980). Reducing the diversity of developmental achievements to a single self-construct not only goes far beyond any existing empirical evidence but strains the boundaries of plausibility. Most people do, after all, have individual cognitive strengths and weaknesses, particularly during the uneven ebbs and flows of childhood and adolescent development.

In addition, a monolithic self-concept provides no more interpretational leverage on mental health problems than does any other single-factor theory, from somatotypes to g (general intelligence). In self theory, if the construct is global self-esteem, mental health problems can only be related to levels that are too high or too low; if the construct is an egolike totality (as in Kegan's position), the maladjusted teenager's "self" can only be seen as immature or in transition. In other words, the specific sorts of adaptation problems that adolescents might have are not seen as corresponding to certain limited disturbances but instead to a general developmental dysfunction. Yet most forms of psychological disorder in childhood and adolescence have their own particular contours and do not totally impair one's present or future mental health prospects. Within the monolithic-self approach, therefore, there is no adequate way of dealing with the varied range of self-concept disturbances that arise most frequently during development.

The model of self-understanding development presented in the previous chapters offers some advantages over these approaches. One of its strengths is that it is comprehensive and multifaceted. Self-understanding as described by the model can be divided into two basic types: the "me" and the "I." Within the "me" persons can differ in the degree to which they focus on each one of the four self-constituents: physical, active, social, and psychological. It is reasonable to expect, for example, that athletes would focus on their physical qualities to a greater extent than adolescents who have little interest in sports or other means of bodily enhancement.

Consider the teenage boy who is always interested in shopping for clothes, trying new ways to wear his hair, and constantly looking in the mirror. What light does the self-understanding model shed on the question of mental health? Suppose that, when asked to describe himself along the lines of a self-understanding interview, the boy replies, "I have brown hair, blue eyes, and I'm five feet, five inches tall." According to our model, this boy's self-definition would be characterized in terms of the physical constituent. Thus, there would be congruence between his behavior and his self-definition; the behavior is supporting this boy's view of himself. Whatever other problems may in fact be posed by his physical preoccupation (such as, whether this interest interferes with other activities), the interest itself (and concomitant behaviors) represent a straightforward expression of his self-image.

Individuals can differ not only in the centrality of the various self-constituents but also in their developmental modes of understanding them. A more meaningful assessment of the adaptiveness of this boy's behavior can be gleaned from learning more about why his physical appearance is so important to him, which would offer a way of discerning the developmental maturity of his understanding of his physical appearance. If his response to the question "Why is it important to know that you look like that?" was "I don't know; I just think how I look is important," or, "Well, the bigger you get, the better you get at sports," it would imply something very different for the boy's social functioning than if he were to reply, "My looks are important to me because I want to start dating." In the former case, the boy's physical attributes are understood to have significance in and of themselves, or with reference to his abilities or activities. In the latter case, the relevance of the self's physical attributes for social appeal and social interactions are emphasized. Each response has a significance within an overall developmental view of self-understanding.

In addition to the "me" component of self-understanding, there are the "I" components, consisting of the senses of continuity, distinctness, and agency. We have argued in previous chapters that these are central aspects of self-understanding, and together form the experience of personal identity. The developments that occur in the various components of the "I" are certain to be involved in adolescent mental health.

For example, consider the adolescent whose understanding of continuity is at a relatively low level of development. His understanding of the self's continuity over time is rooted in observable, physical or behavior characteristics, as in:

HOW DO YOU KNOW YOU'RE THE SAME PERSON YOU WERE FIVE YEARS AGO? It's still me; I don't know; I still look the same, have the same name; I still have the same clothes.

Given this boy's orientation, the changes that emerge during adolescence are severe threats to a consistent sense of self. Because this adolescent relies on mutable physical cues to assure himself that he is still the same person, he is at a disadvantage for being able to appreciate that he is still the same person, despite impending changes. If, as Erikson and James suggest, a stable sense of self is vital to healthy functioning, then this adolescent is at considerable risk for emotional difficulty.

In contrast, at a more age-appropriate level of understanding, continuity is conceptualized more within the social context. Some sense of sameness of self over time can be derived from the recognition by significant others, as for example in "People still respond to me the same way." For the adolescent who expressed this Level 3 understanding of personal continuity, the vicissitudes of her body and the new tasks she must undertake pose no serious threat to her knowledge that she is still the same person. This is not to say that maintaining a sense of continuity is simple for the adolescent at this level of understanding; after all, she will find herself in a variety of social contexts, each of which may hold a different mirror up to her. Furthermore, ruptures in the adolescent's network of friendships and family relationships could be perceived as threatening the very continuity of self. Nevertheless, the adolescent capable of socially based conceptions of continuity is likely to be less vulnerable to the rapid changes that occur in the self. Developmental changes that occur in distinctness and agency are also central in psychological adjustment to adolescence, although we will not give examples here.

Our model allows for (and in fact predicts) some developmental slippage or, as Piaget referred to it, "décalage," among the various components of self-understanding. The empirical findings on normal developmental patterns reported in the previous chapters have indicated that a child or adolescent does not necessarily function at parallel developmental levels in understanding the "me" and the "I." Rather different aspects of self-understanding develop in different ways and at different rates, as a consequence of the different functions that they serve.

For our purposes in this chapter, the developmental discrepancies that we have identified suggest that mental health difficulties might be related to partial, but not holistic, developmental delays in perhaps only one component of self-understanding. In contrast to monolithic-self models, therefore, we would argue that an adolescent's mental health difficulties are usually not related to a broad developmental delay, or to the process of transition between two basic types of self, but instead are reflected only in limited areas of functioning. The value of this approach is that it potentially allows different mental health difficulties to be reflected in different patterns of self-understanding development, rather than attributing all cases of maladaptation to a single type of self-concept flaw.

Adolescent girls with anorexia nervosa and adolescent boys with conduct disorder are the foci of two studies in which patterns of self-understanding were examined. In each case, the role of self-understanding was presumed to be particularly germane to an understanding of some aspect of these populations. We explore the findings of these studies and their meaning in terms of the relevance of self-understanding for mental health. We will consider the implications of the results from the two studies first separately and then together.

Anorexia nervosa and self-understanding

Anorexia nervosa is the clinical term for self-induced starvation, which occurs most frequently among adolescent girls. The bizarre features of the syndrome, a refusal to eat even though the afflicted girl thinks constantly about food, in combination with an apparent increase in the syndrome's incidence over the past 10 years, has resulted in a large clinical literature concerning diagnosis, origins, and treatment (see Garner & Garfinkel, 1985, for a comprehensive review). A number of competing explanations have been offered for the emergence of anorexia nervosa as a relatively common mental health problem, with emphases ranging from biological deficits to cultural values. There do appear to be some commonalities among many clinical accounts concerning the nature of this disorder, with the work of Bruch (1978) best representing this convergence. One point of general agreement is that the anorexic adolescent usually has family relationship problems. In contrast to many families of maladjusted teenagers, however, the anorexic's family is often characterized by "excessive closeness and overintense involvements" (Bruch, 1978, p. 106). Because the relationships to other family members, especially the mother, tend to be suffocatingly tight, the normal tasks of disengagement from the family network is especially difficult.

Adolescents with anorexias also are described frequently in terms of self-concept or self-understanding difficulties (e.g., Garner & Bemis, 1985). Two dimensions of self-understanding are usually purported to be central to the anorexic adolescent's disturbance. One is the sense of agency. Anorexic girls are thought to experience little sense of control over what happens to them in their daily life; they believe they cannot exert their will in a way that will bring about desired ends (Garner & Bemis, 1985).

Second, adolescent girls suffering from anorexia nervosa may have difficulty in perceiving themselves as distinct, autonomous individuals. Bruch (1978) has claimed that the anorexic's inability to experience herself as a separate and efficacious individual is related to distortions in the network of family relationships. Throughout childhood and adolescence, Bruch asserts, the parent ought to serve as a reflecting mirror for the child. By mirroring back the child's emotional and physical cues, the parent encourages the child to accept his or her own feelings and actions. The mothers of anorexic girls fail to fulfill this mirroring role, and instead impose their own thoughts, feelings, and goals upon the developing adolescent. The constricting family relationships compound the difficulty of rejecting this imposition of maternal values, because it threatens the link between self and family. As a consequence, Bruch believes that the daughter never develops an adequate understanding of herself as an independent, individuated person with distinct qualities of her own.

The richness of the clinical writing on anorexia has not spawned a correspondingly valuable body of empirical research. Indeed, a recent review of literature (Schorin, 1985) was unable to find any studies that have described from a developmental perspective the self-concept or self-understanding of anorexics. This is especially surprising, in light of some treatment programs that advocate a developmental approach integrating a concern for the self-concept for the treatment of anorexia (e.g., Strober & Yager, 1985). Thus, a genuine need exists for a developmental investigation of self-understanding in anorexic girls.

In our study (see also Schorin & Hart, in press), we examined whether disturbances in agency and distinctness would be reflected in patterns of self-understanding. Because only these two dimensions of self-understanding had been implicated in clinical reports, our belief was that only development of the sense of agency and distinctness would be affected, with development in the sense of continuity as well as in the "me" showing no distortions associated with the anorexic syndrome.

Two comparison groups of teenage girls were sampled. One consisted of adolescent girls with serious curvature of the spine. This group was selected because, like those with anorexia, they suffer from an affliction that is highly overrepresented among females, are in need of hospital-based treatment, and contend with a condition that involves concern with the appearance of the body. However, for the girls with spinal curvature, this last concern is presumed to be the consequence of a syndrome that originates with the body, rather than a core element of the syndrome itself, as is the case in anorexia nervosa. The other comparison group was comprised of girls with no known physical or psychological illness.

As we expected, the responses generally could be coded using the developmental coding manual we have discussed in previous sections. But the responses elicited by the self-understanding interview were interesting in and of themselves, drawing out many of the themes clinicians believe are characteristic of anorexia. For example, it was frequently clear in various parts of the interviews that the anorexic girls perceived themselves as extensions of their mothers. For some, the powerful influence of the mother on the self was accepted, or viewed positively. For example, in the following example, a 15-year-old anorexic adolescent remarks that she "inherited" several features of self from her mother, and her mother's jokes can change the self:

HOW DID YOU GET TO BE THE WAY YOU ARE? I think I got the caring for people part from my mother I think I inherited that. I think I inherited a good sense of humor too. I was raised with humor. My mother can tell a joke and it changes me.

More usually, however, the responses on the self-understanding interview indicated that the anorexic adolescents felt resentment toward their mothers, who were perceived as overbearing and domineering:

HOW DO YOU THINK YOU GOT TO BE UNCONFIDENT? My mother and I never had a good relationship. I was the only girl in the house from age 8 and she always wanted me to do the work, not the boys. They would do the outside work, I'd do the inside. She was very hard on me and chauvinistic. If I cleaned the whole house but left the bathroom, she'd say, "You didn't clean the bathroom." She's not one to boost your confidence. If I wore a skirt she would tell me it make me look too short. It didn't build confidence. (Age 18)

HOW DID YOU GET TO BE THE WAY YOU ARE? ... My obsession with weight comes from problems at home, my parents have always been very strict. Most of the time I don't like my mother because she's domineering. My parents are domineering.

That's one of the reasons I like my freedom. Like tonight she's telling me I had to eat roast beef. I find myself in my room upset because of what my mother does. I resent my sister. I care about others, but not my family, except my father – I like him. When I found out I had anorexia I felt I had disappointed them. I felt low, they told my grandparents. My mother was previously married. My grandparents are strange in ways, domineering. They won't invite me to California until I'm over my problem. I hear her talking to her friends. It's none of their business. I can see them looking at me to see if I've gotten skinnier. My mother is overreacting. My father is stricter, but I get along with him better because he's not into my life. He'll go into his room if he and I have a problem. I was the queen bee until age five and a half, and my mother had my sister. She had allergies to everything and was crying all the time. My mother never had time. My father was always at work. My mother was always yelling. (Age 15)

THINK OF A TIME WHEN YOU WERE VERY DIFFERENT FROM THE WAY YOU ARE NOW. WHEN WAS THAT? Two or three years ago I was really close to my mother – really inseparable. I wouldn't talk, really, my mother had to tell me to do everything, I just wasn't my own person at all. (Age 14)

In addition to the theme of maternal repression, many anorexic adolescents expressed a desire for independence and personal control over life:

WHAT WOULD BE YOUR SECOND WISH? To be 18, through with college, be a nurse, have it over with. WHY? 'Cause I want to take care of myself, be a nurse. I don't want to go into the hospital again and I won't have to when I'm 18. Really all my life, I've had people telling me what to do. Sometimes they were bad decisions, they made mistakes. If I take care of myself I'll make better decisions, and even if they're bad, I'll blame myself so that will be better because they're my decisions. AND YOUR THIRD WISH? Just to be able to take care of myself and not have anyone tell me what to do. (Age 16)

We also found that the self-understanding interview, originally designed to elicit developmental reasoning, seemed useful in clinical applications as a means for encouraging individuals to talk about topics important to the diagnostician or therapist. The interview proved to be a particularly good medium for encouraging discussions around the problematic issues of distinctness and agency. Our impression was that the anorexic girls were more likely than typical adolescents to discuss fully issues of distinctness and agency in the course of their self-understanding interviews; and this impression was confirmed through a content analysis of responses across the interview (Schorin, 1985). This suggests that our interview questions were tapping emotionally important facets of self-understanding for the anorexic girls in our sample.

Statistical analyses confirmed one of our two main hypotheses concerning the relationship between self-understanding and anorexia. As predicted, anorexic girls conceptualized their agentic selves at a less mature developmental level than did normal teenagers or those with curvature of the spine ($M = 1.6$, $M = 2.1$, and $M = 1.8$ for the anorexic, normal, and curvature of the spine groups, respectively). A Newman-Keuls post-hoc test revealed a significant difference for the comparison of the anorexic to the normal adolescents, but not for comparisons of the adolescents with curvature of the spine to either the anorexic or normal group.

What is striking about this finding is the lack of control it implies for the anorexic's role in becoming the person she is. For example, a typical response for the anorexic girls was "That's the way my family is; that's how I grew up." In this example, the adolescent suggests that she had nothing to do with her self-formation. The direction of influence is exclusively one way, from family to adolescent.

In contrast, normal teenagers were more likely to conceptualize the sense of agency at a higher developmental level, where the motivations and efforts of the self are understood to influence self-formation. Unlike the anorexic girls, the reasoning of the normal adolescents indicates that they do not regard themselves as the passive canvas on which external forces imprint their mark. In addition to the view of a more active self in relation to the social context, the particular aspects of themselves on which the normal controls focus are less concretely observable than what is addressed by the anorexic group.

Contrary to prediction, there were no significant differences among the girls on any measure of the distinctness dimension. Anorexic girls did not reason about distinctness any less maturely than did the control groups.

Finally, although no predictions were made concerning the girls with curvature of the spine, significant differences between them and the normal controls were found in respect to the "me." The spinal curvature group was more likely than the normal group to characterize themselves in terms of the physical self-constituent, and less likely to draw upon the psychological constituent. Although this finding was not hypothesized, it is sensible within the context of the physical problems that adolescents with spinal curvature must confront in their day-to-day lives. Interestingly, the anorexic girls do not have the same physicalistic emphasis in their self-understanding, which may reflect an orientation toward eating and weight as psychological, rather than physiological, concerns.

These results confirm clinical speculation that the agentic dimension of self-understanding is problematic for anorexic girls. In particular, these findings indicate that the anorexic's understanding of agency is less mature than that of normal adolescents.

Although we have claimed the strength of the self-understanding model is in its use as a lens through which to describe and interpret mental health difficulties, we may speculate about the implications of the observed developmental immaturity of anorexic girls for symptomatology. At the levels of self-understanding employed by the girls in this study, the sense of agency is viewed in terms of observable consequences that are either unexplained, or regarded as simple, concrete, cause-and-effect mechanisms, in which the self's role is predetermined. Within such an immature conceptual framework, the sights on which any agentic efforts would be set would necessarily be physicalistic or possibly action oriented. Fixed regimens to effect such goals would be rigidly adhered to as though coming from another source, such that the girl herself had no choice over them.

Accordingly, for the anorexic girl, there exists no other goal than the realization of the ideal body image, which, ironically, she will never reach. The means by which she strives for this all important goal rivet her on activities such as exercising, cooking abundantly for others, and not eating herself. These practices are executed in an automatized, unwavering fashion. Thus, although the study does not offer an explanation as to why the anorexic girl's understanding of agency is immature, nor does it mean to explain anorexia nervosa in terms of this one feature of immature self-understanding alone, it does offer an important piece of information about the way the anorexic girl views herself, which may contribute to the onset of the syndrome.

Conduct disorder

Conduct disorder is the clinical label for patterns of behavior that might be called juvenile delinquency in common parlance. Technically, according to the most recent *Diagnostic and Statistical Manual* of the American Psychiatric Association, the criterion used in the study described in this section of the chapter, conduct disorder is "a repetitive and persistent pattern of conduct in which either the basic rights of others or major age-appropriate societal norms or rules are violated" (p. 45). This particular mental health problem differs in important ways from anorexia nervosa: Conduct disorders usually involve adolescent boys, and are very resistant to treatment (Rosenhan & Seligman 1984), with a very high proportion of adolescents continuing to exhibit manifestations of the same problem throughout adulthood. Adolescents with conduct disorders also come from very different family circumstances: Rather than the upper-middle-class, well-educated, small families of anorexic girls, the typical family is large, poor, with incomplete child-rearing capabilities (Yule, 1978).

There is much less agreement among clinicians and researchers about the origins or treatment of conduct disorders. The lack of consensus is probably best interpreted as an indicator of the multifaceted nature of the problem, rather than a scientific failure to find a single cause or best therapy. Various interacting genetic, psychological, and cultural factors probably form the basis for the development of conduct disorder problems (Rosenhan & Seligman, 1984). Nonetheless, we believe that an emphasis on psychological development, particularly within self-understanding, can contribute to an understanding of conduct disorder.

A recent study by Melcher (1986) provides some preliminary evidence for the interpretive leverage a self-understanding approach can provide. Melcher's goal was to examine the relationships of moral judgment (as assessed by Kohlberg's moral-judgment interview) and self-understanding to conduct disorder. The guiding rationale for her study was that conduct disorder is in part a moral problem, involving as it does the continued violation of societal norms and the rights of others. Drawing upon some recent theoretical work by Blasi (1983), Melcher suspected that the relationship between moral-judgment development and moral behavior is mediated by one's sense of self as reflected in self-understanding. This relationship could work in this way: An adolescent reasoning in an age-typical fashion in moral judgment might use as a moral rule "whatever is 'good' according to my friends and family is morally right" (Stage 3 in Kohlberg's system). However, if this adolescent thinks of the self at Level 1 (categorical), he or she is not especially concerned with whether the self is liked by others (a Level 3 notion). For this reason, the adolescent may decide not to act in accordance with his moral judgment. Melcher's hypothesis was that developmental level of both moral judgment and self-understanding would contribute to the interpretation of conduct disorder in adolescence.

To test her hypothesis, Melcher interviewed a group of adolescents with conduct disorders and a group of normal adolescents. In the first set of analyses on her data, Melcher looked for evidence of main effects for moral judgment and self-understanding. She found no relationship between moral judgment and conduct disorder but did find some evidence for a relationship between conduct disorder and an overall assessment of self-understanding as evidenced by a point-biserial correlation $r = .27, p < .08$. She also found a significant correlation between moral judgment and self-understanding of $r = .43, p < .01$. In a final molar analysis, Melcher found that a weak relationship between the weighted average score for the entire interview and conduct disorder still could be identified, $r = .32, p < .09$, after controlling for moral judgment.

Melcher also examined the possibility that there might be differences between normal adolescents and those with conduct disorders for different questions on the self-understanding interview. Although the emphasis in this book has been on the distinction between questions concerning the "me" versus questions tapping the understanding of the self as "I," Melcher believed that there might be important distinctions among responses to the different "me" questions as well. In Chapter 4 we claimed that to elicit fully a subject's understanding of the self as "me," it was necessary to include questions for self-definition, self-interest, the ideal self, and the self across time. Although we have found in our own research with normal populations considerable developmental homogeneity in responses to these four types of questions, Melcher's hypothesis was that this homogeneity might not characterize her sample of conduct disorder adolescents. Accordingly, she analyzed responses to each of 12 questions pertaining to the self as "me" separately.

Findings from analyses of responses to individual questions concerning the "me" must be cautiously accepted, we believe, because too little is known about how these questions differ among themselves. Yet Melcher's findings from this sort of analysis are readily interpretable. She found that the conduct disorder adolescents had lower average developmental level scores for 3 of the 12 questions she considered: Do you think you'll be the same or different when you're an adult (and how; and why is that important)? Do you think you were the same or different 5 years ago (and how)? What do you want to be like (and why)? All 3 questions concern the self over time: What the self was like in the past, what the self will be like in the future, and what one hopes the self will be like in the future.

The normal adolescents typically responded to these questions with Level 3 responses, indicating their concern with social acceptance. In contrast, Melcher found that the conduct disorder adolescents described their future and ideal selves using Level 1 and Level 2 ideas, which uncovers their lack of concern with the future integration of the self into a network of family, friends, and society.

Together, these findings suggest that if conduct disorder is present, the adolescent's sense of the self as "me" is less connected to the social context. In addition to a developmentally immature conception of the self in the future, Melcher found that such adolescents simply had difficulty envisioning the future of the self at all, as evidenced in these examples:

WILL YOU BE THE SAME OR DIFFERENT AS A PERSON IN FIVE YEARS? My attitudes will change. I could be grouchier, I could be grouchy all the time. IS THAT HOW YOU WILL CHANGE? No. HOW DO YOU THINK YOU'LL BE DIFFERENT? I don't know. It's hard to think ahead like that. WILL YOU BE THE SAME OR DIFFERENT AS AN ADULT? I don't know. WHAT MAKES IT HARD TO ANSWER THAT? Thinking ahead, you don't know what's going to happen in the future. The future might not even come. (p. 96)

DO YOU THINK YOU'LL BE THE SAME OR DIFFERENT AS AN ADULT? I don't know, I have no idea. THINK AHEAD. WILL YOU BE THE SAME OR DIFFERENT? No idea. WHY IS THAT? It's going to be a different world in five to ten years. We may not be living in five to ten years. WHAT IF WE ARE? It's going to be a lot different world . . . if you watch TV about the future and what it's going to be like, you think maybe people will be living on the moon and maybe you'll go up there. I don't know, I really can't tell you. WHAT WILL YOU BE LIKE? We could all die, we could all live. You just can't predict what you'll be like. (pp. 96–7)

These responses reveal the conduct disorder adolescent's lack of temporal perspective on the self. The self in the future is apparently something to which they have given little thought, and when they do project the self into the future, they do so with little concern with the integration of the self into the surrounding social context. In Chapter 1, we claimed that the projection of the self into the future and the construction of a sense of personal continuity are components of personal identity. Although Melcher's research approaches the issue of personal continuity a bit differently than we have in our own work, her findings suggest that adolescents with conduct disorders appear to have difficulties in developing a sense of personal identity that allows for future planning to guide current behavior.

Melcher also found differences between normal adolescents and those with conduct disorders in the developmental level of the agency component of self-understanding. Like the anorexic girls, adolescents with conduct disorders were significantly less mature in their understanding of this aspect of themselves than were the normal adolescents. The typical response among adolescents with conduct disorders revealed a Level 1 notion of agency, a sense that the self is shaped and formed by external forces. For example:

HOW DID YOU GET TO BE THE PERSON THAT YOU ARE? I don't know. . . . It was just me. . . . I don't know, I really don't, it just happened. (p. 98)

Together, the findings from Melcher's study suggest that the conduct disorder adolescent's understanding of self is immature in comparison with that of his agemates. The developmental delay is most evident in an understanding of the self over time and agency. Although these findings must be judged as preliminary, the patterns that emerge are significant. It appears that the adolescent with a conduct disorder, unlike his nondelinquent peers, is not concerned about the future self's appeal to others. Our speculation is that this failure contributes to the perpetuation of the mental health problem. Because the self's future attractiveness to others is not of central importance, the adolescent with a conduct disorder feels few inhibitions about the typical delinquent behaviors that inevitably result in social estrangement. As a consequence, such an adolescent acts in ways that result in social and legal difficulties; these difficulties may perpetuate the developmental delay, because the rejection of the self by others may make it emotionally stressful to consider the self in terms of attractiveness to others. This situation might lead to a solidification of a Level 2 understanding of self, even though this would be developmentally inappropriate.

Again, we would not argue that self-understanding developmental lags are the root cause of conduct disorder in adolescence. Indeed, the continuity of conduct disorder and related mental health problems across the lifespan argues against a claim of only a developmental delay. Our claim is that this developmental delay, whatever its original cause, in turn contributes to the perpetuation of the problem. The longer the adolescent fails to consider the future self and its integration into the social fabric, the more likely it will be that the adolescent will accumulate a burdensome record of school, social, and legal problems. Addressing this self-understanding problem, as well as the developmentally immature sense of agency, may constitute one limited component of a conduct-disorder treatment program.

Conclusions

One of our goals in this chapter was to illustrate the interpretative value that a developmental model of self-understanding has for mental health difficulties in adolescence. In contrast to self-esteem approaches, the self-understanding model emphasizes the individual's understanding of self instead of a positive or negative evaluation of it.

In terms of conduct disorders, the study we reviewed revealed that a developmentally delayed understanding of self appears to be a correlate of conduct disorder. Rather than understanding the self's qualities as affecting one's integration into social relationships and society, the view of the self (particularly in the future) characteristic of adolescents with conduct disorders is concerned with categorical features and comparison with others. The consequence is that the adolescent with a conduct disorder is relatively free from behavioral inhibitions deriving from fears of social estrangement and, as a result, participates in acts that are considered delinquent.

Although this interpretation is somewhat speculative at this point, it is parsimonious in a way that a self-esteem interpretation could not be. It is no doubt true that some delinquent youth have low self-esteem and perform antisocial acts in order to gain attention and to bolster their self-esteem. But it seems to us just as likely that some delinquent adolescents have unreflectively high self-esteem; and because they think so highly of themselves, they are too little concerned about what others think about them. Whatever the status of self-esteem as a contributor to mental health, it is by no means simple or linear, and is in serious need of interpretation. We hope that this chapter indicates the value of a self-understanding approach in guiding such interpretation.

Another of the self-understanding model's advantages over other self-concept models, we have claimed, is that it addresses diverse facets of self-understanding that are interrelated yet also partially independent. These unique features of the model were especially useful in understanding the problems of anorexic girls. As we indicated in the brief literature review preceding our discussion of the study, anorexic girls have usually been characterized as having difficulty with agency and distinctness, with little consensus among clinicians about other self-understanding problems. The research results presented here confirm that anorexics differ from other adolescents in respect to the agency component of self-understanding. In understanding anorexia, then, the developmental model of self-understanding focuses attention on development on a clinically relevant aspect of self-understanding, rather than attributing mental health difficulties to a general deficit in the self-concept. This perspective is sensitive to both typical and atypical development in self-understanding.

The two studies presented in this chapter, in addition to serving as vehicles for demonstrating the interpretative value of our model of self-understanding, also contribute to our knowledge of self-understanding. First, the two studies confirm the psychological reality of the model. Two very different mental health difficulties, one in girls and one in boys, were related in meaningful ways to the distinctions and developments in self-understanding described by our self-understanding model. Three different types of patterns were observed. In both studies, mental health problems were reflected in a developmental delay in understanding an aspect of the self as "I," agency. This confirms the developmental significance of agency awareness, as posited in Chapter 6. Second, the development of the "me" appeared to be delayed in boys with conduct disorders. Finally, although not of central importance in the studies of mental health, differences in the focus of the "me" on one of the four constituents (physical, active, social, and psychological) was found between normal girls and girls with curvature of the spine. Together these findings suggest that the multidimensional nature of the model is necessary in order to account for the variety of ways mental health difficulties are related to self-understanding development.

8 Self-understanding in a Puerto Rican fishing village

With NYDIA LUCCA

Any form of knowledge is an interaction between subject and environment: No concept could be fully functional unless it were closely adapted to the context from which it arose and in which it operates. For social concepts like self-understanding, the nature of the social environment exerts the strongest influence. Many variations in the social environment can affect how the self is construed. Cultures differ, for example, in their perspectives on what is important in one's personal identity, in their views of the ideal self, and even in their modes of drawing boundaries between self and others (Geertz, 1975). The very notion of individuality, including its substance, prerogatives, responsibilities, and desirability, can change dramatically from one social setting to the next (LeVine, 1980). Clearly such social-cultural variations will have an impact on the nature and developmental path of self-understanding in childhood and beyond.

Despite this seemingly obvious conclusion, there has been little comparative research on children's self-conceptions across cultures. The studies that we reviewed in Chapter 2, comprising the bulk of developmentally oriented research on self-concept, were by and large limited to American or Western European school children. Nor, within these already limited samples, was there any attention to possible religious, ethnic, or social-class variations. It is as if developmental researchers have shared a common pair of assumptions: Self is self anywhere in the world; and the conception of self therefore constitutes the same cognitive task.

But there are some reasons to suspect that self-concept development may not follow the same path across cultures. Anthropological research, though not directly exploring children's self-concept development, has reported marked cultural differences in how persons and, by implication, selves are conceived.

Of course, the notions of self and person themselves are not ephemeral cultural artifacts. In every culture people have *some* mode of understanding

158

these basic concepts (Geertz, 1975). Further, because these concepts serve essential human cognitive functions, these modes of understanding no doubt have something in common across cultures. The concept of self, for example, provides people with a critical sense of personal continuity and distinctness, as we have maintained throughout this book. Therefore we might well expect that concepts of self everywhere will necessarily include ideas that establish continuity and distinctness. In fact, LeVine and White (1986, p. 38), surveying the anthropological literature, come to exactly this conclusion: "There are concepts of the person and the self in all cultures. Self-awareness and a sense of one's continuity over time are universal in human experience, and all human adults distinguish between actions of the self as opposed to those of another."

Cross-cultural differences in person and self-conceptions, therefore, cannot be so fundamental as to challenge the very existence or functional roles of these concepts. Rather, such differences must be secondary in nature, pertaining to the ways in which the concepts serve their constant functions. As such, these differences may be confined to a small distinction or set of ideas; or they may be quite broad, encompassing virtually all suppositions on the nature of personhood.

In the reported anthropological data, perhaps the most broad-based cultural difference in how persons are understood concerns their perceived independence versus interdependence. This difference is apparent in the contrasting modes of identifying personal qualities found in Western versus agrarian societies. In Western cultures there is a tendency to abstract personal qualities from their context, whereas in agrarian cultures persons are understood in terms of their contextual features, such as their location in the society's network of social relationships (LeVine & White, 1986).

In a review of cross-cultural studies on the concept of person, Shweder and Bourne (1981) conclude that non-Westerners show "a tendency to *not* abstract out a concept of the inviolate personality free of social role and social relationship – a tendency to not separate out, or distinguish, the individual from the social context" (p. 14). Shweder and Bourne give several examples of this, both from their own research and from the findings of others. One of the most intriguing of these findings is from Clifford Geertz's study of the Balinese. According to Geertz, in Bali there is

a persistent and systematic attempt to stylize all aspects of personal expression to the point where anything idiosyncratic, anything characteristic of the individual merely because he is who he is physically, psychologically, or biographically, is muted in favor of his assigned place in the continuing, and, so it is thought, never-changing pageant that is Balinese life. . . . Physically men come and go – mere incidents in a happenstance history of no genuine importance, even to themselves.

But the masks they wear, the stage they occupy, the parts they play, and most important, the spectacle they mount remain and constitute not the facade but the substance of things, not least the self. (1975, p. 50)

Much the same picture emerges from the more limited body of literature on the relationship between culture and self-concept. In this literature there is also a common portrayal of non-Western conceptions of self as less developed than Western ones (see Shweder & Bourne, 1981, for a discussion of this issue). Indeed, both Baldwin (1905) and Luria (1976) have described cultures in which even adult conceptions of self seem rudimentary and childlike. Luria provides the following excerpts from interviews with peasants in remote Russian villages:

WHAT SHORTCOMINGS ARE YOU AWARE OF IN YOURSELF, AND WHAT WOULD YOU LIKE TO CHANGE ABOUT YOURSELF? Everything's all right with me. I myself don't have any shortcomings, but if others do, I point them out.... As for me, I have only one dress and two robes, and those are all my shortcomings. NO, THAT'S NOT WHAT I'M ASKING YOU ABOUT. TELL ME WHAT KIND OF PERSON YOU ARE NOW AND WHAT YOU WOULD LIKE TO BE. AREN'T THERE ANY DIFFERENCES? I would like to be good, but now I'm bad; I have few clothes, so I can't go to other villages like this. AND WHAT DOES "BE GOOD" MEAN? To have more clothes. (1976, p. 148)

HOW WOULD YOU DESCRIBE YOURSELF? I came here from Uch-Kurgan, I was very poor, and now I'm married and have children. [*Question understood in terms of external conditions of life* – Luria's interpretation.] ARE YOU SATISFIED WITH YOURSELF OR WOULD YOU LIKE TO BE DIFFERENT? It would be good if I had a little more land and could sow more wheat. AND WHAT ARE YOUR SHORTCOMINGS? This year I sowed one pood of wheat.... We've already gathered the hay and will harvest the wheat, and we're gradually fixing the shortcomings. [*Again everything refers to external conditions of life* – Luria's interpretation.] WELL, PEOPLE ARE DIFFERENT – CALM, HOT-TEMPERED, OR SOMETIMES THEIR MEMORY IS POOR. WHAT DO YOU THINK ABOUT YOURSELF? We behave well – if we were bad people, no one would respect us. (1976, p. 150)

Luria believes that these types of self-statements indicate that peasants from remote, preliterate Russian villages have difficulty understanding their own characteristics in any kind of objective sense (p. 151), because their understanding of themselves is interwoven with the specific facts of the social and physical worlds in which they live. Like Geertz's Balinese or LeVine's agrarians, therefore, these peasants cannot abstract personal qualities from their functional roles in the social and physical context. Luria believed that it is only as these peasants become integrated into the collective life of postrevolutionary Russia that they develop the ability for a more detached self-awareness.

Although we accept the general point about contextual biases in the self-understanding of non-Western agrarians, we wonder whether Luria's methods fully uncovered all of his peasant's self-awareness. Judging from the quoted excerpts, Luria's interview hardly tested the limits of subjects' reasoning. Few probe questions (like "Why is that important?") were asked, there are virtually no countersuggestions or other systematic follow-ups; in general, the interview is far more superficial than one administered in clinical fashion. Of course it may be that even a well-probed interview would have failed in this setting due to societal factors inhibiting self-reflection. We have encountered such problems ourselves in attempting to apply our technique to a rural population in Iceland. But still we would be left with the same question: Is the rudimentary nature of the response due to a developmental lag in self-awareness or to a problem in self-expression?

There is no way to answer this question from Luria's data. But in general we believe that it is safest to treat culturally induced variations in response either as socially adaptive alternatives, or as difficulties in communication and expression in the experimental or interview context. The case for developmental lags across cultures is difficult if not impossible to prove, because the systems of meaning from which knowledge derives may be so radically different as to render responses incomparable on any developmental scale.

In the case of Luria's examples, we could imagine them being expanded into far less rudimentary self-statements if the subjects felt encouraged to do so. We can already see in these examples the beginnings of several positions falling within the perspective of our model. Although these examples contain no statements characteristic of the psychological self-scheme, the other three self-schemes (physical, active, and social) are clearly represented. Despite the lack of interviewer probing, several of the excerpts could become interpretable at developmental Levels 1 to 3: Level 1 ("I'm married and have children"), Level 2 ("It would be good if I had a little more land and could sow more wheat"), and Level 3 ("We behave well – if we were bad people, no one would respect us"). This variety of developmental levels and self-schemes that we find present in just these two examples suggests to us that self-understanding in this community is not necessarily impoverished or developmentally retarded.

There remains, however, the likely possibility that the sense of self in small rural settings is qualitatively different on many accounts from the sense of self in Westernized industrial settings. Such differences may spring from a cultural ethic that firmly embeds the self, and persons generally, within their social and physical contexts.

In such cultures, characteristics of self may be understood primarily in terms of their overall social functions, especially those social functions that integrate the individual into a tightly knit network of relationships. We believe that this difference of focus, rather than a "rudimentary" or otherwise impoverished sense of self, is most likely to emerge through cross-cultural investigation. Unfortunately, as noted previously, there is to date few available data on the development of self-concept across cultures.

In the following pages, we describe one exploratory cross-cultural study of self-understanding development. The purpose of this small study was to chart parallels and dissimilarities in the self-understanding of children and adolescents from two very different societies: mainland, urban United States, and a small Puerto Rican fishing village. The two settings differed along virtually every dimension: size, complexity, language, religion, economic status, educational and employment opportunity, family composition, ethnic heritage, and cultural values.

Recent ethnographies (Lucca, 1980; Lucca & Pacheco, 1980) have described the life and cultural perspective of this fishing village. Poverty is omnipresent. Children are ill-clothed, roads are unpaved, health services are nonexistent, and fishing is difficult due to the pollution of the bay bordering the village. Nevertheless, the children of the community seem intent upon adopting the lifestyles of their parents.

Lucca and Pacheco (1980) found that most boys aspire to be fishermen and most girls wish to become wives of fishermen. Accordingly, the social life of the community is characterized by continuity and harmony in family relations, cooperative practices among kin as well as nonkin, and parental expectations that children at an early age will be obedient and will assume serious labor responsibilities. On the average, children and adolescents in this village attend 3 to 4 years of school.

Using the dimensions suggested by Whiting and Whiting (1975) to gauge cultural complexity, Lucca and Pacheco characterized the village as being at a very low level of complexity. This characterization reflects the village's relative lack of occupational specialization, differentiation of settlement pattern, political centralization, social stratification, and religious variation.

The mainland U.S. sample that we used for comparative purposes was drawn from a town in the northeastern United States. Although no formal ethnography of this community has been conducted, a similar northeastern U.S. community, fictionally named "Orchard Town," has been the subject of an extensive sociological and ethnographic documentation (Whiting & Whiting, 1975). Relative to the Puerto Rican fishing village, parents in Orchard Town have tolerant attitudes toward disobedience and aggression in their children. Parents' behavior toward their children, when compared with that found in societies like the fishing village, is democratic rather than domineering or dictatorial. Orchard Town, and like it the community from which our mainland U.S. sample was drawn, can be characterized as complex on the Whitings' scale.

Subjects. The Puerto Rican sample consisted of 48 children and adolescents. The ages of the Puerto Rican subjects ranged from 6 to 15, with most (70%) of the subjects between the ages of 8 and 11 ($M = 10.6$ years, standard deviation (SD) = 2); 25 of the subjects were boys and 23 were girls.

The mainland U.S. sample was comprised of 48 subjects who approximated the age range and gender breakdown of the Puerto Rican sample. The age range of this sample was from 6 to 16, with 67% of the subjects between the ages of 8 and 11 ($M = 10.6$, SD = 2). The sample consisted of 23 boys and 25 girls. The children and adolescents in this sample were from middle-class families, and most students in this community complete 12 or more years of schooling.

Interview procedure. Each child in the study was given the self-understanding interview (Chapter 4). Interviews in Puerto Rico were conducted in Spanish by a native of the community, and interviews in the mainland U.S. sample were conducted in English. The interviews were tape-recorded and later transcribed. The interviews with Puerto Rican subjects were translated into English. Because this study was conducted prior to the development of interview questions tapping the "I" component of self-understanding, only conceptions of the self-as-object were investigated in this research.

Coding procedure. Our first task in coding the responses of the Puerto Rican subjects was to determine whether our self-understanding scoring manual was appropriate for this task – whether these responses matched points in the existing manual without distortion, or whether additional points (or whole levels, for that matter) would need to be added. In large part, though not in every respect, the original manual proved adequate and sufficient.

We quote here from some of the Puerto Rican responses to our interview questions and place them in the context of our original manual. As we will discuss, one significant modification of the manual was needed to accommodate these new responses.

First, we note that the Puerto Rican sample made Level 1 categorical statements about themselves in all the different self-as-object schemes. For instance, in the following example, a child from the fishing village makes a Level 1 reference to her physical characteristics:
WHAT DO YOU LIKE ABOUT YOU? The face, the eyes, and the mouth. WHY? Because these are the most important of all. WHY IS THAT? I don't know. (Age 10)

The following example provides another reference to the physical self-schemes elaborated in ways typical of Level 1. What is distinctive about this example, and many others like it in the Puerto Rican sample, is the reference to the social self-scheme that accompanies the categorical reference to the body:

WHAT ARE YOU LIKE? Good and that's all. I am swarthy. I am short. I am slender. WHY DOES THAT MATTER? I don't know. WHICH OF THESE THINGS IS THE MOST IMPORTANT FOR YOU? Short. WHY? Because in my family they are tall and I am short. (Age 11)

The Puerto Rican children also make reference to their typical activities, again with a Level 1 elaboration. For example:

CAN YOU TELL ME WHAT YOU ARE LIKE? I'm a nice kid. WHY ARE YOU A NICE KID? I help the people. HOW DO YOU HELP THEM? Cleaning the yard, taking care of the animals and taking them outside. FROM ALL THOSE THINGS, WHICH ONE IS THE MOST IMPORTANT? Taking care of the animals. WHY? I like animals very much. WHY ARE EACH ONE OF THOSE THINGS IMPORTANT? Because I like that kind of activity. (Age 12)

In this last example, there is also a reference to preference ("I like animals very much"), which is coded within the psychological self-scheme. The children and adolescents from the Puerto Rican sample also described themselves in terms of their psychological characteristics at higher levels as well. In the first of the following examples, the child describes a limitation on his cognitive ability to understand what his teachers say, a Level 2 concern:

WHAT ARE YOU LIKE? I am so dumb. WHY? Because I don't understand what they teach me. WHY IS IT LIKE THAT? Well, they speak very complicated, and I don't understand very well. (Age 9)

In the following Level 3 example of psychological and social scheme use, the child describes himself in terms of his enjoyment in interacting with his peers. Here the psychological combines with the social:

WHAT ARE YOU LIKE? I'm good. I lend my toys. And I play with the guys, and I enjoy being with the guys. (Age 11)

Most of the responses made by the Puerto Rican children and adolescents could be coded with our existing manual, but one type of response required a modification. The following examples are very common among the responses of the Puerto Rican children and adolescents, yet in our research with hundreds of U.S. children we had rarely heard similar self-descriptions:

FROM ALL THE THINGS THAT YOU ARE, WHICH ONE IS THE MOST IMPORTANT? Be nice and respect people. WHY? Because if I'm bad everybody will hit and hate me. When I would be in danger they would not help me. (Age 12)

CAN YOU TELL ME WHAT YOU ARE LIKE? Good. WHAT DO YOU MEAN BY GOOD? I don't say bad words. I don't say bad words to my father and mother so they don't hit me. (Age 6)

WHAT ARE YOU LIKE? That I behave nice with my mother. I am obedient. They are nice with me, and I am nice with them. WHY IS IT IMPORTANT THAT YOU ARE NICE WITH THEM? Because they, if I behave nice with them, they bring me toys for Three Kings Day, bring me things; and if I obtain a good school average, they bring me toys if I pass the grade. (Age 11)

WHY IS BEING A NICE PERSON GOOD FOR YOU? Because they don't hit me, and I don't behave bad. (Age 6)

FROM THOSE THINGS, TELL ME ABOUT TWO OR THREE. I behave with my parents because they are very nice with me. Also, they spend most of the time working for us. We are six brothers. We eat at my grandma's house. She makes supper for us and also for any unexpected visitor. My parents are very nice with me and my brother. (Age 11)

Common to all these examples is the construal of self through behaviors that elicit positive or negative reactions from others. In none of our current or previous mainland U.S. samples did we find examples of this exact mode of self-understanding. For this reason, our scoring manual contained no category in which such statements could be coded. The manual, however, did contain a category that was logically compatible with this type of reasoning: Level 2 of the social scheme, where one's abilities are considered in light of the reactions of other people. The difference was that the Puerto Rican children were concerned with their *behaviors* (whether they had done something good or bad) in light of others' evaluative reactions, rather than their skills, talents, and abilities. Although this represents a comparison of sort (good versus bad behavior, evaluated through another's eyes), it is more of an implicit one than is a statement about how well one does something and how others judge this accomplishment.

To accommodate this new type of reasoning introduced by the Puerto Rican sample, we added a scoring point to Level 2, social scheme and coded all such responses accordingly. After revising the coding manual to allow for this new type of Level 2 response, the interviews were scored in the standard manner, as described in Chapter 4. Although this modification solved the comparability of scores problem, we nevertheless took note of the variation in reasoning substance that this new scoring point represents. We shall discuss this variation and its cultural significance in our conclusions.

Results

For both samples, there were significant correlations between age and best level (U.S. $r_s = .26, p < .05$ [one-tailed]; P.R. $r_s = .41, p < .01$ [one-tailed]), but not for age and modal level. The likely reason that these age associations were lower than those reported in Chapter 5 was that, in both

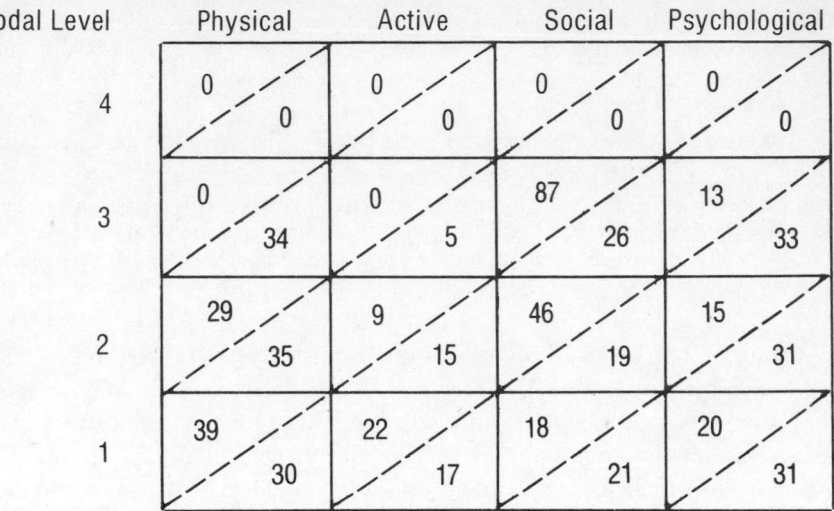

Fig. 8.1. Average percentage of chunks in each of the self-schemes for individuals at each of the four modal levels.
Note: The number in the upper half of each cell is the average for the Puerto Rican sample, and the number in the lower half is the average for the U.S. sample.

samples, subjects were far closer together in age than in our Chapter 5 studies, so that in the present study there was relatively little variation on the age dimension.

Figure 8.1 presents the average percentage of chunks in each of the four self-schemes and at each of the four modal levels for all subjects in the two samples.

As can be seen in Figure 8.1, for the Puerto Rican sample the percentage of physical and active self-scheme statements declined sharply at higher modal levels, with correlations between modal level and percentage of scored chunks in these schemes of $r_s = -.32, p < .05, r_s = -.37, p < .01$, respectively. The percentage of social self-scheme statements, on the other hand, increased dramatically, with a correlation between level and percentage of chunks in that scheme of $r_s = .49, p < .001$. For the U.S. sample, the only significant association was obtained between modal level and percentage of chunks in the active scheme $r_s = -.29, p < .05$.

Table 8.1 presents the number of subjects from each sample at the four developmental self-as-object levels, as measured by both best and modal performance.

As can be seen in Table 8.1, there was a tendency for children and adolescents from the United States to express higher best levels of self-

Table 8.1. *Number of subjects from each sample at developmental levels 1, 2, 3, and 4*

	Level 1		Level 2		Level 3		Level 4	
	Modal	Best	Modal	Best	Modal	Best	Modal	Best
Puerto Rico	18	6	25	22	5	20	0	0
United States	8	0	31	12	9	34	0	2

understanding. Kolmogorov-Smirnov two-sample tests (appropriate for this type of nonparametric comparison) with each of the developmental level measures as the dependent measure and sample as the factor revealed differences between samples for best level K-S $Z=1.6$, $p < .01$. This difference between the samples did not, however, pertain to modal level of self-understanding (K-S $Z=.91$, n.s.).

Because the U.S. sample was slightly older than the Puerto Rican sample, the best-level contrast must be interpreted cautiously, because best level is strongly correlated with age.[1] Nevertheless, the magnitude of the reported contrasts suggest that our mainland sample did score somewhat higher on their best-level statements than did the Puerto Rican sample.

Table 8.2 presents the averages for the two samples for the percentage of chunks in each of the four self-schemes. Consistent with expectations, children and adolescents in the Puerto Rican sample were more likely to characterize the self in terms of its social qualities, as indicated by the higher percentage of chunks in the social scheme $F(1,94)=9.6$, $p < .01$. Also consistent with expectations, children in the mainland U.S. sample had a higher percentage of chunks in the psychological scheme $F(1,94)=12.0$, $p < .001$.

In addition, the Puerto Rican children and adolescents focused more on the characteristics of self leading to punishment and reprimand, as well as on personality traits affecting the self's attractiveness to others. Children

Table 8.2. *Scheme scores for the two samples*

	Self-scheme			
	% Physical	% Active	% Social	% Psychological
Puerto Rico	31	14	36	17
United States	33	14	21	31

and adolescents in the mainland U.S. sample tended more toward describing their own preferences, intellectual qualities, and social astuteness.

Conclusions

The results of this study suggest first of all that our developmental model is useful for characterizing the self-understanding of children and adolescents in an agrarian rural setting, a small Puerto Rican fishing village. The associations between age and developmental level for the Puerto Rican sample were of the same general magnitude as these associations in the mainland United States, indicating that the levels capture similar developmental reorganizations in self-understanding for two very different cultures. We note that in the present study we were able only to investigate the self-as-object; but we have no reason to believe that results with regard to understanding of self-as-subject in the two cultures would be any different.

With respect to developmental levels of self-understanding, the two samples were comparable in most but not in all ways. On the one hand, there appear to be no significant differences in the modal-level scores for the two samples, which suggests that children and adolescents in the U.S. and Puerto Rico tend to think about themselves in comparable ways at similar ages. On the other hand, there was some evidence that mainland U.S. children expressed higher best performances. If so, we attribute this to the mainland children's greater willingness to try out new ideas in the course of the interview. This attitude could well be a function of their greater comfort and ease in the interview setting and would explain the higher best-level scores. Because the mainland children's best-level advantage was not accompanied by a modal-level superiority, we doubt that this finding indicates any developmental gap in self-understanding between the two populations.

The most striking differences between the two samples were variations within rather than between developmental levels. In other words, there were nondevelopmental differences in how a level or a scheme was manifested. For example, the Puerto Rican version of Level 2 in the social scheme was more other-derived and less explicitly comparative than was the mainland U.S. version of Level 2 in the social scheme. The Puerto Rican children were concerned about the effects of their actions on others more than about the relative superiority of these actions vis-à-vis others.

The frequent explicit comparison of the self to others that characterizes Level 2 may describe only children in cultures that encourage individual achievement. In cultures where collective advancement supersedes individual achievement, children may be less likely to think of themselves in terms of "being better at math than the other kids in my class" or being "the worst kickball player in the school." Instead, the Level 2 understanding of self in these more sociocentric cultures may be oriented toward the reactions of others to the self's actions and abilities. The Puerto Rican children made frequent assessments of self based on references to how their families and friends react to their actions.

In our model of self-understanding, the developmental levels provide information that does not necessarily overlap with the self-schemes. In this way, our model departed from previous models, most of which define development in terms that we reserved for our self-schemes (with age, decreasing physical conceptions, increasing psychological ones, and so on). As Figure 8.1 shows, our model's conceptual separation of developmental level from scheme is needed more in characterizing the U.S. sample than the Puerto Rican one. For the Puerto Rican children and adolescents, there was a positive association between modal level and percentage of chunks in three of the self-schemes. In that culture, therefore, level and scheme seem more closely connected than in ours. Maturity of self-understanding is thus linked with a series of standard self-forms as the child passes through successive life phases.

We believe that this finding reflects the interpersonal conformity associated with small rural cultures. Such conformity derives from a press toward tradition and results in a large degree of perceived similarity among individuals at particular life phases. As the Puerto Rican children become adolescents, there may be societal expectations for them to be sensitive to their place in the network of social relationships and thus to take on a stereotyped – what Geertz calls a "stylized" – sense of personal identity. This form of identity, as Geertz writes, will necessarily be less idiosyncratic and more "public" than is common in our culture. Or, as LeVine and White write: "Agrarian cultures have lexicons of life stages, social roles, and local relationships that are often given precedent over idiosyncratic traits in describing a person" (1986, p. 38).

We also found cultural differences between the two samples in usage of the social and psychological self-schemes. The Puerto Rican children relied more heavily on social self-descriptions, whereas mainland U.S. children relied more heavily on psychological ones. Because our small study is one of the first empirical attempts to document cultural differences in children's and adolescents' self-understanding, this finding is important in its own right. Among other things, it demonstrates the developmental origins of trends that have been recently noted in anthropological theory:

The social identities of agrarian peoples are thus constructed in ways not encompassed by Western psychological concepts. They are based on one's location in a network of social linkages rather than on personal qualities defined independently of linkages. This often involves assuming as part of one's identity characteristics of one's family with whom one is linked in the eyes of the community. Although this locational identity is not lost, it changes as one grows older, forges new links and acquires more status. Conformity to the conventions of village life, rather than performance in a role requiring special skill, is central to the acquisition of higher status in adulthood. (LeVine & White, 1986, p. 40)

Differences like those we have been describing no doubt arise from multiple processes of cultural transmission. The two samples in this study live in settings that vary along a number of dimensions: parenting, formal education, and social structure, to name just a few. Expectations parents have for their child almost certainly affect the child's understanding of self. If parents demand academic achievement from a child, that child will evaluate the self, at least at times, in terms of school grades, intelligence, interest in school subjects, and so on. In addition, parents shape their child's sense of self through selecting that child's activities. In a cross-cultural study of sex-role socialization, Edwards and Whiting (1980) found that girls became more nurturant than boys as they grew older. This difference was not a consequence of differences in the way mothers directly interacted with their daughters. Instead, it was traced to the more extensive child-care duties of the girls, duties that were assigned to them by their mothers.

In an even more indirect yet still powerful way, the structure of the social group influences a child's understanding of self. Research by Whiting and Whiting (1975) on the effects of cultural complexity on children's social behavior found that children of complex cultures were more egoistic and less nurturant than children of simple cultures. It is reasonable to assume that their self-understanding reflects this difference, with people from simple cultures more oriented toward their social qualities and responsibilities. Harre (1981) has made such a claim for the self-understanding of Eskimos. Harre claims that, because Eskimos are mainly concerned with the welfare of the collective rather than with that of the individual, the Eskimo language has no direct parallels to our English self-referential statements (like "I am"). Thus, cultural symbol systems such as language communicate and reinforce the child's culturally induced orientation toward the self, inhibiting divergent conceptions of selfhood. This will be particularly evident in tradition-bound cultures like the small rural community that we investigated.

Note

1 Although analyses of covariance have been used by many investigators to control for differences between groups, such as the age difference between the two samples of this study, such analyses violate the intent and assumptions of the technique (Applebaum & McCall, 1983).

9 Self-understanding and social cognition

In this book we have presented a view of self-understanding as a unique conceptual system serving its own special cognitive functions. We have identified the many features of self-understanding that make it unique among other concepts, including its reflexive nature, the dualistic relation between self-as-object and self-as-subject, and its multidimensional constituents.

Our developmental model was designed to capture the uniqueness and complexity of this conceptual system. It divided the self into two major subdivisions, the objective and subjective selves; and within each of these subdivisions it proposed developmental progressions for a number of separate components. Where possible, the model linked these components together into general sequences of developmental levels. For example, developmental trends in the four self-as-object schemes had enough in common to generate one general self-as-object sequence. Some aspects of the self-as-subject progressions also had links to one another as well as to the self-as-object sequence. But many of the conceptual transformations in particular components of the model defied generalization, either within or beyond the model.

Empirically, we found strong positive age trends for the individual sequences proposed by the model, but only moderate associations between the sequences. This result supports the model's proposed developmental progressions while further bearing out the complexity and multidimensional nature of self-understanding. Our system, although an organized conceptual one, contains diversities and multiple functions – as, most notably, in its objective and subjective components. Even where developmental levels are parallel in some respects, they may not be in others; and such divergences no doubt lead to discrepancies in subjects' understanding across the concept's multiple facets.

In its empirical manifestations, then, this conceptual system is clearly not always organized of a piece. As our data show, it is common to reason

171

about different components of the self at different developmental levels. We suspect that, with later development, there is a tendency to consolidate in one's mode of understanding the various components of self, thereby decreasing somewhat the discrepancies we have noted. But there will always be certain functional discrepancies, as well as simple variation of choice.

Cultural context can lead to further discrepancies, as indicated by the variation in Level 2 self-as-object reasoning found consistently in our Puerto Rican data. Such a variation follows logically from values and beliefs held deeply in the culture but nevertheless represents a departure from the central organizing principles of self-understanding development as proposed by the model. The message from such cultural discrepancies is that any conceptual system, including self-understanding, represents a cognizing interaction between subject and environment. Where there are meaningful differences in the cultural environment, we must expect differences in knowledge and its developmental course. In this way, knowledge becomes adaptive and functional. Self-understanding, therefore, may vary in substance and structure across social and cultural settings. We note, however, that the significant variation we found in the small Puerto Rican fishing village was limited to one point in one developmental level, and was largely overshadowed by the remaining patterns of similarity between the two cultural groups.

In self-understanding, therefore, we have a conceptual system with unique features, serving particular functions, and itself containing a complex diversity of components. It is organized around core principles and lawfully reorganized in the course of development; but individuals commonly show some unevenness in using these principles for their own self-examinations. Further, there may be important deviations from the principles themselves where other principles are more compatible with cultural values.

For all of these reasons, we have avoided approaching self-understanding from a "universal-structuralist" perspective, even while we have used structural methods of analysis to define its organizing principles and their developmental trajectories. As noted in Chapter 1, we believe that structural analysis is an invaluable tool for developmentalists, because it enables one to define the core conceptual principles that determine development as they become progressively reorganized. But we strongly prefer to think of such conceptual principles as partial, rather than global, structures. We have taken this direction throughout this book.

The alternative position – other than to abandon the search for organization entirely – would be to posit a few general structures that supposedly pervade all of a child's or adolescent's reasoning, as many within the cognitive-developmental camp have tried to do (see, for example, Kohlberg, 1969; Selman, 1980). The assumption is that, as these general structures evolve into qualitatively new ones, reasoning in many areas will follow. Often researchers have assumed that the sequence of general structures is best captured by Piaget's stages of logical reasoning. The strategy is to place individuals at different stages of development based on performance in Piagetian tasks and then attempt to identify reflections of that stage in the individual's reasoning in the domain of interest. For instance, Noppe (1983) tested children and adolescents on several different formal operational tasks, and also asked them to write self-descriptions. Her hypothesis was that subjects with formal-operational abilities to reason in a hypotheticodeductive mode would describe themselves differently than those capable only of the reality-bound reasoning of concrete operational thinkers. The former, she thought, would be more likely than the latter to describe the self in psychological terms because of their abilities to deduce causes (motives, emotions) from results (behaviors). In this study, however, as in many others like it – including the original Genevan experimental attempts decades ago – the posited relations across tasks turned out to be weak or nonexistent.

Our own position is that the search for general structures responsible for development across diverse domains fails to respect the unique features and functions of knowledge in each domain. Piagetian formal-operational reasoning tasks, for instance, assess an individual's ability to deduce general principles about the physical world. Although there may be some commonalities between thinking about the physical world and social relationships, social reasoning differs in one fundamental respect (Damon, 1979).

In the course of social interaction, individuals intentionally alter their actions in order to coordinate them with the actions of others. The child, whether talking with his parents or playing with friends, must construct knowledge about the relationships between self and other within the awareness that one's own actions can radically affect the nature and direction of the ongoing social interaction. Acquiring knowledge about the physical world proceeds differently: The child learns that the wind blows and the sun shines without intentional coordination with the child's actions or participation. There is a basic distinction, therefore, between social and physical reasoning. The developmental connections between these two broad domains are likely to be relatively weak, as a consequence of the previously mentioned fundamental difference (Damon, 1977). For this reason, then,

Noppe's failure to find strong or meaningful relationships between formal operational thinking and self-description in the study we have described seems to us predictable.

Although it is not surprising that there is little evidence for a direct connection between the developmental trajectories of physical cognition and self-understanding, we do expect self-understanding development to be partially related to development in other social-cognitive areas, for self-understanding is itself a social-cognitive concept. Like other concepts within the social domain, the process of constructing knowledge about the self occurs within a network of relationships in which different persons intentionally modify their actions in reaction to the actions of others. This concept, in fact, has been a point of departure for virtually every major theorist who has written on the social self (e.g., Baldwin, 1902; Mead, 1934; Mahler et al., 1975).

But even within the social domain there are important distinctions in the structure and function of different types of knowledge. The most commonly studied social-cognitive concepts in developmental psychology focus on interpersonal interaction, relationships, and regulations: friendship, authority, morality, person perception, and role taking, to name just a few. Primarily, the child's understanding of these interpersonal relationships and regulations functions to facilitate effective participation in social interaction and in society (Damon, 1983). Although self-understanding too serves this goal, it is distinct from these interpersonal concepts in that it aids in the differentiation of the individual from society (as we discussed in Chapter 1). For this reason, self-understanding development is unlikely to be identical with development of the interpersonal concepts. Empirically, then, we would predict that self-understanding developmental levels would exhibit only a moderate degree of association with developmental levels of interpersonal concepts.

To examine the developmental relationships between self-understanding and some key interpersonal concepts, we conducted a small study with 38 children, approximately equally divided by grade (kindergarten, 1, 3, and 5) and sex. The children were interviewed on four topics: self-understanding, positive justice, authority, and friendship. The interview procedures and coding manuals for positive justice and authority were from earlier work on these topics (Damon, 1977). An understanding of friendship was elicited and coded using parts of Selman's (1980) interview and coding manual. The order of the presentation of interview topics was randomized to prevent possible order effects. The results of this small study are summarized in Table 9.1.

These intercorrelations indicate that higher developmental levels of self-

Table 9.1. *Correlations among best-level scores for self-understanding, positive justice, authority, and friendship*

	Positive justice	Authority	Friendship
Self-understanding	.49(38)*	.34(34)**	.38(37)**
Positive justice		.48(33)*	.38(36)**
Authority			.51(33)*

*$p < .01$;
**$p < .05$.

understanding are likely to be associated with higher developmental levels of reasoning about positive justice, authority, and friendship. Yet it is clear from the moderate magnitude of the associations in Table 9.1 that the development of self-understanding is not reducible to the development of these other social concepts, or to any single common source. Nor, as we have maintained previously (Damon, 1977, 1979, 1980) are the social concepts themselves reducible to each other or to core principles that they may have in common.

Self-understanding development, then, is related to but also distinct from the development of interpersonal reasoning. We have argued this view because self-understanding is a social concept with an individuating function not shared by most other social concepts: It serves not only to integrate the individual into society, but also to differentiate the individual from all others. As we noted in Chapter 1, a core component of each person's sense of self is a sense of individuality.

But there is another area of social cognition – person perception – that also shares this individuating function. Our knowledge of another person is not composed solely of characteristics the individual has in common with others. Like self-understanding, our knowledge of another must also include the features that serve to identify that person uniquely. Knowing others, therefore, is a cognitive activity with some close links to knowing the self (which follows also from the basic realization that the self and other are both persons).

This link between knowing self and others has long been noted in social and developmental psychology. In fact, we have argued early in this book that psychology has made too much of this link, blurring the contrasts between conceptual systems with some radically different features and functions. But neither do we wish to blur the commonalities between these two forms of construing persons. Our claim is that self-understanding and other-understanding (or "person perception," as it is called in the field) share the common function of identifying individuals, and thus have a common bond. But, at the same time, because one knows the self in many intimate ways unimaginable in person perception generally, the two conceptual systems are in many ways different. These two social-cognitive concepts, therefore, stand in a uniquely close yet fundamentally separate relation to one another. To explicate this complex and developmentally important relation further, we will present a detailed conceptual analysis and one further set of findings.

Person perception and self-understanding

Person perception has long interested social and developmental psychologists, for the very good reason that it is a central part of one's social-cognitive repertoire. The way in which one understands people directly influences one's social communications and interactions and changes greatly over the course of the lifespan. Particularly in the last 10 years, when social-cognitive study has become a popular topic, there have been numerous attempts to document varying patterns of person perception within and across individuals.

Each person is of course unique, and there are special problems and challenges in acquiring knowledge of any individual. Further, each individual whom one knows stands in a special position relative to oneself. That is, one has different relationships with different individuals: Some relationships are intimate, others distant; some domineering, others egalitarian; some competitive, others cooperative; and so on. Certainly the special nature of one's relation with a particular person flavors one's knowledge of that person, just as the special nature of an individual's personal characteristics poses unique demands for one's attempts to acquire knowledge of that individual. A key part of understanding persons lies in recognizing the differences among them both in terms of their relationships to oneself and in terms of their own individual makeups apart from oneself.

Among the universe of persons, there is one whose position in relation to oneself is totally different from all others, and who therefore presents a radically different type of cognitive task for one's understanding. This person is of course oneself. When one attempts to know other persons, one is on the outside looking in; when one attempts to know the self, one is on the inside looking both outward and inward. One has access to the self in a manner impossible with any other person, no matter how intimate the relationship. Further, one has feelings and attitudes about the self unmatched by one's emotions toward others, and these feelings and attitudes may well affect the manner in which one processes information about the self and others. The challenge of "knowing thyself" is unique in the endeavor of person perception.

Despite the seemingly apparent idiosyncrasies of self-perception, psychologists studying person perception have often failed to make a distinction between person perception generally and self-perception in particular. The initial inclination has been to assume that the process of understanding others is similar to the process of understanding the self. Developmental studies have attempted to show that the same general developmental descriptions apply to children's changing conceptions of both self and other over time (Montemayor & Eisen, 1977; Rotenberg, 1982). Such studies have been successful in obtaining empirical evidence in support of this position. However, they have done so by employing developmental descriptions at such a high level of abstraction that they would apply to almost any cognitive-developmental phenomenon. The most common examples of such descriptions are Werner's (1957) notion of increasing differentiation and hierarchical integration, or Flavell's (1977) notion that development proceeds from "surface" (overt properties) to "depth" (covert properties). Although these characterizations do capture age-related trends in both understanding self and understanding others, much of the unique quality of both developmental tasks eludes them.

The bias in favor of assuming similarities between self- and other-understanding derives from a long tradition within psychology. In fact, some of the most influential theories of social development are based on the notion that self- and other-conceptions go hand in hand in the course of development (Baldwin, 1902; Kohlberg, 1969). Baldwin (1902) attributed the existence of social phenomena such as the sense of justice to the identical relationship between the understanding of self and the understanding of others. According to Baldwin, the sense of justice depends on an awareness that others have the same desires as does the self:

One's interests, the things he wants in life, are the things which, by the same very thought, he allows others, also the right to want; and if he insists upon the gratification of his own wants at the expense of the legitimate wants of the "other," then he in so far does violence to his sympathies and to his sense of justice. (p. 21)

Following Baldwin (1902) and Mead (1934), Kohlberg (1969) assumes an identical relationship between the evolution of an understanding of self and other as a result of the developmental process involved in which an understanding of self is used to inform an understanding of others, and vice versa. The interpenetration of self- and other-understanding yields a social or shared self, because, when one thinks of others, the injuries of others are in part experienced as one's own. This empathy arising from the synchronous development of self- and other-understanding is, according to Kohlberg, the motivation underlying morality.

Whether self-understanding and other-understanding develop synchronously is an empirical question with important ramifications. Should the two types of understanding not develop in a parallel fashion, then the theories of Baldwin and Kohlberg and other authors who explain the social nature of humans in terms of a parallel development of self and other would need to be reevaluated.

A more mundane reason for examining the relationship between self- and other-understanding is to evaluate the need to investigate the development of each of the two types of understanding independently. If self- and other-understanding do develop in an exactly parallel fashion, then a researcher would have only to investigate one type of understanding to know the development of the other type. Some authors have, indeed, reached the conclusion that the two types of understanding are essentially similar. For instance, in discussing the results of their study investigating self-understanding, Montemayor and Eisen (1977) described their findings as basically similar to those emerging from the study of the development of an understanding of other people. It is precisely this question that concerns us in the remainder of this chapter: Is self-understanding development the same as the development of an understanding of others? We shall begin by examining the two theoretical traditions that have considered the issue in greatest detail.

Imitation theory

According to classic imitation theory, the development of self-understanding parallels the development of an understanding of others. This position has received its clearest exposition in the work of Baldwin (1902), who sought to explain the child's socialization and acquisition of competencies necessary to function in society through the process of imitation:

All were born helpless; all have been educated. Each has been taught; each is to become a teacher. Each learns new things by doing what he sees others do; and each improves on what the other does only by doing what he has already learned. Each teaches simply by doing and rules the others by his example. (p. 80)

For Baldwin, as well as for other imitation theorists (Guillaume, 1926/1971; Kohlberg, 1969; Piaget, 1965/1932), the onset of imitation marks the beginning of selfhood. There are three stages in the process of becoming a self, according to Baldwin. In the projective stage, which emerges during the first 6 or 7 months of life, the child is not aware of a distinction between the self and others. The child's perception of the world is composed of projects, or images, that are assumed to be of personal origin. Projects, or images, of people are particularly interesting to the child for two reasons: First, people are more unpredictable than objects, and second, there is a growing affective involvement with people.

In the subjective stage, which appears late in the first year of life along with the third stage, the child turns his or her attention inward toward the internal sensations. This happens as a result of imitation. As the child continues to watch other people, he or she becomes aware that the other performs interesting actions. In an effort to renew the interesting perceptions that accompany the actions exhibited by others, the child attempts to recreate or imitate those actions. However, in the course of imitation, the child experiences a significant difference between the actions of the other and those the child recreates. In experiencing his or her own actions, the child is aware of kinesthetic and volitional components that accompany that action. But when observing another perform an action, the child experiences only the visual perceptions associated with a movement. The differing experiential components to the same actions result in self-awareness; the child begins to see that the self and the other are different, and that the self is the locus of subjective experiences such as kinesthetic feedback and volition.

At the third stage in the process of becoming a self, the ejective stage, the inner sensations, emotions, and pleasures that were associated only with the self at the previous stage are seen to be applicable to one's understanding of another or are ejected into the other: "Other people's bodies, says the child to himself, have experiences in them much as mine has" (Baldwin, 1902, p. 14).

This third stage obviously must follow the subjective stage, because the inner experiences accompanying an action are most easily discovered within the self. But once these inner sensations are identified by the child as belonging to certain actions, the child assumes that these same sensations are felt by others when they act accordingly. Once this basic correspondence of "dialectic" is established between the self and other, one's understanding of self and the other are basically identical. One comes to think new things about the self by applying thoughts and characteristics of others to the self. Baldwin (1902) offered this example:

Last year I thought of my friend W as a man who had great skill on the bicycle and who wrote readily on the typewriter. But now, this year, I have learned to do both these things. I have taken the elements formerly recognized in W's personality, and by imitative learning brought them over to myself. I now think of myself as one who rides a "wheel" and writes on a "machine." (p. 16)

Conversely, what one thinks of the self is ejected: "When I have a headache I cannot see a person riding, jumping, etc., without attributing to him the throbbing which such action would produce in my own head"

(Baldwin, 1902, p. 18n.). Because what one learns about the self is, by the process of ejection, an addition to what one knows about others, and what one knows about others becomes meaningful for understanding the self, what a person thinks of "another is – not stands for, or represents, or anything else than is – his thought of himself, until he adds to it a further interpretation; the further interpretation is in turn first himself, then is – again nothing short of this is – his thought of the other" (p. 89).

On several points, Baldwin's (1902) theory of the development of self- and other-understanding falls short. First, Baldwin never explains how one comes to have an accurate understanding of another person. Although one can reasonably assume that the other experiences the same class of inner sensations and emotions that the self experiences, one cannot easily discern which particular sensations and emotions the other is currently experiencing. Thus, in the example of ejecting one's headache into another who is riding a horse, the attribution is likely to be wrong. Indeed, even young children are aware that the self's current sensations and perceptions do not necessarily correspond to the other's subjective state. The imitation thesis fails to depict the ontogenesis of accurate ejection or attribution, or what is more frequently termed role taking.

Baldwin's assertion that imitation is the mechanism of self- and other-understanding development has also received criticism in large part because Baldwin never developed what he meant by imitation. Dewey (1898) claimed that all Baldwin's theory does is identify a similarity without explaining it, because Baldwin's "imitation" has no specific meaning or mechanism:

I do not see that we know any more of the psychology of the sense of personality and of (the other) society than we did before. . . . Baldwin's method in simply sending us from the (other) society, fails as a matter of fact to establish even this interdependence. (p. 401)

Of course, Baldwin's failure to detail the psychological mechanisms involved in imitation does not mean that he was wrong. His thesis concerning the interrelationship of self- and other-understanding due to imitation might simply need elaboration, as some of his followers have attempted to do. (e.g., Guillaume, 1926/1971). Furthermore, despite the problems that we have outlined, Baldwin's theory has gained the acceptance of a number of psychologists including Piaget (1965/1932), Kolhberg (1969), Loevinger (1977), and Lewis and Brooks-Gunn (1979), which indicates that the imitation thesis is of some explanatory value.

Attribution theory

Beginning from a social-psychological rather than a developmental perspective, Jones and Nisbett (1972) have elaborated the basic tenets of

Heider (1958) into a theory relevant to the issue of developmental similarities and dissimilarities of self- and other-understanding. They begin with the assumption that the self's and other's actions are the only data from which an understanding of self and other may be inductively constructed, and that these actions are perceived in much the same way that nonsocial objects are perceived.

In Jones and Nisbett's theory, the actions of the self and other are interpreted differently for two reasons: There are different data available about the self and other, and there are differences between the way one processes information about the self and other. With regard to the first point, Jones and Nisbett (1972) assert that there is more and better data available for perceiving and interpreting the self's actions than is available for perceiving and interpreting the actions of another. The self knows what experiences accompany the actions of the self but cannot know with any certainty the experiences accompanying the actions of another because the other's feelings can only be inferred and not known:

The observer's (self's) knowledge about the actor's (other's) feelings is limited to inferences of two types: attempts to read inner experience from physiognomic and gestural ones, and judgments based on the observer's knowledge of what others and he himself have felt in similar situations. . . . Knowledge of the actor's feeling states is therefore never direct, usually sketchy, and sometimes wrong. (p. 89)

Similarly, one usually knows the intent of one's actions, whereas the intentions of another can only be unreliably inferred.

A third information difference is that one usually has knowledge of the temporal precursors of one's own acts, whereas in considering the actions of another, one frequently has no idea what circumstances preceded them. Thus, when thinking about the self, one tends to think that the self's actions are contingent upon a temporal sequence of events, whereas one regards the other's actions as simply the result of a disposition.

A final difference between the data available to interpret the self's actions and the data available to interpret the actions of another concerns the variability of behavior: "The actor's (self's) knowledge about the variability of his previous conduct – associated, in his mind, with different situational requirements – often preempts the possibility of a dispositional attribution" (p. 85). In interpreting another's action, one frequently has little idea about the variability of the other's behavior. Again, therefore, a dispositional attribution might be preferred for understanding the actions of the other.

Not only are there differing amounts of information available to an individual for interpreting the actions of the self and the other, but the information that is common both to the knowledge of the self's and other's actions may be also interpreted differently. Jones and Nisbett (1972) argue that the self perceives its own behavior "To be a response to environmental cues that trigger, guide, and terminate it" (p. 89). In contrast, for the individual observing another's actions, "The focal commanding stimulus is the actor's behavior" (p. 6), and the individual is likely to assume that the actor is the cause of the behavior. The individual is likely to view the self's actions as caused by environmental factors, rather than by dispositions, simply because the self literally cannot see itself perform an action very well and, therefore, the self's attention cannot be diverted from environmental contingencies by the perceptual attractiveness of the act.

From the attribution perspective, then, the understanding of self and other will not be similar, nor will they develop synchronously because the two types of understanding are based on different information and because self and other are oriented toward different features of the action context. Self-understanding is focused on the environmental contingencies that control actions and, therefore, should be constituted of knowledge of these causal contexts – for instance, "I am nice to my mother when she buys me candy and none of my brothers are around to see me act nice." On the other hand, an understanding of other people should be composed of stable dispositions such as "He is always friendly" or "She is always nice."

Criticism of the attribution paradigm has focused on the assumption that the other can be known simply by inferring or attributing dispositions on the basis of the other's behaviors. Hamlyn (1974) has asserted that another person's behavior could not possibly make sense, or be interpreted, unless the self understands what a person is: "In order to construe a facial expression as one, say, of joy, one would have to know first that the expression was one manifested by some thing that could indeed manifest joy – by, that is, a person" (p. 6). This basic knowledge of what constitutes a person cannot be gained in the nonsocial inductive manner postulated by attributionists. As Peters (1974), Hamlyn (1974), and Damon (1979) among others have pointed out, social knowledge, including an understanding of other people, cannot be gained apart from social interaction. Reciprocity, the give-and-take of relationships, constitutes the distinguishing characteristic of sociality; it must be experienced by the child in order to understand it. Still, once the basic knowledge of personhood is gained, there is no reason that the attribution perspective developed by Jones and Nisbett could not be an accurate description of the process by which self- and other-understanding is accumulated.

Empirical research

In one of the best-known studies of person-perception development, Lively and Bromley (1973) asked children from ages 7 to 15 years to write descriptions of people they knew. In one analysis of the data, the authors divided the descriptions into "peripheral" and "central" statements. Peripheral statements described the other in terms of physical appearance, name, age, activities, possessions, likes and dislikes, social roles, and kinship and social relationships. These types of statements in fact correspond quite closely to the self-as-object Level 1 in our self-understanding model. Central statements describe the other in terms of personality traits, general habits, motives, needs, values, and attitudes. Lively and Bromley's data analysis revealed that the proportional usage of central statements increases with age, and the proportional usage of peripheral statements decreases. These results parallel findings summarized in Chapter 5 for our model of self-understanding development – in particular, the movement away from the characteristics treated in a categorical manner (e.g., appearance, name, typical activities) toward a more organized understanding of personal characteristics.

Barenboim (1981) posited a three-level progression in the development of the understanding of others. At the first level, the child describes other people in terms of behavioral comparisons (e.g., "Jimmy is the fastest runner in the class"). The use of behavioral comparisons leads to the development of psychological constructs in the description of other people, as the child begins to infer stable dispositions that produce the observed behaviors (e.g., "John does well in class because he is smart"). As the child becomes adept at making psychological inferences in the description of other people, he or she begins to make psychological comparisons between people (e.g., "Joan is much friendlier than Fred").

To test this hypothetical sequence in the development of understanding other people, Barenboim interviewed children in the age groups of 6, 8, and 10 years of age, asking each child to describe three people he or she knew well. The same children were interviewed 1 year later at which time each was asked to describe three different people. Comparisons between the age groups revealed that there was a significant increase in the use of behavioral comparisons between the ages of 6 and 8, and a significant decrease in the use of behavioral comparisons between the ages of 9 and 11. Psychological constructs began to rise in frequency only between the 10- and 11-year-old children. Analysis of the changes occurring within subjects between Time 1 and Time 2 indicated that all but two followed the proposed developmental sequence.

These results do substantiate the developmental sequence hypothesized by Barenboim. However, even though the sequence as depicted may describe a developmental phenomenon, it is not a comprehensive description of the development of an understanding of others. As Barenboim (1981) himself has admitted, the sequence does not characterize all of the subject's actual descriptions: "The non-analyzed residual category contains a large percentage of subjects' statements" (p. 137). Perhaps the most valuable aspect of Barenboim's study is that it reveals that behavioral comparisons become an important aspect of understanding of others, just as was found in the case of self-understanding.

The studies by Livesly and Bromley and by Barenboim indicate that there are some developmental similarities between an understanding of self and others. Other studies, however, suggest that there may be differences between these two types of understanding. Such studies frequently derive from the attribution hypothesis predicting that the self will be described in terms of environmental conditions that may cause a particular action whereas the other will be characterized in terms of cross-situational traits or dispositions. Usually this research involves an experimental manipulation with adult subjects.

For example, Nisbett, Caputo, Legant, and Marecek (1973) reported that an adult recounting his or her own actions in a number of experimental situations is more likely to attribute his or her behavior to situational cause and free will, while ascribing the roots of another's behavior in the same situation to personality traits and dispositions. Taylor and Fiske (1975) found that simply the difference in spatial orientation affected the interpretation of another person's behavior. Someone sitting behind the actor perceived the actor's actions as he or she would perceive the self's (i.e., as elicited by the environment); but when facing the other person performing the acts, the causes of the other's acts were more frequently attributed to personality traits and dispositions.

This attribution research suggests that descriptions of others should more frequently include psychological characteristics, because of the tendency to attribute personality traits and dispositions to others. But developmental research seems to indicate just the opposite. In their development study (described in part previously) Livesly and Bromley (1973) asked children from ages 7 to 15 to write descriptions of themselves and other people they knew. With 7-year-old children, the category of likes and dislikes was by far the most frequently used in self-descriptions, but the same category was rarely used in the description of others. Categories of interests and hobbies, and intellectual aptitudes and abilities, followed the same trend; 7-year-olds used these categories more frequently for self-description than for other-description. Adolescents added still more differences to the schism between conceptions of self and other, using categories of motivation and arousal, and orientation, more frequently when describing the self than in describing others. In a very similar study, Secord and Peevers

(1974) reported that self-descriptions contained more references to preferences, beliefs, and abilities, whereas other-descriptions mentioned superficial characteristics or role categories. Taken together, these last two studies suggest a tendency for children to think of the self in more psychological terms than when thinking about the other, a tendency that becomes even more pronounced in adolescence.

In our own small study of the relationship between self-understanding and person perception, conducted with the same children who participated in the social-cognitive study described in the first part of this chapter, we examined several hypotheses. The brief literature review that we presented suggested to us that there should be both similarities and differences between the developmental paths of the two domains. We expected that the same developmental reorganizations that occur in self-understanding would also be present in an understanding of others. Differences between self-understanding and an understanding of others could emerge in two ways: First, there might be scheme-score differences between self-understanding and an understanding of others (e.g., self-understanding might be more psychologically oriented than an understanding of others), and second, there might be differences between the two types of understanding not captured by our developmental manual that could be identified through a qualitative analysis of a subset of the data. Any apparent differences between self-understanding and an understanding of others identified in this analysis of a subset of the data could then be tested against the entire data set.

This study was conducted early in our investigation, before the self-as-subject questions designed for the Chapter 6 studies had been refined. For this reason, the present study compares subjects' understanding of the objective self with their understanding of the objective other. Conceivably it could be of great interest to compare subjects' understandings of subjective features of self and others, because subjectivity may have more of a privileged role in self-understanding than in other-understanding. But this interesting issue must await further inquiry.

In the present study, each child was interviewed three times: with the self-as-object questions of our self-understanding interview (see Chapters 4 and 5), and with two sets of queries about significant and well-known "others" in the child's life – friends and parents.

The friend interview was designed to elicit the child's conception of his or her best friend, using a set of questions that parallels the self-definition questions on the self-understanding interview (e.g., "What kind of person is your best friend?"). We chose a close friend as one target for the child to describe because Livesly and Bromley (1973) suggested that self- and other-descriptions are most likely to be similar when the other is a well-liked peer. We expected that minimizing the discrepancies in this way would allow a clearer analysis of possible differences between self-conceptions and other-conceptions.

In addition to the basic questions that induce a child to define a friend, the friend interview also included several questions designed to elicit the child's theory of person knowledge, for example: "How did you get to know all these things about . . . ? Is there anything that has happened that lets you know what kind of person ———— really is? In general, how can you get to know another person your age? Or anybody? Do you know yourself or your friend better? Why? Are there things you know about yourself that you could never know about your friends? Is this an important difference?"

The parent interview was identical to the friend interview, except that the child's conception of one of his or her parents was elicited. The parent as a target for an other-description should magnify discrepancies between self and other due to maturity and status differences, while still allowing the child to describe a person he or she knows well. The magnified difference, we expected, would allow an analysis of the extent to which an unlike other may be understood in the same terms as the self.

Probe questions for the friend and parent interviews focused on the meaning and importance of a characteristic mentioned by the subject, just as with the self-understanding interview. For instance, if a child said that her friend was "nice," the interviewer would ask, "What does that mean?" and, "Why is that important?"

In addition to the standard questions on the self, friend, and parent interviews, children were also asked to respond to several questions concerning their beliefs about how they got to learn about themselves: "Now that you've told me a lot of things about yourself, can you tell me how you got to know all these things about yourself? Is there anything special that has happened that really showed to yourself what kind of person you are? What does your friend think about you? Do you agree? What if your friend thought that you were . . . [opposite of one of the characteristics offered by the child in response to the self-definition questions]? What would you think about yourself then? Who would be right? What does your father or mother think about you? Do you agree? . . . "

To compare subjects' responses across the three interviews, we needed a common scoring instrument. For this purpose, we chose the developmental coding manual that we constructed for the self-understanding interview (see Chapter 4); but we initially needed to determine whether this scoring manual could be appropriately used for coding responses to the friend and parent interviews. As indicated previously, there was good reason to believe that it would be: Other investigators had used the same scoring system for coding both descriptions of self and other (e.g., Lively & Bromley, 1973; Secord & Peevers, 1974). A qualitative analysis indicated that descriptions of the self and other were sufficiently comparable to allow the use of the same coding manual. Although subjects offered descriptions of their friends and parents that were sometimes different from their descriptions of themselves, descriptions of others could be coded by the developmental and scheme criteria presented in the self-as-object sections of the self-understanding scoring manual.

The use of the self-understanding coding manual for coding the self, friend, and parent interviews, therefore, permitted developmental-level and scheme-score comparisons. However, because some subjects did not offer codible responses to all three interviews, data from a few of the subjects were omitted from some of the analyses.

As expected, both best-level and modal-level scores for self-understanding were correlated with age: r_s (33) = .59, $p <$ .001, and r_s (33) = .31, $p <$ .05 (one-tailed). Best-level and modal-level scores assigned to the friend interview were also correlated with age: r_s (25) = .43, $p <$ .05, and r_s (25) = .31, $p <$ .05 (one-tailed). Interestingly, however, neither best-level nor modal-level scores on the parent interview were correlated with age: r_s = .16, n.s., and r_s = .04, n.s., respectively). An ANOVA revealed no significant differences among the three types of descriptions with respect to either of the developmental level scores; in other words, there was no consistent trend for children to use higher-level reasoning for describing the self, or the friend, or the parent.

There was some modest developmental consistency across interviews with respect to the most advanced form of reasoning used (best level) but not with respect to typical (modal) reasoning. The correlations between best-level scores for the different interviews were: self-understanding and friend, r_s (25) = .45, $p <$ .05, self-understanding and parent, r_s (24) = .24, n.s., and best friend and parent, r_s (24) = .47, $p <$ .05.

These results suggest some developmental links between self-understanding and person perception; but these links extend only to best level of performance, and even there are not especially strong. Further, the pattern of results suggests that the child's knowledge of the best friend has unique qualities. It is like the child's understanding of self, in that the two conceptions share developmental commonalities. Yet it is also developmentally linked to an understanding of the parent, whereas self-understanding is not.

The scheme scores for the three interviews were also examined. The proportion of each subject's spontaneous statements coded as physical, active, social, and psychological were examined in a series of repeated-measure ANOVAs. No significant differences were found among the three interviews in the proportion of reasoning characteristic of any of the four schemes. This means, for instance, that the children in this study did not use psychological characteristics more frequently to describe themselves than to describe their friends or parents. Nor were there any significant correlations among the proportion of statements coded in a particular scheme on one interview and the proportion of statements coded in the same scheme on the other two interviews. Only 1 out of the 12 calculated correlations barely attained the .05 level of significance, likely a chance result.

In our previously mentioned qualitative analysis of the three sets of interview responses, we noticed that descriptions of friends and parents contained a striking number of self-referent descriptions. In other words, subjects frequently described others in terms of others' effects on the self. We provide two examples of this common phenomenon:

WHAT DO YOU THINK IS THE MOST IMPORTANT THING TO SAY ABOUT THE KIND OF PERSON YOUR MOM IS? She's easy to handle; nothing to it. WHAT DO YOU MEAN "EASY TO HANDLE"? Like if I want to go over to my friend's house, I usually can trick her into saying yes. Like I'll say, "Mom, can I go over to Brad's house?" or something and she says, "Sure." She doesn't know what we're doing, so fine. (Grade 3)

WHAT ELSE DO YOU MEAN WHEN YOU SAY SHE'S NICE? She cleans up my bedroom. WHY DOES THAT SHOW THAT SHE'S NICE? I don't know. (Grade 4)

In addition to receiving a code based upon our developmental coding manual, these types of responses also were coded as "Self-Reference in Other-Descriptions." To permit comparisons with self-understanding responses, another category, labeled "Other-Reference in Self-Description," was constructed. We present an example of an other-reference in a self-description:

WHAT'S THE MOST IMPORTANT THING TO KNOW ABOUT YOU? That I am nice. WHY IS THAT THE MOST IMPORTANT THING TO KNOW ABOUT YOU? Because then I give my mother things.

The purpose of these two "specific-person reference" scoring categories is to allow an analysis of subjects' tendencies to ascribe characteristics to a person (either self or other) in accord with these characteristics' effects on particular individuals.

There were significantly more specific-person references (self-references) in descriptions of friends and parents. An ANOVA of the total number of specific-person references made in each description, with means of 0.53, 2.24, and 2.9 in the self, friend, and parent descriptions respectively, revealed a significant effect due to the person being described ($F = 11.43$,

$p < .01$). Furthermore, a Newman-Keuls post-hoc analysis revealed that there were more specific-person references, again principally self-references, in descriptions of parents than in descriptions of self ($p < .05$) or of peers ($p < .01$). There were no developmental trends in subjects' tendencies to make specific-person references made on any of the three interviews.

These findings, in conjunction with the findings of the other studies reviewed, indicate that neither the attribution nor the imitation paradigm is wholly correct. The attribution paradigm cannot account for the pattern of developmental links and similarities that clearly exist between self- and other-understanding. To capture this pattern, a developmental orientation toward shared organizing principles of knowledge is needed. We have tried to bring such an orientation to this investigation as well as to our other explorations in social-cognitive development. This orientation borrows much from the structural-developmental approach, but does not go so far as to posit universal rules that permeate knowledge in all its forms. Rather, it looks for instances of specificity and generality both within and across domains.

The imitation thesis, an example of a more globalistic approach, cannot account for either the developmental or the nondevelopmental differences between self- and other-understanding. It cannot account for the tendency of subjects to understand others in terms of their effects on the self, as demonstrated in our findings concerning self-reference in other-descriptions, nor can it account for the tendency to attribute the roots of one's own behavior to the environment while attributing the roots of another's behavior to personality characteristics, as reported in the attribution research.

Because self-references are as common in descriptions made by adolescents as those of younger children (Honess, 1980), we do not believe that the self-referencing phenomenon can be explained in terms of egocentrism, as some authors have suggested (Scarlett, Press, & Crockett, 1971; Secord & Peevers, 1974). Rather, we believe that the explanation for the self-referencing phenomenon lies in an egoistic, rather than egocentric, explanation.

At least part of one's understanding of another person must always be concerned with how that person's qualities directly affect the self, which is our most direct window into others' behavior. It is also, of course, the view with the most personal impact, and thus the one likely to make the most lasting impression. When a child, therefore, thinks of her parents as "nice," very likely this refers to the nice things that the parents do for the child. In contrast, when one thinks of the self, there is little reason to link the meaning of a particular self-characteristic to its effects on another person. For example, when a child thinks of the self as being nice, it makes little difference to the perceived degree of the self's niceness whether the self is especially nice to friends and not so nice to siblings, or vice versa. We believe this to be an indication of a basic difference in perspective between the understanding of self and other.

References

Aboud, F. (1979). "Self: an identity, a concept, or a sense?" In *Soviet and Western perspectives in social psychology*, ed. L. Strickland. New York: Pergamon Press.

Aboud, F., and S. Skerry. (1983). "Self and ethnic concepts in relation to ethnic constancy." *Canadian Journal of Behavioral Science* 15: 3–34.

Allport, G. W. (1942). *The use of personal documents in a psychological science*. New York: Report of the Social Science Research Council.

Alston, W. (1977). "Self-intervention and the structure of motivation." In *The self: psychological and philosophical issues*, ed. T. Mischel. Oxford: Blackwell.

Amsterdam, B. (1972). "Mirror self-image reactions before age two." *Developmental Psychobiology* 5: 297–305.

Applebaum, M., and R. McCall. (1983). "Design and analysis in developmental psychology." In *Handbook of child psychology*, vol. 1, ed. W. Kessen. New York: Wiley.

Baldwin, J. M. (1902). *Social and ethical interpretations in mental life*. New York: Macmillan.

———. (1905). "Sketch of the history of psychology." *Psychological Review* 12: 144–55.

Barenboim, C. (1981). "The development of person perception in childhood and adolescence: from behavioral consequences to psychological constructs to psychological comparisons." *Child Development* 52: 129–44.

Bem, D., and A. Allen. (1974). "On predicting some of the people some of the time: the search for cross-situational consistencies in behavior." *Psychological Review* 81: 506–20.

Bernstein, R. M. (1980). "The development of the self-system during adolescence." *Journal of Genetic Psychology* 136: 231–45.

Blasi, A. (1983). "Moral cognition and moral action: a theoretical perspective." *Developmental Review* 3: 178–210.

———. (1986). "The self as subject: its dimensions and development." Unpublished manuscript, University of Massachusetts, Boston.

Brainerd, C. (1978). *Piaget's theory*. Englewood Cliffs, N.J.: Prentice-Hall.

Bretherton, I., S. McNew, and M. Beeghly-Smith. (1981). "Early person knowledge as expressed in gestural and verbal communication: when do infants acquire a 'Theory of Mind'?" In *Infant social cognition: empirical and theoretical considerations*, ed. M. Lamb and L. Sherrod. Hillsdale, N.J.: Lawrence Erlbaum Associates.

Brim, O. (1976). "Life span development of the theory of oneself: implications for child development." In *Advances in child development and behavior*, vol. 2, ed. H. Reese. New York: Academic Press.

Bromley, D. (1977). "Natural language and the development of the self." In *Nebraska symposium on motivation*, vol. 25, ed. C. Keasey. Lincoln: University of Nebraska Press.

Broughton, J. M. (1978a). "Development of concepts of self, mind, reality, and knowledge." In *Social Cognition*, ed. W. Damon. San Francisco: Jossey-Bass.

———. (1978b). "The cognitive-developmental approach to morality: a reply to Kurtines and Greif." *Journal of Moral Education* 7: 81–96.

———. (1980). "The divided self in adolescence." *Human Development* 24: 13–32.

Bruch, H. (1978). *The golden cage: the enigma of anorexia nervosa*. Cambridge, Mass: Harvard University Press.

Bruner, J. S. (1973). "The organization of early skilled action." *Child Development* 44: 1–11.

Buhler, C. (1930). *The first year of life*. New York: John Day.

Butterworth, G., and P. Light. (1982). *Social cognition: studies of the development of understanding*. Chicago: University of Chicago Press.

Campos, J., K. Barrett, M. Lamb, H. Goldsmith, and C. Stenberg. (1983). "Socioemotional development." In *Handbook of child psychology*, vol. 2, ed. M. Haith and J. Campos. New York: Wiley.

Chandler, M., M. Boyes, L. Ball, and S. Hala. (1987). "The conservation of selfhood: a developmental analysis of children's changing conceptions of self-continuity." In *Self and identity*, ed. T. Honess and R. Krysia. New York: Routledge & Kegan Paul.

Cicchetti, D. (1984). "The emergence of developmental psychopathology." *Child Development* 55: 1–7.

Clarke-Stewart, A., S. Friedman, and J. Koch. (1985). *Child development: a topical approach*. New York: Wiley.

Cohen, J. (1968). "Weighted kappa: nominal scale agreement with provision for scaled disagreement or partial credit." *Psychological Bulletin* 70: 213–20.

Colby, A., L. Kohlberg, J. Gibbs, and M. Lieberman. (1983). "A longitudinal study of moral judgment." *Monographs of the Society for Research in Child Development* 48, nos. 1–2 (serial no. 200).

Coopersmith, S. (1967). *The antecedents of self-esteem*. San Francisco: W. H. Freeman.

Damon, W. (1977). *The social world of the child*. San Francisco: Jossey-Bass.

———. (1979). "Why study social cognitive development?" *Human Development* 22: 206–11.

———. (1980). "Patterns of change in children's social reasoning: a two-year longitudinal study." *Child Development* 51: 1010–17.

———. (1983a). *Social and personality development*. New York: Norton.

———. (1983b). "The nature of social-cognitive change in the developing child." In *The relationship between social and cognitive development*, ed. W. Overton. Hillsdale, N.J.: Lawrence Erlbaum Associates.

Damon, W., and D. Hart. (1982). "The development of self-understanding from infancy through adolescence." *Child Development* 53: 841–64.

Darwin, C. (1877). "A biographical sketch of an infant." *Mind* 2: 285–94.

Dewey, J. (1898). A review of *Social and ethical interpretations in mental development*, by James M. Baldwin. *Philosophical Review* 7: 398–409.

Dixon, J. C. (1957). "Development of self-recognition." *Journal of Genetic Psychology* 91: 251–6.

Dusek, J. B., and J. F. Flaherty. (1981). "The development of the self-concept during the adolescent years." *Monographs of the Society for Research in Child Development* 46, no. 4 (serial no. 191).

Edwards, C., and B. Whiting. (1980). "Differential socialization of girls and boys in light of cross-cultural research." *New Directions in Child Development* 8: 45–57.

Epstein, S. (1973). "The self-concept revisited or a theory of a theory." *American Psychologist* 28: 405–16.

Erikson, E. (1950). *Childhood and society*. New York: Norton.

———. (1956). "The problem of ego identity." *Journal of the American Psychiatric Association* 4: 56–121.

———. (1968). *Identity: youth and crisis*. New York: Norton.

———. (1982). *The life cycle completed*. New York: Norton.

Feldman, D. H. (1980). *Beyond universals in cognitive development*. Norwood, N.J.: Ablex.

Ferguson, G. (1966). *Statistical analysis in psychology and education*. New York: McGraw-Hill.

Fischer, K. (1980). "A theory of cognitive development: the control and construction of hierarchies of skills." *Psychological Review* 87: 477–531.

———. (1983). "Illuminating the processes of moral development [Review of *A longitudinal study of moral judgment*, by A. Colby et al.]." *Monographs of the Society for Research in Child Development* 48, nos. 1–2 (serial no. 200).

Fischer, K., and D. Bullock, (1981). "Patterns of data: sequence, synchrony, and constraint in cognitive development." In *New directions for child development*, no. 12, *Cognitive development*, ed. K. W. Fischer. San Francisco: Jossey-Bass.

Flavell, J. (1977). *Cognitive development*. Englewood Cliffs, N.J.: Prentice-Hall.

Flavell, J., and L. Ross. (1981). *Social cognitive development: frontiers and possible futures*. Cambridge: Cambridge University Press.

Freud, S. (1922). *Group psychology and the development of the ego*. New York: Norton.

Froman, T., and L. Hubert. (1980). "Application of prediction analysis to developmental priority." *Psychological Bulletin* 87: 136–46.

Gallup, G. G. (1977). "Self-recognition in primates: a comparative approach to the bidirectional properties of consciousness." *American Psychologist* 32: 329–38.

Gardner, H. (1983). *Frames of mind*. New York: Basic Books.

Garner, D., and K. Bemis. (1985). "Cognitive therapy for anorexia nervosa." In *Handbook of psychotherapy for anorexia nervosa and bulimia*, ed. D. Garner and P. Garfinkel. New York: Guilford Press.

Garner, D., and P. Garfinkel, eds. (1985). *Handbook of psychotherapy for anorexia nervosa and bulimia*. New York: Guilford Press.

Geertz, C. (1973). *The interpretation of cultures*. Chicago: University of Chicago Press.

———. (1975). "On the nature of anthropological understanding." *American Scientist* 63: 47–53.

Gergen, K. (1965). "Interaction goals and personalistic feedback as factors affecting the presentation of self." *Journal of Personality and Social Psychology* 1: 413–24.

———. (1977). "The social construction of self-knowledge." In *The self: psychological and philosophical issues*, ed. T. Mischel. Totowa, N.J.: Rowman and Littlefield.

———. (1984). "Theory of the self: impasse and evolution." In *Advances in experimental social psychology*, vol. 17, ed. L. Berkowitz. New York: Academic Press.

Glick, J., and A. Clarke-Stewart. (1978). *The development of social understanding*. New York: Gardner Press.

Goldman-Rakic, P., A. Isseroff, M. Schwartz, and N. Bugbee. (1983). "The neurobiology of cognitive development." In *Handbook of child psychology*, vol. 2, ed. M. Haith and J. Campos. New York: Wiley.

Gordon, C. (1968). "Self-conceptions: configurations of content." In *The self in social interaction*, vol. 1, ed. C. Gordon and K. Gergen. New York: Wiley.

Guardo, C., and J. Bohan. (1971). "Development of a sense of self-identity in children." *Child Development* 42: 1909–21.

Guillaume, P. (1971). *Imitation in children*. Chicago: University of Chicago Press. (Original work published 1926)

Hamlyn, D. (1974). "Person-perception and our understanding of others." In *Understanding other persons*, ed. T. Mischel. Oxford: Blackwell.

Harre, R. (1981). "Psychological variety." In *Indigenous psychologies*, ed. P. Heelas and A. Lock. New York: Academic Press.

Harris, P. L. (1983). "Infant cognition." In *Handbook of child psychology*, vol. 2, ed. M. Haith and J. Campos. New York: Wiley.

Hart, D., and W. Damon. (1984). "Naive epistemologies of self and other." Paper presented at the Southeastern Conference on Human Development, Athens, Georgia.

———. (1986). "Developmental trends in self-understanding." *Social Cognition* 4: 388–407.

Hart, D., N. Lucca-Irizarry, and W. Damon. (1985). "The development of self-understanding in Puerto Rico and the United States." Paper presented at the meeting of the Society for Research in Child Development, Toronto, Canada, April.

Hart, D., J. Maloney, and W. Damon. (1987). "The meaning and development of personal identity." In *Self and identity*, ed. T. Honess and K. Yardley. New York: Routledge & Kegan Paul.

Harter, S. (1982). "The perceived competence scale for children." *Child Development* 53: 87–97.

———. (1983). "The development of the self and the self-system." In *Handbook of child psychology*, vol. 4, ed. M. Hetherington. New York: Wiley.

———. (1986). "Cognitive-developmental processes in the integration of concepts about emotions and the self." *Social Cognition* 4: 119–51.

Hartup, W. (1983). "Peer relations." In *Handbook of child psychology* vol. 4, ed. M. Hetherington. New York: Wiley.

Heider, F. (1958). *The psychology of interpersonal relations*. New York: Wiley.

Hildebrand, D., M. Laing, and A. Rosenthal. (1977). *Prediction analysis of cross classifications*. New York: Wiley.

Hill, J. P. (1980). "The family." In *Toward adolescence: the middle school years. The seventy-ninth yearbook of the National Society for the Study of Education*, ed. M. Johnson. Chicago: University of Chicago Press.

———. (1981). Commentary on *The development of the self-concept during the adolescent years*, by J. Dusek and J. Flaherty. *Monographs of the Society for Research in Child Development* 44, no. 4 (serial no. 191).

Honess, T. (1980). "Self-reference in children's descriptions of peers." *Child Development* 51: 476–80.

Howard, G., and C. Conway. "Can there be an empirical science of volitional action?" *American Psychologist* 41: 1241–51.

Hume, D. (1978). *A treatise of human nature*, ed. L. A. Selby-Bigge and P. H. Nidditch. Oxford: Clarendon Press. (Originally published 1738)

Humphrey, T. (1964). "Some correlations between the appearance of human fetal reflexes and the development of the nervous system." In *Growth and maturation of the brain: progress in brain research*, vol. 4, ed. D. P. Purpera and J. P. Schade. Amsterdam: Elsevier.

James, W. (1890). *The principles of psychology*. New York: Holt.

———. (1910). "A suggestion about mysticism." *Journal of Philosophy, Psychology, and Scientific Methods* 7: 85–92.

———. (1961). *Psychology: the briefer course*. New York: Harper & Row. (Originally published 1892)

———. (1948). *Psychology*. New York: World Publishing Co.

Jessor, R. (1983). The stability of change. In *Human development: an interactional perspective*, ed. D. Magnusson and V. L. Allen. Orlando, Fla: Academic Press.

Johnson, C. N., and H. Wellman. (1982). "Children's developing conceptions of the mind and brain." *Child Development* 53: 222–34.

Jones, E. E., and R. E. Nisbett. (1972). "The actor and observer: divergent perceptions of the causes of behavior." In *Attribution: perceiving the causes of behavior*, ed. E. E. Jones et al. Morristown, N.J.: General Learning Press.

Josselson, R. (1973). "Psychodynamic aspects of identity formation in college women." *Journal of Youth and Adolescence* 2: 3–52.

Kagan, J. (1981). *The second year of life*. Cambridge, Mass: Harvard University Press.

Kegan, R. (1982). *The evolving self: problem and process in human development*. Cambridge, Mass.: Harvard University Press.

———. (1985). "The loss of Pete's dragon." In *The development of the self*, ed. R. Leahy. New York: Academic Press.

Keller, A., L. Ford, and J. Meacham. (1978). "Dimensions of self-concept in preschool children." *Developmental Psychology* 14: 483–9.

Kohlberg, L. (1969). "Stage and sequence: the cognitive-developmental approach to socialization." In *Handbook of socialization theory and research,* ed. D. A. Goslin. Chicago: Rand McNally.

Kohlberg, L., and C. Armon. (1984). "Three types of stage models used in the study of adult development." In *Beyond formal operations: late adolescent and adult cognitive development*, ed. M. Commons, F. Richards, and C. Armon. New York: Praeger.

Kohlberg, L., and C. Gilligan. (1971). "The adolescent as a philosopher: the discovery of the self in a postconventional world." *Daedalus* 100: 1051–86.

Kokenes, B. (1974). "Grade level differences in factors of self-esteem." *Developmental Psychology* 10: 954–8.

Kuhn, D. (1976). "Short-term longitudinal evidence for the sequentiality of Kohlberg's early stages of moral judgment." *Developmental Psychology* 10: 590–600.

Kuhn, M., and T. McPartland. (1954). "An empirical investigation of self attitudes." *American Sociological Review* 19: 68–76.

Kurtines, W., and E. Greif (1974)." The development of moral thought: review and evaluation of Kohlberg's approach." *Psychological Bulletin* 81: 453–70.

Laing, R. D. (1968). *The divided self*. New York: Penguin Books.

Leahy, R. (1985). *The development of the self*. New York: Academic Press.

Leahy, R., and N. Kogan. (In press). "Social cognition and identity achievement." In *Development in young adulthood: characteristics and competencies in education, work, and social life*, ed. S. Messerick. San Francisco: Jossey-Bass.

LeVine, R. (1980). "Anthropology and child development." In *Anthropological perspectives on child development*, ed. C. Super and S. Harkness. San Francisco: Jossey-Bass.

LeVine, R., and M. White. (1986). *Human conditions: the cultural basis for educational development*. New York: Routledge & Kegan Paul.

Lewin, K. (1935). *A dynamic theory of personality*. New York: McGraw-Hill.

Lewis, M, and J. Brooks-Gunn. (1979). *Social cognition and the acquisition of self*. New York: Plenum.

Lively, W., and D. Bromley. (1973). *Person perception in childhood and adolescence*. New York: Wiley.

Loevinger, J. (1977). *Ego development*. San Francisco: Jossey-Bass.

Loevinger, J., R. Wessler, and C. Redmore. (1970). *Measuring ego development*. San Francisco: Jossey-Bass.

Lowenthal, M., M. Thurner, and D. Chiriboga. (1975). *Four stages of life*. San Francisco: Jossey-Bass.

Lucca, N. (1980). "The study of fishing communities: a critical review of the literature." Unpublished qualifying paper, Harvard University.

Lucca, N., and A. Pacheco. (1980). "Metas y pautas par la crianza en una comunidad pesquera en Puerto Rico." *La Torre*, December.

Luria, A. R. (1976). *Cognitive development: its cultural and social foundations*, trans. M. Lopez-Morillas and L. Solotaroff. Cambridge, Mass.: Harvard University Press.

Maccoby, E. (1980). *Social development: psychological growth and the parent–child relationship*. New York: Harcourt Brace.

Mahler, M., F. Pine, and A. Bergman. (1975). *The psychological birth of the human infant*. New York: Basic Books.

Marcia, J. (1966). "Development and validation of ego identity status." *Journal of Personality and Social Psychology* 35: 551–8.

———. (1980). "Identity in adolescence." In *Handbook of adolescent psychology*, ed. J. Adelson. New York: Wiley.

Markus, H. (1977). "Self-schemata and processing information about the self." *Journal of Personality and Social Psychology* 35: 63–78.

McGuire, W., and A. Padawer-Singer. (1976). "Trait salience in the spontaneous self-concept." *Journal of Personality and Social Psychology* 33: 743–54.

Mead, G. H. (1934). *Mind, self and society*. Chicago: University of Chicago Press.

Melcher, B. (1986). "Moral reasoning, self-identity, and moral action: a study of conduct disorder in adolescence." Ph.D. diss., University of Pittsburgh.

Mohr, D. (1978). "Development of attributes of personal identity." *Developmental Psychology* 4: 427–8.

Montemayor, R., and M. Eisen. (1977). "The development of self-conceptions from childhood to adolescence." *Developmental Psychology* 13: 314–9.

Morse, S., and K. Gergen. (1970). "Social comparison, self-consistency, and the presentation of self." *Journal of Personality and Social Psychology* 16: 148–56.

Nisbett, R., C. Caputo, P. Legant, and J. Marecek. (1973). "Behavior as seen by the actor and as seen by the observer." *Journal of Personality and Social Psychology* 27: 154–64.

Noppe, Ilene. (1983). "A cognitive developmental perspective on the adolescent self-concept." *Journal of Early Adolescence* 3: 275–86.

Nowicki, S., and B. Strickland. (1973). "A locus of control instrument for children." *Journal of Consulting and Clinical Psychology* 40: 148–54.

Nozick, R. (1981). *Philosophical explanations*. Cambridge, Mass.: Harvard University Press.

Papousek, H., and M. Papousek. (1974). "Mirror-image and self-recognition in young human infants: I. A new method of experimental analysis." *Developmental Psychobiology* 7: 149–57.

Parfit, D. (1971a). "Personal identity." *Philosophical Review* 80: 3–27.

———. (1971b). "On the importance of self-identity." *Journal of Philosophy* 68: 683–90.

Parmelee, A., and M. Sigman. (1983). "Perinatal brain development and behavior." In *Handbook of child psychology*, vol. 2, ed. M. Haith and J. Campos. New York: Wiley.

Parten, M. (1932). "Social play among preschool children." *Journal of Abnormal and Social Psychology* 28: 243–68.

Peevers, B. (1987). "The self as observer of the self: a developmental analysis of the subjective self." In *Self and identity: perspectives across the lifespan*, ed. T. Honess and R. Krysia. New York: Routledge & Kegan Paul.

Peevers, B, and P. Secord. (1973). "Developmental changes in attributions of descriptive concepts to persons." *Journal of Personality and Social Psychology* 26: 120–8.

Peters, R. (1974). "Personal understanding and personal relationships." In *Understanding other persons*, ed. T. Mischel. Oxford; Blackwell.

Piaget, J. (1965). *The moral judgment of the child*. New York: Free Press. (Originally published 1932)

———. (1967). *Six psychological studies*. New York: Vintage Books.

———. (1969). *The child's conception of the world*. Totowa, N.J.: Littlefield, Adams, & Co. (Originally published 1929)

———. (1983). "Piaget's theory." In *Handbook of child psychology*, vol. 1, ed. P. Mussen. New York: Wiley.

Piers, E., and D. Harris. (1969). *The Piers-Harris children's self-concept scale*. Nashville, Tenn.: Counselor Recordings and Tests.

Preyer, W. (1893). *The mind of the child*. New York: Appleton.

Rest, J. (1983). "Morality." In *Handbook of child psychology*, vol. 3, ed. J. Flavell and E. Markman. New York: Wiley.

Rosenberg, M. (1965). *Society and the adolescent self-image*. Princeton, N.J.: Princeton University Press.

———. (1979). *Conceiving the self*. New York: Basic Books.

———. (1985). "Self-concept and psychological well-being in adolescence." In *The development of the self*, ed. R. Leahy. New York: Academic Press.

Rosenhan, D., and M. Seligman. (1984). *Abnormal psychology*. New York: Norton.

Rotenberg, K. J. (1982). "Development of character constancy of self and other." *Child Development* 53: 505–15.

Ruble, D. (1983). "The development of social comparison processes and their role in achievement-related self-socialization." In *Social cognitive development: a social-cultural perspective*, ed. E. Higgins, D. Ruble, and W. Hartup. Cambridge: Cambridge University Press.

Rutter, M., and N. Garmezy. (1983). "Developmental psychopathology." In *Handbook of child psychology*, vol. 4, ed. M. Hetherington. New York: Wiley.

Saltzstein, H. (1983). "Critical issues in Kohlberg's theory of moral reasoning [Commentary on "A longitudinal study of moral judgment"]." *Monographs of the Society for Research in Child Development* 48, nos. 1–2 (serial no. 200).

Sarbin, T. (1962). "A preface to a psychological analysis of the self." *Psychological Review* 59: 11–22.

Sartre, J.-P. (1947). *Baudelaire*. Paris: Gallimard.

Scarlett, H., A. Press, and W. Crockett. (1971). "Children's descriptions of peers: a Wernerian developmental analysis." *Child Development* 42: 439–53.

Schorin, M. (1985). "Self-understanding development in anorexic female adolescents." Ph.D. diss., Clark University, Worcester, Mass.

Schorin, M., and D. Hart. (In press). "Psychotherapeutic implications of the development of self-understanding." In *Cognitive development and child psychotherapy*, ed. S. Shirko. New York: Plenum.

Secord, P. (1984). "Determinism, free will, and self-intervention: a psychological perspective." *New Ideas in Psychology* 2: 25–33.

Secord, P., and B. Peevers. (1974). "The development of person concepts." In *Understanding other persons*, ed. T. Mischel. Oxford: Blackwell.

Selman, R. (1980). *The growth of interpersonal understanding*. New York: Academic Press.

Shantz, C. (1983). "Social cognition." In *Handbook of child psychology*, vol. 3, ed. J. Flavell and E. Markman. New York: Wiley.

Shoemaker, S. (1963). *Self-knowledge and self-identity*. Ithaca, N.Y.: Cornell University Press.

Shoemaker, S., and R. Swinburne. (1984). *Personal identity*. Oxford: Blackwell.

Shweder, R., and E. Bourne. (1981). *Does the concept of the person vary cross-culturally?* Technical Report No. 6, Cognitive Science, University of Michigan, Ann Arbor.

Snarey, J., L. Kohlberg, and G. Noam. (1983). "Ego development in perspective: structural stage, functional phase, and cultural age-period models." *Developmental Review* 3: 303–38.

Snyder, S., and D. Feldman. (1977). "Internal and external influences on cognitive development change." *Child Development* 48: 937–43.

———. (1980). "Individual developmental transitions: a film metaphor." In *Beyond universals in cognitive development*, ed. D. H. Feldman. Norwood, N.J.: Ablex.

———. (1984). "Phases of transition in cognitive development: evidence from the domain of spatial representation." *Child Development* 55: 981–9.

Snyder, S., and J. Norcini. (1982). "An interaction of internal and external disequilibrium in moral reasoning development." Paper presented at the Seventh Biennial Southeastern Conference on Human Development, Baltimore, Md.

Spragens, T. A. (1973). *The dilemma of contemporary political theory: toward a postbehavioral science of politics*. New York: Dunellen.

Sroufe, A., and M. Rutter. (1984). The domain of developmental psychopathology. *Child Development* 55: 17–29.

Sternberg, R. J. (1984). *Beyond I.Q.: a triarchic theory of human intelligence*. Cambridge: Cambridge University Press.

Strober, M., and J. Yager. (1985). "A developmental perspective on the treatment of anorexia nervosa in adolescents." In *Handbook of psychotherapy for anorexia nervosa and bulimia*, ed. D. Garner and P. Garfinkel. New York: Guilford Press.

Swinburne, R. (1973–4). "Personal identity." *Proceedings of the Aristotelian Society* 74: 231–48.

Taylor, S., and S. Fiske. (1975). "Point of view and perceptions of causality." *Journal of Personality and Social Psychology* 32: 439–45.

Trevarthen, C. (1974). "Conversations with a two-month-old." *New Scientist* 62: 230–5.

———. (1977). "Descriptive analyses of infant communicative behavior." In *Studies in mother–infant interaction*, ed. H. R. Schaffer. New York: Academic Press.

Turiel, E. (1975). "The development of social concepts: mores, customs, and conventions." In *Moral development: current theory and research*, ed. D. Depalma and J. Foley. Hillsdale, N.J.: Lawrence Erlbaum Associates.

———. (1983). *The development of social knowledge*. Cambridge: Cambridge University Press.

———. (1983). "Domains and categories in social-cognitive development." In *The relationship between social and cognitive development*, ed. W. Overton. Hillsdale, N.J.: Lawrence Erlbaum Associates.

Vallacher, R., D. Wegner, and H. Hoine. (1980). "A postscript on application." In *The self in social psychology*, ed. D. Wegner and R. Vallacher. New York: Oxford University Press.

Wellman, H. (1986). "First steps in the child's theorizing about the mind." Paper presented at the International Conference on Developing Theories of Mind, Toronto, Canada.

Werner, H. (1948). *The comparative psychology of mental development*. New York: Harper & Row.

———. (1957). "The concept of development from a comparative and organismic point of view." In *The concept of development*, ed. D. B. Harris. Minneapolis: University of Minnesota Press.

White, R. (1972). *The enterprise of living: growth and organization in personality*. New York: Holt, Rinehart & Winston.

Whiting, B., and J. Whiting. (1975). *Children of six cultures*. Cambridge, Mass.: Harvard University Press.

Wiggins, D. (1980). *Sameness and substance*. Oxford: Oxford University Press.

Williams, B. (1970). "The self and the future." *Philosophical Review* 79: 161–80.

———. (1973). *Problems of the self*. Cambridge: Cambridge University Press.

Wylie, R. (1979). *The self concept: theory and research on selected topics*, rev. ed., vol. 2. Lincoln: University of Nebraska Press.

———. (1974). *The self-concept: a review of methodological considerations and measuring instruments*. Lincoln: University of Nebraska Press.

Youniss, J. (1975). "Another perspective on social cognition." In *Minnesota symposia on child psychology*, vol. 9., ed. A. Pick. Minneapolis: University of Minnesota Press.

Yule, W. (1978). "Behavioral treatment of children and adolescents with conduct disorders." In *Aggression and anti-social behavior in childhood and adolescence*, ed. L. Herson, M. Berger, and D. Shaffer. Oxford: Pergamon Press.

Author index

Aboud, F., 34, 39, 125, 191
Allen, A., 111–12, 191
Allport, G. W., 2, 191
Alston, W., 4, 191
Amsterdam, B., 28, 33–4, 191
Applebaum, M., 170, 191
Armon, C., 104, 195

Baldwin, J. M., 25, 160, 174, 177–80, 191
Ball, L., 34, 39, 192
Barenboim, C., 183–4, 191
Beeghly-Smith, M., 98, 191
Bem, D., 111–12, 191
Bemis, K., 148, 193
Bergman, A., 18, 34, 195
Bernstein, R. M., 33, 35, 47, 191
Blasi, A., 2, 9, 131, 137, 153, 191
Bohan, J., 34, 38, 126, 193
Bourne, E., 159, 160, 197
Boyes, M., 34, 39, 192
Brainerd, C., 103, 191
Bretherton, I., 98, 191
Brim, O., 13, 191
Bromley, D., 33, 43, 114–15, 182, 184–5, 187, 191, 195
Brooks-Gunn, J., 27, 29, 33–4, 59, 180, 195
Broughton, J. M., 32–5, 46, 79, 133, 141, 191–2
Bruch, H., 47–8, 192
Bruner, J. S., 13, 192
Buhler, C., 23, 192
Bullock, D., 105, 193
Butterworth, G., 13, 192

Campos, J., 21, 192
Caputo, C., 184, 196
Chandler, M., 34, 39, 192
Chiriboga, D., 139, 195
Cicchetti, D., 141–2, 192
Clark-Stewart, A., 12, 192–3
Cohen, J., 89, 192

Colby, A., 122, 192
Conway, C., 130, 194
Coopersmith, S., 15, 142–4, 192
Crockett, W., 189, 197

Damon, W., vii, viii, xii, 4, 12, 13, 16, 17, 79–80, 89, 91, 98, 104, 107, 124, 126–7, 138, 173–5, 182, 192, 194
Darwin, C., 26, 192
Dewey, J., 180, 192
Dixon, J. C., 27, 33, 192
Dusek, J. B., 114, 192

Edwards, C., 170, 192
Eisen, M., 34, 50, 54, 177–8, 196
Epstein, S., 2, 192
Erikson, E., 16, 124–5, 192–3

Feldman, D. H., 4, 11, 12, 16, 89, 104–9, 193, 197
Ferguson, G., 91, 193
Fischer, K., 4, 11, 13, 16, 54, 104–5, 108, 144, 193
Fiske, S., 184, 198
Flaherty, J. F., 114, 192
Flavell, J., 16, 54, 103, 177, 193
Ford, L., 33, 41, 114, 195
Freud, S., 54, 193
Froman, T., 93, 193

Gallup, G. G., 28, 193
Gardner, H., 4, 11, 12, 16, 104, 193
Garfinkel, P., 147, 193
Garmezy, N., 140, 197
Garner, D., 147–8, 193
Geertz, C., ix, 125, 158–60, 193
Gergen, K., 110, 116, 193, 196
Gilligan, C., 54, 195
Glick, J., 12, 193
Goldman-Rakic, P., 24, 193
Gordon, C., 50, 114, 193

Greif, E., 78–9, 195
Guardo, C., 34, 38, 126, 193
Guillaume, P., 178, 180, 193

Hala, S., 34, 39, 192
Hamlyn, D., 182, 193
Harre, R., 170, 193
Harris, D., 15, 196
Harris, P. L., 25, 194
Hart, D., xii, 4, 91, 98, 107, 124, 126–9,
  138, 148, 192, 194, 197
Harter, S., 14, 21, 35, 48, 54, 115, 125,
  144, 194
Hartup, W., 143, 194
Heider, F., 181, 194
Hildebrand, D., 91, 194
Hill, J. P., 115, 140, 194
Hoine, H., 139, 198
Honess, T., 189, 194
Howard, G., 130, 194
Hubert, L., 93, 193
Hume, D., 4, 194
Humphrey, T., 24, 194

James, W., viii, 5, 7, 17, 124, 130, 194
Jessor, R., 17, 194
Johnson, C. N., 33, 36, 194
Jones, E. E., 180–1, 194
Josselson, R., 124, 194

Kagan, J., 22–5, 33, 195
Kegan, R., 104, 144, 195
Keller, A., 33, 41, 114, 195
Kogan, N., 125, 195
Kohlberg, L., 54, 104–5, 173, 177–8, 180,
  195, 197
Kokenes, B., 114, 195
Kuhn, D., 90, 195
Kurtines, W., 78–9, 195

Laing, M., 91, 194
Laing, R. D., 124, 195
Leahy, R., xii, 125, 141, 143, 195
Legant, P., 184, 196
LeVine, R., ix, 158–9, 169–70, 195
Lewin, K., 77, 195
Lewis, M., 27, 29, 33–4, 59, 180, 195
Light, P., 13, 192
Livesly, W., 33, 43, 114, 182, 184–5, 187,
  195
Loevinger, J., 137, 180, 195
Lowenthal, M., 139, 195
Lucca, N., 162, 195
Lucca-Irizarry, N., xii, 194
Luria, A. R., 160, 195

McCall, R., 170, 191
Maccoby, E., 132, 195

McGuire, W., 33, 40, 196
McNew, S., 98, 191
Mahler, M., 18–22, 34, 174, 195
Maloney, J., 124, 126, 194
Marcia, J., 16, 124, 196
Marecek, J., 184, 196
Markus, H., 111, 196
Meacham, J., 33, 41, 114, 195
Mead, G. H., viii, 9, 124, 131, 174, 177,
  196
Melcher, B., 153–5, 196
Mohr, D., 33, 41, 196
Montemayor, R., 34, 50, 54, 177–8, 196
Morse, S., 110, 196

Nisbett, R. E., 180–1, 184, 194, 196
Noam, G., 104, 197
Noppe, I., 173, 196
Norcini, J., 107, 109, 197
Nowicki, S., 132–3, 136, 196
Nozick, R., 2, 7, 8, 196

Pacheco, A., 162, 195
Padawer-Singer, A., 33, 40, 196
Papousek, H., 30, 196
Popousek, M., 30, 196
Parfit, D., 2, 7, 8, 124, 196
Parmelee, A., 24, 196
Parten, M., 89, 196
Peevers, B., 33–5, 42, 46–7, 97, 114, 184–5,
  187, 189, 196, 197
Peters, R., 12, 182, 196
Piaget, J., 11, 78–80, 129, 178, 180, 196
Piers, E., 15, 196
Pine, F., 18, 33, 195
Press, A., 189, 197
Preyer, W., 27, 196

Redmore, C., 137, 195
Rest, J., 89, 196
Rosenberg, M., 15, 35, 50, 98, 140, 144,
  197
Rosenhan, D., 152–3, 197
Rosenthal, A., 91, 194
Ross, L., 16, 193
Rotenberg, K. J., 177, 197
Ruble, D., 33, 43, 62, 197
Rutter, M., 17, 140, 197, 198

Saltzstein, H., 105, 197
Sarbin, T., 2, 3, 197
Sartre, J.-P., 8, 197
Scarlett, H., 189, 197
Schorin, M., 148, 150, 197
Secord, P., 33–5, 42, 46–7, 97, 114, 129,
  184–5, 187, 189, 196, 197
Seligman, M., 152–3, 197

Selman, R., 13, 33, 35, 37, 133, 142, 173–4, 197
Shantz, C., 12, 13, 197
Shoemaker, S., 7, 197
Shweder, R., 159–60, 197
Sigman, M., 24, 196
Skerry, S., 34, 39, 191
Snarey, J., 104, 197
Snyder, S., 89, 104–9, 197
Spragens, T. A., 130, 197
Sroufe, A., 17, 198
Sternberg, R. J., 4, 11, 198
Strickland, B., 132–3, 136, 196
Strober, M., 148, 198
Swinburne, R., 7, 8, 197, 198

Taylor, S., 184, 198
Thurner, M., 139, 195
Trevarthen, C., 13, 198
Turiel, E., 4, 11, 12, 104, 198

Vallacher, R., 139, 198

Wegner, D., 139, 198
Wellman, H., 33, 36, 194, 198
Werner, H., 177, 198
Wessler, R., 137, 195
White, M., 159, 169–70, 195
White, R., 44, 198
Whiting, B., 162, 170, 192, 198
Whiting, J., 162, 170, 198
Wiggins, D., 7, 198
Williams, B., 7, 124, 198
Wylie, R., 14, 15, 98, 143, 198

Yager, J., 48, 198
Youniss, J., 13, 198
Yule, W., 152, 198

Subject index

abstraction
  self-evaluation, adolescents, 47–8
  self-understanding model, 54–5
active self-scheme
  adolescents, 51
  children, 41–3, 51
  comparative assessments, 62–3
  cross-sectional studies, 91–4, 96–7
  interpersonal implications, 65–6
  longitudinal findings, 101–3
  versus physical self-scheme, 42
  Puerto Rican study, 161, 166
  self-statements, 60
  self-understanding interview, 84
  self-understanding model, 55–69
  and systematic beliefs, 68
affect, and self-esteem, 14–17
age factors
  adolescence, 48
  cross-sectional studies, 91, 95
  identity development, 39
  "me" dimension, 57
  self-concept stability, 114
  dimensions of self, children, 38–9
  self-recognition, infants, 30–1
agency sense, 6
  adolescents, 47
  anorexia nervosa, 148–52
  and autonomy, 6
  conduct disorder, 155
  development of, 133–6
  empirical findings, 123–38
  James's analysis, 130–1
  research problems, 132–4
  self-understanding interview, 82, 84
  self-understanding model, 55–6, 70–1
agrarian societies, 159–70
Albanian children, 23
anorexia nervosa, 147–52
Aristotelian tradition, 130
attribution theory, 180–2, 184–5, 189

Baconian revolution, 130
Baldwin's theory, 25–6, 177–80
Balinese culture, 159–60
behavioral comparisons, 183
beliefs, 67–9
Bem and Allen's approach, 111–12
biological approaches, 22–5
Blasi's work, 137
body image
  versus activities, self, 41–2
  adolescents, 50
body movement, 131
brain transplant problem, 7

central self-statements, 183
chunks, 83–6, 166–7
clinical interview, *see* interview method
"closest continuer" theory, 8
cognition, 11; *see also* social cognition
commitment, 125
comparative self-assessments
  and self-concept, 43
  self-understanding model, 61–3
competence, 43
conduct disorder, 152–6
"consolidation of personality," 21
consolidation–transition model, 106–9
contingencies, facial recognition, 27–31
continuity sense, *see* self-continuity
contradictory self-statements, 49
covert properties, 177
cross-sectional findings, 88–98
cultural factors
  comparative self-assessments, 62
  Puerto Rican study, 158–70
  self-understanding, 172

Damon and Hart's self-understanding
  model, 107–9
dendrite branching theory, 24
"depth" properties, 177

"differentiation" developmental phase, 19, 177
dispositional attribution, 181–2
distinctness sense
  anorexia nervosa, 148–52
  children's understanding, 126–9
  empirical findings, 123–38
  and personal identity, 8, 124–6
  self-understanding interview, 82–4
  self-understanding model, 55–6, 74–6
dualism, and self, 14

egocentrism, 189
ejective developmental phase, 179–80
emotions, and self-esteem, 14–16
Erikson's theory, 16
Eskimo culture, 170
existential functions, self, 8–9
external locus-of-control, 132

facial recognition, 26–32
feature clues, self-recognition, 27–9
Flavell's theory, 177
friend interview, 185–9
friendship, 143

gender
  cross-sectional studies, 94, 96
  as dimension of self, 38
  and self-recognition, infants, 30–1
Gergen's theory, 110
global-stage approaches, 104
gradual-transformation model, 107–9

hierarchization, 54–5, 177

"I" concept
  adolescents, 44–6
  and existential self, 8–11
  infants, 31–2
  James's theory, 5–11
  and mental health, 145–6
  self-understanding model, 55–6
  and volition, 130–1
identity formation, *see* personal identity
ideological commitment, 125
idiographic approach, 112
imitation
  and person perception, 189–90
  self-development, 25
  theory of, 178–80
individual differences, 112, 140
individuality
  dimension of self, children, 38, 40
  and "self," 2–3
  self-concept formation, 40–1

individuation, 13
infancy
  self-recognition paradigm, 26–32
  social-cognitive research, 26–35
intelligence, 11
intentional relations, 13
internal locus-of-control, 132
interpersonal interactions
  and self-development, 174–5
  self-understanding model, 64–7
  social cognition, 13
interrater reliability, 88–90, 134–5
interview method, 77–86; *see also* self-
    understanding interview
  clinical settings, 150
  evaluation, 78–80
  self-concept stability, 113–14, 116
  and testing effect, 116

James, William, theory, 5–11, 130–1
juvenile delinquency, 152–6

Kagan's theory, 22–5
Kappa statistic, 89–90
Kohlberg's approach, 104–5, 108, 122, 178

locus-of-control, 132–3
logical-positivist approach, 77–8
longitudinal findings, 98–122, 134–8
  personal identity, 126–9
  self-concept stability, 109–22

Mahler's theory, 18–22
maturational explanations, 22–5
Mead's theory, 9–11, 131
"me" concept
  adolescents, 44–5
  conduct disorder, 154–5
  infants, 31–2
  James's view, 5–10
  and mental health, 145–6
  self-understanding model, 55–69
mental health
  adolescents, 139–57
  developmental context, 141–2
  self-understanding role, 140
mirror images, 26–9
morality
  and conduct disorder, 153
  developmental influence, 71
  relevance to personal identity, 124
  and self-conception, 177–8
moral-stage theory, 104–5
motivation
  adolescents, 49, 71
  and self-knowledge, 36

motor movements, 131
"multiple intelligences," 11
myelinization theory, 24

"negative bias," 106–9
neurological approaches, 23–4
nonconscious experience, 45
"normal autistic" phase, 19
Nozick's theory, 8

object constancy, 21
objective self, *see* "me" concept
Orchard Town, 162

parent interview, 186–9
peer relations, 143
peripheral self-statements, 183
personal continuity, *see* self-continuity
personal identity
  children, research, 38
  and continuity, 124–6
  deficits in, 124–5
  and distinctness, 124–6
  and "I" concept, 7–10
  James's theory, 7
  philosophical perspectives, 124–6
  psychological issues, 124–6
  Puerto Rican study, 169
  and self-understanding, 16
"person perception"
  empirical research, 182–90
  imitation paradigm, 189–90
  versus self-perception, 177, 184–90
  and self-understanding, 176–81
physical self-scheme
  versus activity dimension, 42
  age factors, 39
  children, 32–3, 36–9, 41–2
  comparative assessments, 62
  cross-sectional studies, 91–4, 96–7
  infants, 30
  interpersonal implications, 65
  longitudinal findings, 101–3
  Puerto Rican study, 161, 166
  self-statements, 59–60
  self-understanding interview, 84
  self-understanding model, 55–69
Piaget's theory, 11, 78, 173
picture study, 30
"playmate recognition" stage, 27–8
"positive bias," 106–9
"practicing subphase," 20
preschoolers, active self, 42
pride, 50–1
projective developmental phase, 178–9
psychoanalysis, 18–22
psychological adaptation, *see* mental health

psychological constructs, 183, 185
psychological self-scheme
  adolescents, 51
  children, 39–42
  comparative assessments, 63–4
  cross-sectional studies, 91–4, 96–8
  interpersonal implications, 66–7
  interview effects, 116
  longitudinal findings, 101–3, 116
  Puerto Rican study, 164, 166
  self-statements, 61
  self-understanding interview, 84
  self-understanding model, 55–69
  and systematic beliefs, 69
Puerto Rican study, 62, 158–70, 172

"rapprochement," 20
rating scales, 115
reflection experience
  adolescence, 44
  methodological difficulties, 138
  and the self, 6–7, 9–11
reliability, interview method, 88–90
rural settings, 159–62

Sarbin's theory, 3–4
scoring manual, 83–6
"self," definition, 2–5
self-as-object, 55–69; *see also* "me" concept
self-as-subject, 69–76, 88–122; *see also* "I"
  concept
self-awareness, 22–5
self-concept
  adolescents, 50–1
  definition, 2–11
  individuality function, 40–1
  James's theory, 5–6
  longitudinal findings, 109–22
  and mental health, 142–7
  stability of, 109–22
self-continuity
  children's understanding, 126–9
  conduct disorder, 155–6
  dimension of self, children, 38–40
  empirical findings, 123–38
  and mental health, 146–7
  and personal identity, 8, 124–6
  self-understanding interview, 82, 84
  self-understanding model, 55–6, 72–4
self-differentiation, 48
self-esteem
  adolescents, 50–1
  affective components, 14–15
  and mental health, 142–3, 156–7
  predictive value, 15
  scales, 15
  and self-understanding, 14–16

stability, 110–11
self-evaluation
  adolescents, 47
  self-understanding interview, 81–2
self-interest, 82
self-knowledge, 31, 51
self-perception, 177–8
self-recognition
  infancy research, 26–32
  and neuronal maturation, 25
self-reflection, *see* reflection experience
self-understanding interview, 77–86
  characteristics, 77–86
  clinical application, 150
  internal consistency, 90
  interrater reliability, 88–90
  test–retest reliability, 90–1
semantic differential, 114–15
Sentence Completion Test, 137
separation–individuation, 18–22
sequential stage models, 103–4
sex roles, *see* gender
shame, 50–1
smiling sign, 30
Snyder and Feldman's model, 105–9
social cognition, 25–52, 171–91
  childhood research, 32–44
  empirical research, 182–90
  infancy research, 26–32
  and person perception, 176–8
  and self-perception, 177–8
  and self-understanding, 11–14, 171–90
  study of, 12–13
social comparisons, 43
social interaction
  and self-knowledge, 23
  self-understanding model, 73
  social-cognitive approach, 25

social self-scheme
  adolescents, 50–1
  agrarian societies, 169–70
  children, 43–4
  comparative assessments, 63
  conduct disorder, 154
  cross-sectional studies, 91–4, 96–9
  interpersonal implications, 66
  longitudinal findings, 101–3
  Puerto Rican study, 161, 164–70
  self-statements, 60–1
  self-understanding interview, 84
  self-understanding model, 55–69
speech, 23–4
stage models, 103–4
Sternberg's "tripartite theory," 11
story dilemmas, 37
structural-developmental approach, 77–8,
  172
subjective development stage, 179
subjective self, *see* "I" concept
"surface" properties, 177
"surface to depth" dimension, 54
symbiotic developmental phase, 19

television, 29–30
test–retest reliability, 90–1
"tripartite theory," 11

videotapes, 29–30
volition; *see also* agency sense
  adolescents, 44–7
  and self-knowledge, 36, 44

Werner's theory, 177
Western culture, 159
"withdrawal recognition" stage, 28
work commitment, 125

"This book by Damon and Hart is a welcome book. It offers an excellent picture of the state of the art with respect to theory and research on the development of self-understanding. The authors clarify the role, function, and importance of self-understanding and its development. They succeed in relating past and contemporary theory and empirical findings dealing with the self, the self-concept, and self-understanding."   *–Human Development*

"[The book] provides a valuable framework for stimulating new research and theory on the diversity of self-understanding. Its reasonable arguments and clear style make it broadly accessible and should ensure that it will have a wide influence on research on the development of self."
                                                    –Contemporary Psychology

"…[Damon and Hart's] work marks a significant contribution to the field and will serve as a heuristic guide to the other studies of the development of self-concept."   *–Merrill-Palmer Quarterly*

"Damon and Hart have written a thought-provoking and worthwhile book: it illustrates the value (and potential limitations) of asking developing children probing and sensitive questions."
                              –The International Journal of Social Psychiatry

"The authors set themselves the bold task of taking a comprehensive look at their subject from a developmental perspective. There can be no doubt of the depth, expertise and rigour of this work.... I have gained deeper understanding of a subject which has always troubled me and concepts which will be clinically useful."   *–The British Journal of Psychiatry*

William Damon is Professor and Chair of Education at Brown University.
Daniel Hart is Associate Professor of Psychology at Rutgers University.

CAMBRIDGE

UNIVERSITY

PRESS

ISBN 0-521-42499-2